Praise for *Free Agent Learning*

"*Free Agent Learning* explores how students might become co-designers and stewards of learning experiences that extend beyond school walls and receive credit for anytime, anywhere, passion-driven learning. Evans explains how having a meaningful choice in the path and pace of the learning process is important to students based on Speak Up data from surveying students since 2004. She lifts up a fundamental principle—a majority of students want to be in control of when and how they learn. An important consideration is how education systems will need to evolve to shift power to the learner, in hopes students can build agency over the path and pace of their learning with a focus on purpose and student goals, and underscores how advanced digital learning can support this vision."

—Susan Patrick,
President & CEO, Aurora Institute

"As educators and researchers debate the problems on mental health that ready access to smartphones creates for students, Julie Evans explores the flipside: the unbridled access to engaging learning opportunities this access unleashes. How to balance the positives that Evans outlines in this book with the observed challenges makes this volume more than worth it."

—Michael Horn,
Author, *From Reopen to Reinvent*

"Vital skills like collaboration and leadership can be learned and coached—but not taught. *Free Agent Learning* describes how we can support young people in 'experiential learning' that involves both doing and reflection."

—Chris Dede,
Timothy E. Wirth Professor in
Learning Technologies, Harvard
Graduate School of Education

"For decades, home schooling families have used any moment of the day, any place in the world to 'school' their children; the rest of us are just now catching up. As a brilliant education researcher, Julie examines in detail how students today learn outside of this place called school and how these learning experiences prepare them to be engaged, self-motivated, lifelong learners. This book provides a blueprint of *free agent learning* for teachers, leaders, and parents to draw upon and encourage personalized, interest-based learning as the learning norm as opposed to the exception."

—Julie Young,
Vice President Education,
Arizona State University,
Outreach and Student Services

FREE AGENT
LEARNING

FREE AGENT LEARNING

Leveraging Students' Self-Directed Learning to Transform K–12 Education

JULIE A. EVANS

JB JOSSEY-BASS™

A Wiley Brand

Jossey-Bass
A Wiley Imprint
111 River St, Hoboken, NJ 07030
www.josseybass.com

Printed in the United States of America
Simultaneously published in Canada

Jossey-Bass books and products are available through most bookstores. To contact Jossey-Bass directly, call our Customer Care Department within the U.S. at 800–956–7739, outside the U.S. at +1 317 572 3986, or fax +1 317 572 4002.

Wiley also publishes its books in a variety of electronic formats and by print-on-demand. Some material included with standard print versions of this book may not be included in e-books or in print-on-demand. If this book refers to media such as a CD or DVD that is not included in the version you purchased, you may download this material at http://booksupport.wiley.com. For more information about Wiley products, visit www.wiley.com.

Library of Congress Cataloging-in-Publication Data

Names: Evans, Julie (Education entrepreneur) author.
Title: Free agent learning : leveraging students' self-directed learning to
    transform K-12 education / Julie Evans.
Description: First edition. | Hoboken, NJ : Jossey-Bass, [2023] | Includes
    index.
Identifiers: LCCN 2022029595 (print) | LCCN 2022029596 (ebook) | ISBN
    9781119789826 (hardback) | ISBN 9781119789840 (adobe pdf) | ISBN
    9781119789833 (epub)
Subjects: LCSH: Self-managed learning. | Autonomy (Psychology) |
    Individualized instruction.
Classification: LCC LB1066 .E93 2023 (print) | LCC LB1066 (ebook) | DDC
    370.15/23—dc23/eng/20220729
LC record available at https://lccn.loc.gov/2022029595
LC ebook record available at https://lccn.loc.gov/2022029596

Cover Design: Wiley
Cover Image: © SofiaV/Shutterstock

FIRST EDITION

SKY10035966_091222

To my favorite Free Agent Learners:
Elizabeth, David and Matthew

Contents

About the Author

Dr. Julie A. Evans is the Chief Executive Officer of Project Tomorrow (www.tomorrow.org) and the founder of the heralded Speak Up Research Project, which annually collects and reports on the authentic views of K-12 students, parents, and educators nationwide on key education issues. Dr. Evans serves as the chief researcher on the Speak Up Project as well as leading national research efforts on the impact of emerging learning models and interventions in both K-12 and higher education. Her work includes helping education leaders embrace change and innovation in education and learning how to effectively leverage the voices and views of their local stakeholders, including students, as an asset in education transformation efforts.

Dr. Evans's background includes executive and management positions with a Fortune 500 multinational information technology company and two education technology start-ups prior to joining Project Tomorrow. As a national thought leader and influencer, she brings to discussions about the future of education a unique perspective because of her experiences working in both the for-profit and nonprofit sectors as well as within education. Dr. Evans is a graduate of Brown University and earned her doctorate in educational leadership from the University of California San Diego and California State University San Marcos. She is a frequent facilitator, speaker, and writer on new learning models within education, most notably around digital learning. Among her many accolades and awards, Dr. Evans was named in April 2020 as the winner of EdTech Digest's National Leader award.

Acknowledgments

This book is the result of nearly 20 years of research and reflection on the how K-12 students use technology to support their learning, both when they are in school and when they are self-directing learning outside of school. Thus, there are many people who have been part of this journey with me and have had a direct or indirect hand in getting these important insights about Free Agent Learning to this stage. I appreciate each of you, and you hold a special place in my heart for your contributions to this work.

It should not be surprising that my first acknowledgment must be to the over 4 million K-12 students who have shared their views on school and learning through Project Tomorrow's research activities, most notably the Speak Up Research Project. Through your completion of a Speak Up survey or participation in the hundreds of focus groups and panel discussions I have facilitated over the past 20 years, I am especially grateful for your willingness to share your authentic, no-spin zone feedback on your classroom learning experiences, and how you have embraced technology to support your self-directed learning activities outside of school. I also want to thank you for your bottomless well of optimism that schools can improve and your belief that your ideas can make a real difference, if only someone would listen. It has been a true privilege to provide a way through the Speak Up Research Project for your views to have a tangible impact on local, state, and national programs and policies on education. A special thank-you is due to the students who shared with me their own personal Free Agent Learning experiences to serve as examples and representations of the many varied ways that students are self-directing their own learning. To all students, I urge you to keep speaking up and sharing your ideas about education. Your voices are more important than ever!

I would also like to acknowledge the many teachers, school principals, district leaders, and parents who every day encourage and empower our nation's youth to speak up and share their ideas about how to improve school and learning for all students. Special thanks are due to the many school and district leaders who each year facilitate the opportunity for their communities to participate in the national Speak Up Research Project, providing a way for the voices of their students (and other stakeholders such as teachers and parents) to be a valuable input into local planning. You are not only building student agency, but you are paying it forward in terms of creating a new momentum around the value of student voice and choice in education decisions. Thank you for your efforts to improve education through your valuation of students' ideas.

Many thanks must be extended as well to the school and district leaders who over the years have shared with me their own experiential insights about how to bridge the gap between the too often disparate aspects of students' learning lives at home and at school. I am especially appreciative of the education leaders who shared with me through the experience of writing this book their own ideas about how school and district leaders, can utilize this new knowledge about Free Agent Learning to create a more inclusive culture in their schools and communities.

None of this work on Free Agent Learning or even the Speak Up Research Project would be possible without the incredible team of innovators who have been part of the Project Tomorrow family over the past 20 years. Many thanks are due to the original members of the NetDay and subsequently, the Project Tomorrow Board of Directors, who always enthusiastically supported the Speak Up Research

Project and continue to lend their considerable time, talents, and treasures to sustain this important work. I am also very appreciative of the many corporate, nonprofit, association, and philanthropic partners that have provided financial support, guidance, and advice as scaffolding for the research work of Project Tomorrow. Your friendship and willingness to engage in this work with us is a gift that I will always cherish. My deepest appreciation is for the many team colleagues from both the NetDay and Project Tomorrow eras who through their hard work and dedication turned my "big crazy idea" into a reality with the design and implementation of the Speak Up Research Project. You have shared my vision over the past 20 years and thus, in so many ways, this book about Free Agent Learning is your legacy as well.

Throughout all my years of research on digital learning, my favorite study team has often been my own children, Elizabeth, David, and Matthew. They have been participants in this digital learning revolution, and while they often chided me with, "I don't want to be a research statistic," it has been the greatest experience of my life to learn along with them. Finally, I would like to recognize my greatest cheerleader, my husband Ron, whose love and support throughout this book journey has made this all possible.

Introduction

It was during middle school that Samantha developed a personal interest in learning more about the stock market. Her curiosity about the stock market was not the result, however, of something she studied at school or a homework assignment. Rather, being a socially aware eighth grader, Samantha kept up on current events. In particular, the social justice movement stimulated her interest in learning more about how wealth is acquired and leveraged for societal good. Understanding the ups and downs of the stock market and its impact on the economy was derivative of that interest. To satisfy her curiosity to learn more about the connection between the stock market and the economy, she googled information about the various markets, read online stock reports about companies that caught her eye, watched cable business shows such as *Mad Money* and *Squawk Box*, and followed financial news reporters and commentators on social media. As her interest-driven knowledge increased, Samantha expanded her self-directed learning to include the foreign exchange markets, and ultimately to start using her allowance and babysitting proceeds to make some small investments and trades herself.

Her personal access to technology not only helped her learn about the stock market, but it also proved to be invaluable in managing her nascent trading career, in addition to supporting her schoolwork life. Samantha used the calendar function with the Google suite to get reminders about tomorrow's math test and next week's book report for English class and to keep track of critical financial industry events including when Apple was announcing its quarterly earnings.

Electronic worksheets were useful for documenting her lab results in science class as well as helping her plan and track her stock trades. As Samantha explained to me, her self-directed learning about the stock market was not simply a hobby, but rather, it was preparing her to be successful in the future, most notably in terms of developing financial literacy and personal capabilities for making informed decisions about money. Empowered by her personal access to the Internet and a wide range of digital resources and tools, Samantha turned a curiosity to learn about the workings of the stock market into an educational and life preparation experience that was beyond what she was learning in school, and in many ways through a more meaningful learning process. And her intrinsic motivation for more information and knowledge continues to grow.

When I spoke with her in October 2020 as part of a virtual panel discussion, Samantha was starting to research and learn about Bitcoin. On that day, Samantha was also very proud that one of her early morning 10 cent trades on a stock that she had heavily researched was already up $2 by noon. There was no class in her middle school or unit of study in the prescribed curriculum that was helping students like Samantha develop real-world financial literacy or having contextually relevant experiences like this to learn about the ins and outs of the financial world. And while not every student may share Samantha's personal interest in this topic, curiosity is a human condition and thus, it is not unreasonable to assume that our young people have other learning interests that are beyond what is happening in their classrooms. Empowered with personal access to technology and an intrinsic motivation to learn more about the stock market, Samantha felt a personal imperative to address what she perceived as a gap in her education by taking her educational destiny into her own hands to pursue intellectual curiosities, academic interests, and career preparation goals on her own outside of school. Samantha is a Free Agent Learner.

Free Agent Learnership, the subject of this book, is the process by which students self-direct highly personalized learning experiences outside of school around topics and subjects of strong interest or academic passion for them as independent learners and owners of their own educational destiny. I call the students who are engaged in these self-directed, interest-driven learning pursuits "Free Agent Learners." The name is a take-off on a term commonly used in professional sports. In the professional sports world, Free Agents are athletes who are not bound by commitments or artificial structures that restrict their actions or limit their ability for example to negotiate better contracts with other teams. Central to an athlete's free agency is their self-determination, their ability to make their own choices relative to the direction of their career. The professional athlete who has Free Agent status has the capacity to pursue their own goals, whether that is to play for the highest bidder for their talents or for the team in their hometown. Likewise, students are Free Agents regarding their learning today because they now can also exercise greater self-determination when it comes to learning. Learning for today's K-12 students is not limited to the classroom or the after-school program but rather happens across a variety of settings and through a seamless flow of practices from morning to night. The increasingly ubiquitous availability and access of digital tools and resources such as social media, mobile devices, online communities, and digital games is the fuel that is propelling this new learning paradigm of Free Agent Learning. Students' learning potential is no longer restrained by the knowledge of their teacher, the resources within their classroom, or their ability to visit a local library or museum. A world of knowledge and learning experiences can now be accessed with a few clicks or swipes on their personal smartphone. Empowered with access to technology and a passionate motivation for highly contextualized learning experiences, students are now "Free Agents" in the sense that they can drive their own educational destiny just as professional athletes with free agency have the capacity to direct their own career fate. Most importantly, the experiences that students are having outside of school, driving their own learning experiences, using a wide range of digital tools and resources, and using those experiences to prepare for their future success, are influencing their expectations for in-school learning as well. For today's education leaders, understanding Free Agent Learning is not just about gaining an appreciation for their students' out-of-school activities, but rather, it is an essential input in the ongoing process of transformation of K-12 education to ensure that all students are well prepared to become tomorrow's innovators, leaders, and engaged citizens of the world.

In my role as Chief Executive Officer of Project Tomorrow®, a national education nonprofit organization, I have been studying the role of technology in supporting student outcomes and teacher effectiveness for nearly 25 years. Starting in 2003, those research efforts were consolidated into a groundbreaking new initiative that not only provides annual national reporting on the digital learning trends but affords an efficient and effective way for K-12 schools and districts to understand the views and values of their local stakeholders on the use of technology within learning. Each year, Project Tomorrow through our Speak Up Research Project® provides a suite of online surveys for K-12 leaders to utilize to collect feedback from their students, parents, teachers, and principals and other district administrators. Any K-12 school or district can use the Speak Up surveys, and Project Tomorrow provides access to all locally collected data with appropriate state and national comparative data for benchmarking. By design, Speak Up is a free service with a mission to help all education leaders realize the benefits of incorporating the views of their stakeholders into local planning and decision-making. Central to the Speak Up Research Project is a unique focus on listening to the ideas of K-12 students about their own learning experiences, both in school and out of school. The nationally aggregated Speak Up data and insights about digital learning trends is widely shared through national reports, infographics, briefings, and conference presentations. The data and insights about Free Agent Learning shared in this book are derivatives of the Speak Up Research Project.

My personal journey to identify and appreciate the phenomenon of Free Agent Learning started in spring 2003. During a three-month period, I conducted focus groups with middle school and high school students in five of our nation's most challenged urban and rural communities to learn how students were using digital tools to support their learning, both in and out of school. The existing literature on the student perspective was limited to a few case studies, mostly involving students in suburban communities. I felt a strong need to hear from students in less advantageous situations about their digital learning experiences. I learned three fundamental truths from those student discussions that transformed my professional practice and my world vision. First, like the students in the suburban communities, these students in the less resourced communities I visited were using a wide range of technologies to support self-directed learning outside of school. This was especially poignant given that most of the students I met with did not have Internet access or computers in their homes in 2003, but they had the resourcefulness and personal drive to seek out places and people who could provide them with technology access on a regular basis. This reality obviously challenged the prevailing views and assumptions about the Digital Divide. Second, the students felt frustrated and disappointed with the lack of sophistication in how their teachers were using digital tools, content, and resources in school to support their learning potential and with their teachers' seeming unwillingness to listen to their experientially based ideas about digital learning. Third, the students believed that their future success beyond high school absolutely depended on closing the digital disconnect between their aspirations for digital learning and the deficiencies that they saw in their learning environments. A 12th grade girl from Rosedale, Mississippi, summed up her peers' perspective succinctly when she asked me, "Why is it that our teachers do not realize that when they hold back on using technology in class, they are holding back our future?" Through the shared experiences of these students across five very different communities, it was obvious to me that our K-12 schools and districts, as well as our nation, needed a better way to understand the views and values of our students regarding their learning experiences and the role of technology within those experiences. And that the views of students, especially based on their experiences with using technology for self-directed learning, could be an asset for transforming student learning experiences in schools. Since that time, the Speak Up Research Project has continued to collect and report on the ideas of students, as well as parents, teachers, and administrators, and the research findings are used annually to inform local, state, and national policies and programs on education and digital learning. It has been my honor and privilege to facilitate opportunities for students in particular to have a greater voice in education decisions through the Speak Up process.

Remarkably, the Speak Up results each year continue to validate the same three truths I uncovered in 2003: Students use technology regularly outside of school to self-direct learning around areas of personal interest, they are frustrated by the continuing lack of sophistication in how digital tools are used in their classroom, and they feel a strong personal imperative to take matters into their own hands to ensure they are well prepared for their future success. The students I talked with in 2003 were certainly Free Agent Learners. You will see that they share similar motivations for self-directed, interest-driven learning with the students you will learn about in this book. Despite the significant investments that have been made in classroom technology and teacher professional learning, especially since the COVID pandemic, the Speak Up Research continues to document each year that students' aspirations for more effective learning experiences in school, what I refer to as the Student Vision for Learning, is still not fully realized in most schools and communities. The goal for this book, therefore, is to provide education leaders with new information about students' self-directed learning experiences, especially with technology, that can be translated into actionable knowledge to close the gap between students' expectations for more effective learning and their current in-classroom experiences. To that end, the book is organized into two primary sections. Chapters 1 through 5 focus on understanding Free Agent Learning motivations and behaviors; chapters 6 through 10 provide insights about why it is important for today's education leaders to appreciate Free Agent Learning and ideas for how to incorporate this new knowledge into your school and district plans. Speak Up research findings are used throughout the book to substantiate the way students are using technology to empower self-directed learning and their frustrations with current classroom learning practices. Additionally, the book leans into several key educational theories and frameworks that provide validation for Free Agent Learning. Included in various chapters are authentic vignettes about students and their self-directed learning experiences that will provide further understanding of the motivations and aspirations of Free Agent Learners and hopefully inspire education leaders to inquire about their own students' views and values on self-directed learning. Student names have of course been changed in the narrative to protect their privacy and identities.

Too often in education, conversations about improving learning experiences for students devolve into a binary choice between making incremental changes or undertaking a wholesale transformation of classroom practices. Both are usually unsustainable for different reasons. Small changes though easy to implement often do not yield tangible outcomes that make a significant difference and thus are frequently abandoned when budgets are squeezed or key staff leave the school or district. Widespread adoption of new practices requires very careful planning, a high degree of buy-in from stakeholders, and a significant amount of patience before real results are evident. A lack of patience and/or the ability to articulate measurable benefits or outcomes is too often the death knell for innovative initiatives in education. *Free Agent Learning: Leveraging Students' Self-Directed Learning to Transform K–12 Education* provides a new research-based road map for education leaders interested in improving learning experiences for their students by recognizing that students' self-directed, interest-driven learning outside of school can provide the impetus for rethinking and reengineering classroom practices and school cultures. But it starts with being open to new ideas and setting aside existing assumptions and out-of-date conventional wisdom about your students, their use of technology outside of school, and their expectations for in-school learning. Consequently, the quote attributed to the French novelist Marcel Proust, *"The voyage of discovery is not in seeking new landscapes, but in having new eyes"* is an appropriate send-off as you begin your voyage of discovery about Free Agent Learning. For the sake of Samantha and all students who are Free Agent Learners, my wish is for you to approach this book and the study of students' self-directed, interest-driven learning with new eyes.

Chapter 1

Understanding the Student Vision for Learning

L earning for today's K–12 student is not limited to the classroom or the afterschool program but rather happens across a variety of settings and through a seamless flow of practices from morning to night. The increasingly ubiquitous availability and access of digital tools and resources such as social media, mobile devices, online communities, and digital games is the fuel that is propelling a new learning paradigm, Free Agent Learning.

Free Agent Learning acknowledges that school is no longer the sole repository of knowledge and embraces the concept that students increasingly have the agency and the means to adopt new self-directed, interest-driven behaviors outside of school. Yet, for the most part, these self-directed, interest-driven digital learning experiences, which are fundamentally beyond the sponsorship of teachers or other adults in formalized learning environments, are still often discounted and devalued as trivial by educators. Existing research on student learning with technology focuses primarily on how students are using digital tools and resources under the direction of teachers or other adults in both formal and informal settings. However, emerging research from Project Tomorrow presents a case for how students are actually using digital and new media tools to self-direct learning around academic interests and personal curiosities about their world. I call these students "Free Agent Learners."

Evidence of students' interest-driven digital learning validates the need for education leaders to think past traditional learning settings and to appreciate the ways that students are self-directing meaningful learning experiences without the sponsorship of teachers and other adults. Beyond the classroom and school building walls, students are developing their own learning ecosystems and networks that highly value collaboration, knowledge sharing, and peer mentoring. Their interest-driven participation with digital tools results in personal identification as learners and experts and in the development of the workplace-ready skills that are the desired outcomes of state educational standards and what employers are increasingly demanding of new employees.

Additionally, these self-directed learning behaviors are not limited to students of privilege or those students with certain demographic qualifications. Rather, the use of digital tools, content, and resources by students outside of school to self-direct learning appears to be a universal phenomenon characterized by a strong orientation to the purposeful motivations driving the behaviors. The existence of this phenomenon has significant implications for addressing equity considerations in education. Most notably, this brings to the forefront the need for students to have access to technology and the Internet outside of school not only to do homework or participate in remote learning but to be able to pursue interest-driven, highly personalized learning experiences if desired.

A key *aha* moment for education leaders to realize is that today's students are not waiting for their teachers to transform the classroom learning experience to better fit their needs for skill development, to help prepare them for an uncertain future, or even to answer their questions about science, history, or politics. That ship has sailed. Armed with Internet connectivity in their pocket, backpack, or palm of their hand, students have the capacity now to self-direct learning around academic passions or personal curiosity about their world.

They are using a variety of digital tools, content, and resources and developing a host of new learning behaviors to support these interest-driven activities. At the center of this self-directed learning is a series of highly developed purposes that are propelling today's students to take their educational destiny into their own hands, quite literally. An opportunity exists for educators to learn from these student experiences and use that knowledge to spearhead a new morning in education, a morning that values students' self-directed learning experiences and aims to create in-school experiences that are innovative, relevant, and purposeful.

A Free Agent Learning Experience: Chad

As a senior in high school, Chad enjoyed every day in his physics class. The teacher was personable and knowledgeable, and Chad was one of those students teachers love; he was like a sponge soaking up everything in the curriculum. To cover all of the required content in this introduction to physics course, the high school teacher moved quickly though the prescribed pacing guide to ensure that the class covered all of the topics in the state curriculum. This meant that not every subject or chapter in the class textbook was covered. This is the reality in many K–12 classrooms.

In Chad's physics class, one of the chapters in the course textbook that was skipped was on quantum mechanics. Though not assigned or covered in the class, Chad read that chapter on his own and found the content very compelling. His curiosity propelled him to want to learn more about quantum mechanics, the science of examining how matter and light work at the atomic and subatomic level.[1] To address that very personal learning need, Chad did some research online and found an online forum about quantum mechanics. The participants in the forum included college professors and students in higher education physics programs. While observing the interactions and communications on the forum, Chad noted that many of the participants kept mentioning the same textbook, David J. Griffiths' *Introduction to Quantum Mechanics*.[2] At that time, Chad was not aware that this textbook was the standard in many college-level physics courses, but he thought it might be a good resource to support his personally directed learning path about quantum mechanics. Chad did some investigative work and found that he could buy a used copy of the Griffiths text on Amazon. He bought that book and used it to initiate a new, interest-driven educational process on quantum mechanics on his own beyond the sponsorship or facilitation of this teacher. This learning process was not to satisfy a course requirement, nor to specifically help his grade in his physics class. And it was definitely not a homework assignment.

For Chad, this experience was about learning something that he was interested in, pure and simple. He was able to do this on his own time, unencumbered by the traditional structural components of school that sometimes bog down the learning experience such as restricted learning time, a focus on testing results, and adherence to a standardized curriculum or pacing guide. And he was able to pursue an academic passion that had high personal resonance for him. This self-directed learning process was also highly efficient for Chad. As Chad explained it, he certainly could have asked his high school physics teacher about quantum mechanics, and he is sure that the teacher would have welcomed the opportunity to provide information. But Chad was not looking for a lecture on quantum mechanics or even questions about why he was interested in an academic topic that was beyond the high school curriculum. Chad was very specifically seeking a self-directed learning experience that could be highly personalized to his interests, and one in which he could self-direct and manage the learning process. Like many high school seniors, Chad had a full plate for activities taking up his time every day beyond his academic course load, including community service activities and working on his college applications. He needed an efficient learning process that would fit into his overall 24/7 learning day, whether that was at 10 p.m. on a Tuesday night or 3 p.m. on Sunday afternoon; just not necessarily second-period physics class on a Wednesday. His self-directed, interest-driven learning involved the purposeful use of digital resources and was focused on a topic of academic curiosity.

The key here is that Chad had a very clear purpose in mind when pursuing the self-initiated learning. As we will discuss further in this book, purpose is a powerful stimulant for Free Agent Learning. Taking place outside of school, in his own personal environment, Chad was in charge of his own learning destiny on quantum mechanics. Chad was a Free Agent Learner. Today, Chad is a college professor and researcher studying artificial intelligence and robotics.

The Four Learning Environments for Students

As we will discuss further, Chad's story is not unusual. The learning process for students has always taken place across four distinct environments (see Table 1.1 later in this chapter). Most adults find it easy to identify three of those learning spaces: school-based learning, homework, and extracurricular programs. The fourth learning space, the self-directed, interest-driven space described in our example about Chad, is the one that most educators are challenged identifying.

School-Based Learning

The three traditional environments that adults easily recognize are typified by a learning process that is guided, sponsored, or facilitated by a teacher or another education guardian in the student's life. Consequently, when asked to identify questions about what, where, how, or when students learn, the first impulse for most adults will be

5

Table 1.1 Characteristics of the four environments for student learning.

Environment characteristics	Environment #1: School-based learning	Environment #2: Homework	Environment #3: Extracurricular programs	Environment #4: Self-directed, interest-driven learning
Location	In person or virtual classroom	At home or beyond physical classroom space	At school or in another learning space such as a community recreation center	Wherever the student is
Goal	Facilitate learning activities that will prepare students with knowledge they need to be successful in the future as deemed by education authorities or policy leaders.	Provide students with activities to support the classroom instruction. This may include remediation or repetition activities as well as flipped learning experiences.	Provide students with enrichment or alternative learning activities that supplement in-school learning. These are often focused on particular topic areas or discrete skill development.	Provide students with learning experiences that meet their particular needs or curiosities.
Source of learning direction	Teacher-directed and -sponsored	Teacher-directed and -sponsored	Adult-directed and -sponsored	Student self-directed
Structure	Formalized structure with curriculum and standards driving learning process.	Learning activities are structured to align with classroom goals. Students may have flexibility in terms of where this happens, but often these types of learning activities have a due date for completion.	Learning activities are structured around program goals or desired student outcomes.	Informal learning structure that is set by the students themselves or by the types of learning experiences they choose.

Focus of expertise	Teacher as content and pedagogy expert.	Teacher as content and pedagogy expert.	Adult program leader as content and pedagogy leader.	Diffused levels of expertise depending on the sources that the students use for their self-directed learning.
Framework for technology use	Technology is used primarily as an engagement tool or source of content to support classroom instruction and management. In remote learning, technology serves as learning platform.	Technology is used to facilitate homework assignment completions and to facilitate communications between school and home.	Technology is used as an engagement tool and depending on the program may be used to support the program activities and goals.	Technology facilitates students' access to learning content and resources and levels the playing field for students to self-direct their own learning.
Frequency of technology use	Technology use is usually sporadic and not integrated effectively into a seamless flow of classroom or instructional activities.	Students often use technology to support homework activities even if it is not assigned as such.	Technology use frequency is dependent on the program learning activities and goals.	Technology is the foundation for the self-directed learning, and thus usage is frequent but also highly purposeful.
Value of the learning environment by educators	Highly valued as the most important learning experience.	Despite mixed research on the value of homework experiences, teachers continue to assign it and parents continue to expect homework to be assigned.	Learning experience is highly valued as a supplement to classroom instruction, not as a replacement.	Not valued as valid learning.

to point to a school or classroom setting, the first of the traditional learning environments. Education has traditionally given the classroom teacher the primary responsibility for sponsoring or facilitating learning experiences for their students. That is exactly what was happening in Chad's physics class. The teacher, probably very effectively, was teaching the key concepts of physics so that the students could successfully gain the knowledge needed, either to satisfy a graduation requirement or even to potentially enhance their ability to be successful in a college physics course. The learning experience may have included hands-on labs and engaging inquiry-based discussions to help connect the theoretical academic content to real-world situations such as recommended by the College Board.[3] The form and function of these types of experiences are what we all traditionally consider learning.

Homework

It is quite probable that Chad's physics teacher may have also assigned homework to their students to help reinforce those key learning topics and support students' remediation on some of the difficult course concepts. That homework may have included reading assigned chapters in the textbook or writing up notes from the in-class lab. Despite debates and conflicting research on the value of homework as a learning modality, most teachers continue to assign homework or out-of-school directed learning as part of their everyday instructional practice. Some teachers have taken the homework modality and flipped it so that many aspects of the traditional in-classroom learning experience such as listening to a lecture or watching a demonstration or lab happens at home with classroom time spent on more collaborative or interactive activities. This innovation, popularized by Jonathan Bergmann and Aaron Sams, is often referred to as the Flipped Classroom model of teaching and learning.[4] So, for example, using this model, a physics teacher may create a video of their lecture on thermodynamics or a demonstration of gravity at work for students to watch at home as a homework assignment, and then class time can be used to support project-based learning activities, discussions, or teacher-supported remediation work. Whether it is through traditional homework or potentially a Flipped Classroom implementation, this process of students engaging with teacher-assigned, time-specific learning content outside of the classroom represents the second traditional learning environment for students.

Extracurricular Programs

The third traditional learning environment for students is an extra-curricular program that takes place after school, on a weekend day, or during school breaks. Schools have long valued and encouraged students (and their parents) to participate in these types of extracurricular, enrichment learning opportunities and an entire sector of K–12 education is devoted to providing students with these types of out-of-school learning programs. One nonprofit organization, the Afterschool Alliance, promotes, supports, and advocates for effective out-of-school learning experiences for students.[5] Chad's teacher may have encouraged their students to participate in such extracurricular activities to help the students extend their learning such as through participation in the highly regarded PLTW (formerly known as Project Lead the Way) programs, which introduce students to STEM fields through real-world learning experiences and skill development activities.[6]

Many of the organizations or programs that support this third learning environment have evolved over time to meet the changing needs of students. For example, 4-H started as a way to provide hands-on learning experiences for students around agricultural topics. Today, the organization considers its mission to provide a wider universe of STEM learning opportunities for students through its out-of-school programming, in-school enrichment experiences, clubs, and camps including addressing computer science and coding as new focus areas.[7]

While some aspects of these types of learning experiences may certainly have elements of self-directed learning, the overall flow, content, and learning process are still primarily adult-sponsored and facilitated. Also, students need to formally join a school or community-based program to reap the benefits of these experiences. There is a planned action that is required for participation. Similarly, like school, extracurricular programs have a time and place component. The 4-H chapter meets every Saturday at 10 a.m., for example, and the learning experience happens primarily during this dedicated time period. Unlike school, which has a universality of access and compliance requirement, afterschool, Saturday, or summer programs are really only available to students who know about them and/or have the resources to participate, whether that is financial, time, or transportation. Despite all of the good work that has been done to promote and value these learning experiences, they are simply not easily available to all students.

Self-Directed, Interest-Driven Learning

Chad's pursuit of external sources of knowledge beyond his teacher is an example of the fourth environment for learning, where students pursue self-directed, interest-driven experiences to satisfy a particular learning purpose. This type of learning is not adult-sponsored, -facilitated, or -directed, but rather the impetus for this learning experience is generated by the students themselves. The students define the learning purpose for these experiences and instigate the process on their own terms and at their own discretion regarding pace and place outside of school. And their motivations are driven by an intrinsic passion to learn something that is of meaning to them.

Self-directed learning around areas of personal interest is not a new type of learning. For example, the public library system is a manifestation of people's interest in self-directed learning. Before having everyday access to learning content through one's personal smartphone, the most accessible way for anyone, formal or informal student, whether they were 8 years old or 80 years old, to pursue an interest in learning more about dinosaurs, the history of England, or even physics was to go to their local library, find a book on that subject, and check out the book with a promise to return it in two weeks, for example. We probably have all experienced this type of limited self-directed learning and benefited from the learning experience.

The limitations on this version of interest-driven learning are many, however. Did that local library have books on the topic that you were interested in learning about? And if it did, was it available for you to check out to read when you wanted to pursue that self-directed learning, or was it already being used at that time by someone else? Was the collection of books or other learning content the most appropriate for your interest or even the best representation of the content available? Those types of content vetting and curation decisions were not made by you but by someone else, most likely the librarian purchasing the books. Your access to that learning material would also be limited by the time limit set by the library for borrowing a book. Your learning time therefore would be restricted to a few days, maybe a few weeks, but not forever. The library owned the content; you were simply leasing access to it for a finite period of time. And before virtual libraries or online databases of content, you had to physically go to a library building to access the learning content. This inherently limits the access to only those people, including students, who could navigate transportation options to

11

get to the physical library location, whether that library is in your hometown or many miles away. Additionally, libraries are not usually open 24/7 to accommodate self-directed learning curiosities or even have open hours that support students. This is true of many libraries nationwide as local municipalities struggle with funding their local libraries. This is even true in the city of Philadelphia where Benjamin Franklin started the first public library. Today, for example, in West Philadelphia, one of the poorest neighborhoods in the city, the public libraries are not open on Saturday or Sunday, days that may be most convenient not only for student-age learners but also for adult learners interested in pursuing this type of self-directed learning.

Power and Technology in the Four Learning Environments

There are two additional aspects that illuminate key differences across the four domains of learning. The first has to do with power, the second with technology.

Power

Much has been discussed and written for years about the distribution of or lack of distributed power in the average classroom. Teachers are considered to exert power over students through their selections of class materials to use, the lesson plans and learning activities they implement in the classroom, and the level of student discourse and discussion that is allowed to take place. Students correspondingly exert their power by engaging or not engaging in the classroom learning activities and their responsiveness to various teaching processes.

Most recently, a common flashpoint for these power distribution conversations has been around student choice within school-based learning. From longstanding Speak Up Research, we know that a majority of students in grades 6–12 say that they like learning when they can be in control of when and how they learn.[8] The element of having a meaningful choice in the path and pace of the learning process is important to students. And yet, only one-third of middle and high school teachers say they are very comfortable providing students with choices in their learning process. The reasons that teachers give for their reluctance to embrace choice within their classroom vary. Some point to curriculum standards as the culprit. Others worry about how to logistically facilitate student choices within large class sizes without losing control of the learning process. And yet, others are even more candid and express their belief that their training and expertise makes them the best arbitrator of what constitutes effective learning and that their students simply are not equipped to make these decisions for themselves.

In the fourth learning domain, where students pursue self-directed, interest-driven learning, the power shifts explicitly from teacher or adult education guardian to the students themselves. In that learning modality, students have untethered control over the pace and path of their learning as well as the purpose. They have a level of choice and self-efficacy that is rarely available in their school-based learning, homework, or afterschool programs.

Technology

Access and use of technology in the fourth domain, self-directed learning by students, also separates this domain from the three traditional learning environments. The use of digital content, tools, and resources is very much present across all domains. This is especially true as a result of the COVID pandemic and the need to shift learning from physical classrooms to virtual classrooms. Before spring 2020, most teachers utilized technology in their classroom as primarily an engagement tool to entice students into learning, and/or sporadically to use a particular resource (such as a video, online article, or digital game) to support a lesson or unit of study. Educators have long emphasized the engagement factor when talking about the value or benefit of technology use within learning. So, for example, many teachers over the past few years have adopted easy-to-use online quiz tools to engage their students in the learning process. The inclusion of a NASA video or NPR podcast within a lesson may represent a more advanced use case than using a Kahoot quiz as a motivator. The bottom line is that only a reduced subset of teachers, across all grade levels and content areas, had been seamlessly integrating technology within their everyday curriculum after reengineering their lessons to take advantage of the best aspects of digital learning tools.

The pandemic forced not only a physical switch from physical classroom to online space, but it also repositioned technology as a learning platform for the remote lessons and class discussions. Technology now had a larger, more important function within the classroom—to ensure continuity of learning through tablet, laptop, and Chromebook screens. Consequently, teacher technology skills increased during this time with more teachers reporting greater familiarity and comfort with certain aspects of technology usage. What was unclear, however, was whether the increased use of the digital tools would be sustained in the physical classrooms and whether teachers' mindsets had been permanently changed about the value of using technology within their everyday practices. A by-product of the pandemic is certainly the increased access that students have to technology outside of school as facilitated through the distribution of digital learning devices and mobile hotspots to support Internet connectivity. Similarly, it is unclear whether that increased home access means that more teachers will be assigning digital homework now or whether extracurricular programming is now more readily available online than before.

What is different in this fourth environment, however, is that students' self-directed, interest-driven learning has long been fueled by students' personal access to online content, resources, and tools, most notably through their personal smartphone and ubiquitous Wi-Fi connectivity. Technology is the enabler for Free Agent Learning that has opened up new opportunities for more students to be like Chad and pursue academic passions on their own terms. While increased classroom access to and usage of technology is changing many aspects of the learning processes in the classroom and in extracurricular and enrichment programs outside of the classroom, it has a long way to go to catch up to the types of learning experiences that students are having on their own, where they are in control of the learning process, have unprecedented opportunities to exercise agency, and see themselves as successful learners outside of school.

Comparing the Four Learning Environments at a Glance

The contrast between the in-school learning experience and the self-directed, out-of-school experience for most students is stark. The rich learning experiences that many students are having outside of school do not resemble in any way their classroom experience, their homework-type learning, or even what they are experiencing in many afterschool programs. Free Agent Learning is fundamentally different because it places the student in charge of their own learning. That is facilitated through the effective use of a multitude of digital tools, resources, and content that the student personally identifies, vets, and curates to support their learning purposes and passions. Access to technology is the ultimate enabler for granting more students, from elementary through high school, the opportunity to be a Free Agent Learner. Free Agent Learning, however, is not limited to only the K-12 schooling years. Opportunities are expanded for all when technology is used effectively to support self-directed learning, whether that is in formal or informal education settings. Table 1.1 summarizes the four environments for student learning.

The Origins of the Student Vision for Learning

Students' experiences against all four of these environments or domains have contributed to students' aspirations for more effective learning experiences overall. In some cases, they have helped to clarify what students like about different learning modalities; in other cases, they exemplify what needs to change to best meet students' needs and preferences. Students' increased access to digital tools, content, and resources outside of school is a driving force in the expansion of self-directed learning and in the way that students want to experience learning in general. Smartphone usage by middle and high school students, including those from low-income communities, has surpassed a tipping point. With ready access to the Internet now in their pocket or backpack, it should not be surprising that students feel that they can drive their own educational destiny with a swipe, a click, or voice command. More importantly, they are demonstrating by their self-directed digital learning actions that they are indeed interested in learning about the world around them and developing the types of skills that will prepare them for future success.

From these interactions with digital content, tools, and resources for learning on their own, students have developed their own preferred vision for learning. It is not codified by the students as this Student Vision for Learning, though. You will not see students carrying banners or wearing T-shirts that give voice to their ideas on how to improve learning. But the Student Vision for Learning is embedded in the DNA of how students talk about better learning environments and most notably, how to improve school-based learning.

It is important to understand, however, that the Student Vision for Learning is not simply aspirational. It is not merely a wish list of intangible, pie-in-the-sky ideas. Rather, the students' model for how to improve learning environments is highly predicated on their own experiences with learning, both in school and on their own. These experiences have resulted in students' having deep insights about the power of collaborative learning, the immense capacity of new learning environments when they are untethered to traditional methodologies or resources, and the unparalleled relevancy of learning experiences that marry academic content with real-world context while developing greater student agency along the way. This vision is also in many ways a reflection of their discontent with their learning processes in the traditional classroom. And it is a mirror into the students' experiences with self-directed, interest-driven learning.

A key distinguishing characteristic of the Student Vision for Learning is self-determination of their personal learning pathway or process. As discussed earlier, in many ways, technology has been the fuel for enabling students to become self-directed learners. The ability to self-direct one's own learning in school is very different than when a student is at home freely engaging with learning content through the use of their smartphone or laptop and a Wi-Fi connection. In school settings, students have relatively little control or power over their learning journey or pathways.

Let us take an example from a high school English language arts class. In this class, for their capstone assignment in the study of the novel *The Great Gatsby*, students are provided with four choices: simulate an interview between the author, F. Scott Fitzgerald, and one of his characters about key lessons learned from the book's events; write a poem that describes a character, a setting, or an event in the novel; draw a map of the geographical settings for the novel's events using information provided by the author; or create a slide show with contemporary images that represent the key themes from the novel. While each option provides an alternative to the typical English class essay or book report, the students' choices are still limited

17

to what the teacher has determined as authentic representations of what constitutes knowledge about the novel, not what the students may believe is the best way for them to show what they know. And the choice of the classic Fitzgerald novel was predetermined by the teacher or the school curriculum standards, not based on student interest or preference or even on whether the story narrative is still relevant for today's students.

In a self-directed, self-determined learning experience, students have the freedom to choose not only the learning content but the best tools for facilitating that knowledge acquisition process. Additionally, the arbiter of what constitutes knowledge is viewed through the lens of the individual student and their lived experiences. For example, students are regularly watching YouTube videos to learn how to do something that interests them (47% of middle school students). Additionally, over one-quarter of middle school students (28%) have their own YouTube channel to showcase their self-created videos. For some of these students the process of video creation and posting is the end goal—to showcase a talent, a skill, interest areas, or newly acquired knowledge. For 12% of these middle school students, however, it is about getting feedback on their content from an authentic public audience. It should not be surprising therefore that 44% of students in grades 6–8 and 51% of students in grades 9–12 say they are learning valuable skills for their future through their independent, self-directed interactions using YouTube. Correspondingly, a similar percentage of middle and high school students (43%) say the skills they are learning in school are valuable for their future success. And to the dismay of many English teachers, one-third of students in grades 6–8 (37%) say they learn more from watching a video than reading a book. While this may seem counterintuitive to many, Steven Johnson in his book *Everything Bad Is Good for You* advances the idea that rather than pop culture eroding our ability to think or make good decisions, the use of video, games, and other multimedia may be strengthening our cognitive abilities.[9] History teachers in particular seem to be endorsing this same concept. In a recent study conducted by Project Tomorrow on the use of pop culture within high school history courses, 84% of teachers said that the effective use of videos and other multimedia assets was effective in stimulating more in-depth class discussions with their students.[10]

To understand the Student Vision for Learning, it is important to emphasize again that for most students today, learning is a 24/7 enterprise. The construct that learning only happens during the traditional school day is no longer valid. The majority of students in grades 3–12 have access to information and knowledge at their fingertips through a ubiquitously Internet-connected mobile device in the palm of their hand. This access has transformed the way students access information, but in addition, it has also created a new empowering ethos around learning wherein students believe they have a right and a responsibility to self-direct their own learning enterprise. At its best, a student's learning day is comprised of a seamless set of engaging educational interactions with teachers, classmates, parents, and experts, some near and some far away. Conceptually, these interactions happen both in the traditional physical worlds of classrooms, libraries, and community centers and in the virtual spaces of social media, multiplayer online games, and video content development. But the reality is that the traditional school day only encompasses a small part of the learning continuum that students experience every day. And despite well-documented calls for the need for education transformation and some highly publicized examples, the cadence and structure of most students' learning days look remarkably similar to that of their parents—with one important distinction.

The school and classroom have lost their long-held positioning as the exclusive purveyor of knowledge and even social interactions. Out of school, students are engaging with myriad informal, spontaneous, and self-directed learning experiences happening throughout the day. Increasingly, students acknowledge that these self-directed learning experiences, empowered through the use of technology, are more significant than what happens in their period 2 American history class. And despite how schools are rebranding themselves as focusing on college and career preparation, most students feel that their untethered learning that is not bound by the limits of their teachers' knowledge or the resources of their local physical community is the best way for them to be prepared for inclusion in a global society. Access to digital tools and the Internet outside of schools provide an easy and convenient way for students not only to supplement what they are learning in school but also to be able to self-direct a new, personalized learning process around areas of their own interest and address individualized purposes. In many ways, how students are utilizing mobile devices, online resources, and social media on their own to access content, to communicate and collaborate with experts, and to develop workplace skills is a truer representation of the potential of technology than what is exhibited today in many classrooms.

Studying the Evolution of the Student Vision for Learning

The examination of how students are empowering a new vision for learning through their self-directed, digital learning experiences beyond the sponsorship or facilitation of their teachers has the potential to provide significant new insights into what could be possible in our classrooms. Appreciation of these insights requires that the views of students are respected and listened to not just because of their status as technology savants but as essential stewards of their own learning innovations.

For almost twenty years, Project Tomorrow's Speak Up National Research Project has provided the nation with a unique window into how technology is currently being used (or not) to drive student achievement, teacher effectiveness, and overall educational productivity in K–12 schools. Most notably, the Speak Up findings first documented and continue to reveal each year the increasingly significant disconnect between the values and aspirations of our nation's students about how the effective use of technology can improve the learning process and student outcomes and the values and aspirations of their less technology-comfortable teachers and administrators. Students, regardless of community demographics, socioeconomic backgrounds, gender, and grade, tell us year after year that the unsophisticated use of digital tools, content, and resources in school is in fact holding back their education and in many ways disengaging them from learning. In many communities and states, this hard realization that today's classroom environment does not mirror the way today's students are accessing learning content and experiences outside of school or what they need to be well prepared to participate, thrive, and compete in a global, informative-intensive economy and society is exacerbating what many business, policy, and education leaders say is a relevancy crisis in American education.

The Speak Up findings paint a vivid picture of the ongoing disconnect between students' aspirations for learning and types of learning experiences they are having in school every day. While the Student Vision for Learning is not predicated on the use of technology exclusively, this new vision provides a solid demonstration case for how digital tools, content, and resources can help educator actors create more meaningful and appropriate learning experiences for today's students. Understanding the Student Vision for Learning is also a prerequisite for appreciating the behaviors and motivations of students as Free Agent Learners. In many ways, these Free Agent Learners, as the central characters in this book, represent a Digital Advance Team for the rest of us, rapidly assimilating and adapting the new technologies used in their personal lives to drive increased productivity in their self-directed learning.

Decomposing the Student Vision for Learning into the Four Essential Elements

Empowered with digital access to a world of information and knowledge, learning for today's students blurs the traditional boundaries of formal and informal education. Increasingly, students are tapping into the Internet and other digital resources to self-direct learning outside of school. Beyond the control of their teachers, these self-directed learning experiences are having a profound impact on students' expectations for school. This is a concept that may be new for many school and district leaders: the idea that students' out of school learning experiences—especially when those experiences are self-directed—may influence the students' hopes for in-school learning.

As an example, students who are actively engaged with creating, editing, and posting videos on YouTube as a form of self-directed learning are more likely than other students to say that having learning opportunities in school where they can use media creation tools to share content with others is important to them. This example not only underscores the importance for school and district leaders of gaining a new appreciation for this new student culture of Free Agent Learning but also of understanding that students' experiences with learning beyond the classroom is an important input to transforming our traditional education institutions to better meet the needs of today's students.

The Student Vision for Learning is predicated on students' learning experiences across all four learning environments. However, the experience that students are having outside of school, self-directing learning around areas of personal interest and purpose, is strongly evident in the four essential elements that define the Student Vision for Learning. Based on the analysis of almost 20 years of Speak Up Research, I have identified the following four components as encompassing the students' vision for a more effective learning environment:

- **Social-based learning**—students want to leverage communications and collaboration tools to create and personalize networks of experts to inform their education process and to support shared problem-solving experiences.

- **Untethered learning**—students envision learning experiences that transcend the classroom walls to expand their access to knowledge and experts so that their education is not limited by resource constraints, traditional funding streams, geography, local community assets, or even the knowledge or skills of their teachers.

- **Contextualized learning**—students desire stronger connections between academic content and real-world issues and events with a goal to drive learning productivity as well as the development of the college, career, and citizenry skills they need for future success.

- **Self-directed learning**—students believe that the types of learning experiences where they can control (at least to some degree) the *what, where, how,* and *why* of the experience will help them develop agency and efficacy as a life long learner.

Some may be surprised to not see technology use explicitly identified as a component of the Student Vision for Learning. Students see technology use with a different lens than adults. The Speak Up Research has long documented that most educators, teachers, and administrators will often cite increased student engagement as the primary benefit or outcome of digital learning, but the students' list of benefits and outcomes is very different. Students see technology as a facilitator of learning experiences that result in increased academic outcomes, development of future-ready skills, and that enables greater personalization of the learning process. Like the Student Vision itself, these views on the value of technology use in learning are based on students' lived experiences using technology for self-directed learning.

23

As will be further discussed in later chapters, students' use of technology to support Free Agent Learning is highly purposeful. Thus, students are bringing that same ethos of purpose into their vision for improved learning environments in school. For example, students are already using online and social media tools to support highly purposeful socially based learning outside of school, and so it is not necessary to call out technology use explicitly; it is already baked into the vision.

While each of the four essential elements represents some dramatically new approach to teaching and learning in a classroom setting, for the students, the incorporation of the digital tools and applications is merely a natural extension of the way they are currently living and learning outside of that classroom. This presents a unique opportunity for schools and districts. Understanding how today's students want to bring the best elements of their informal, self-directed learning into the classroom can help education leaders plan for how to fully take advantage of digital tools to support new models of learning and improve the overall learning experience for students. The key to unlock this opportunity is a long overdue realization that students' ideas on how to leverage technology within learning can provide meaningful insights for administrators and even present a clear pathway for implementation. At its core, Free Agent Learning is the closest manifestation of the Student Vision for Learning and thus worthy of further exploration, discovery, and discussion in our subsequent chapters.

Connecting the Dots

- Learning for students is a 24/7 enterprise. School is just one small part of their overall learning ecosystem.
- With self-directed learning, which takes place beyond the sponsorship or facilitation of educators, students are in control of their pace, place, and purpose of their learning.

- Technology enables and empowers students to take their educational destiny into their own hands with self-directed, interest-driven learning.

- Based upon experiences with self-directed learning, students articulate their own perspective on what constitutes effective learning today. The Student Vision for Learning encompasses four types of learning experiences: socially based learning, untethered learning, contextually rich learning, and self-directed learning.

- Free Agent Learning is an actualization of the Student Vision for Learning.

Now, Think about This!

1. Thinking about the types of learning experiences students are having in your classrooms today, how closely aligned are those instructional activities with the Student Vision for Learning? Will students recognize their vision for learning in your classrooms?

2. What obstacles or barriers prevent you and your colleagues from building learning experiences around the Student Vision for Learning?

3. What benefits or outcomes do you think are possible if learning experiences in your school, district, or community incorporated some or all of the Student Vision components?

4. What is one thing that you can do today or tomorrow to elevate awareness and appreciation for the Student Vision for Learning within your school, district, or community?

Understanding the Student Vision for Learning

Notes

1. https://www.britannica.com/science/quantum-mechanics-physics.
2. https://en.wikipedia.org/wiki/Introduction_to_Quantum_Mechanics_ (book).
3. https://apcentral.collegeboard.org/courses/ap-physics-1?course=ap-physics-1-algebra-based.
4. https://www.amazon.com/Flip-Your-Classroom-Reaching-Student/ dp/1564843157.
5. https://www.afterschoolalliance.org.
6. https://www.pltw.org.
7. https://4-h.org/about/history.
8. https://tomorrow.org/speakup/speakup_data_findings.html.
9. https://www.amazon.com/gp/product/1594481946?tag= randohouseinc18625-20.
10. https://certell.org/resources/projecttomorrow.pdf.

Chapter 2

Defining Free Agent Learnership

Free Agent Learnership is the process by which students self-direct highly personalized learning experiences outside of school around topics and subjects of strong interest or academic passion for them as independent learners and owners of their own educational destiny. Digital tools, content, and resources enable students to adopt the Free Agent Learnership mindset and related behaviors more easily and efficiently within their 24/7 universe of learning experiences. The increasingly ubiquitous access that students from kindergarten through high school have to technology potentially levels the playing field for more students to engage in self-directed, interest-driven learning outside of school and enjoy the benefits of those learning experiences. But the reality is that those advantages have not been spread equitably for all. This will be further discussed in Chapter 9 including why Free Agent Learnership is important to addressing the equity challenges in our schools and communities. Free Agent Learnership becomes a way for students, on their own, to actualize the Student Vision for Learning in their own educational life even if their school environment is slow to incorporate the essential elements of that vision.

To set the table for understanding Free Agent Learnership, in this chapter I will first leverage the Speak Up Research Project data findings to document students' increased personal access to technology. While that growth has been significant in the last few years, technology access on its own is not the instigator for the motivations or the behaviors around self-directed learning. Rather, I have identified four key attributes or characteristics of Free Agent Learnership that distinguish this new phenomenon from students' use of technology to support assigned schoolwork goals or their everyday use of digital and social media for entertainment and friend management: place independence, power ownership, purposeful technology use, and passionate motivations. To understand the relationship between these four attributes of Free Agent Learning and student motivations, I will also share key insights from several respected education frameworks and theories to provide a context for not only the appreciation of students' self-directed learning behaviors but also how those activities help students address three basic psychological human needs: autonomy, competence, and relatedness.

The Link between the Growth in Technology Usage and Free Agent Learning

Research organizations such as Project Tomorrow have long documented students' use of digital tools, content, and resources to support learning in school. The Speak Up Research Project has also reported on the longitudinal growth in students' access to technology in school and the trend lines associated with teachers' adoption of technology to support classroom instruction, partly as a result of the COVID pandemic and the sudden shift to remote, virtual learning in spring 2020. While heightened national attention was placed on the role of technology in learning during the pandemic, technology was already being widely used to support student learning in classrooms long before the sudden shift to remote learning. Two preexisting conditions had already initiated the increase in technology use within classroom learning: expanded access to digital tools in the classroom and a plethora of education technology products and content aligned to K–12 curriculum and standards. The pandemic-induced dependence on technology simply accelerated an existing trend line.

The longitudinal data findings from Speak Up illustrate the growth in technology usage over time in the classroom. For example, 35% of teachers in 2014 reported using digital games to support learning in their classroom. During the 2020–2021 school year, 6 in 10 teachers noted that digital games were now part of their instructional practice with students. And of course, the increase in the use of digital content such as online games was only possible because of the increased emphasis within K–12 districts on one-to-one programs where every student is assigned a digital learning device (tablet, laptop, Chromebook) to support classroom instruction. In 2014, only 25% of classroom teachers reported that their students were assigned a personal device to use for learning. That percentage increased to 45% during the 2017–2018 school year.

The pandemic and the need to provide learning continuity while school buildings were closed significantly accelerated the adoption of 1:1 programs in schools. Armed with federal and state funding to support remote learning, school districts bought unprecedented numbers of devices and distributed those along with mobile hotspots to their students. The most recent Speak Up findings indicate that 9 in 10 school principals now say their students each are assigned an Internet-enabled tablet, laptop, or Chromebook to use to support classroom learning activities as well as being able to use that same school-owned device at home for homework or online learning as needed.

The increased access and usage of technology in the classroom over the past few years certainly represents an impressive achievement. Many policymakers and education leaders continue to congratulate themselves on empowering the implementation of new learning models in the classroom with this sudden influx of devices and online resources in schools. Some have even gone so far as to prophesy that school transformation such as with a greater emphasis on personalized learning may be an unintended silver lining from the pandemic—that the way technology is being used today may foretell a new era in education in the future.

What most people have missed, however, is that students themselves, long before the pandemic, had already transformed their learning through the self-directed, interest-driven digital learning activities they were engaged with far beyond the classroom. Long before schools embraced 1:1 programs, students were enjoying 1:1 access to a world of learning content through their own personal smartphone in their pockets. And they were blending their own learning or creating hybrid learning environments by mixing and matching digital and traditional learning modalities to support personal goals. Despite the good intentions of school and district leaders, students were simply not waiting for schools to catch up regarding how to use technology effectively to support purposeful learning. Equipped with a very clear vision for the type of personalized learning experience that would be most meaningful and an almost ubiquitous access to the Internet, students embraced Free Agent Learning long before the pandemic and the sudden shift to digital learning. With a single-minded focus on school-based, teacher-directed learning only, most adults, however, were simply unaware of how students were driving their own learning destiny outside of school. Or they were blinded by their own preconceptions of what constituted effective learning.

And yet, several signposts were there to help educators see the reality of student technology usage. As with school technology usage, access to a digital device has been an important driver in fueling self-directed learning. The Speak Up research findings document that evolution as well. In 2011, 50% of high school students reported having a personal smartphone. By 2014, the personal smartphone access had grown to include 82% of high school students and 68% of middle school students. However, 2018 was certainly a watershed year in terms of students having their own personal smartphone that they could use for communications, information, and engagement.

Speak Up data findings from 340,927 students in grades K–12 indicate that 2018 was the first year that over 50% of students in grade 4 reported having their own iPhone or a similar always connected device. In that same year, 8 in 10 middle school students also reported being smartphone users, as did 92% of high school students.

For middle school and high school students (and increasingly elementary students) having a personal smartphone has certainly reached a tipping point, with no statistical differentiation based on community type, home poverty levels, or geography.[1] This is not to say that every student has the latest device versions from Apple or Samsung. But the important distinction is that the students universally have Internet-connected devices with a Wi-Fi connection to access a world of information and interactions with their thumbs. Since that time, these Internet-connected phones have become more and more ubiquitous in the hands of our children and youth, just as they are with adults. It was inevitable, therefore, that students would leverage this access for self-directed learning even if these devices were not allowed to be used in school. For the students, a smartphone is a digital learning device, even if their schools do not recognize it as such. The always-on, always-connected, always-available devices empower students with universal access to seek out information on a whim, pose a question to a network of experts, or share their own thinking on any topic using the hot social media tool of the day. This highly individualized experience and the convenience of the access provides a fertile field for students' self-directed learning.

But access to technology does not define or explain Free Agent Learning. While technology access certainly enables or empowers the types of self-directed, interest-driven learning activities embraced by many students today, it is more important for today's school and district leaders to look beyond the shock and awe often associated with reports on students' technology usage and to immerse themselves in understanding the *why* of Free Agent Learnership. What motivates a student, for example, to seek out information on their own, not as part of a school assignment, about the ethical implications of using horseshoe crab blood in biomedical research? Why might a student prefer to use YouTube to research future careers or college majors versus asking for help from their school guidance counselor? How can getting feedback from an online audience on their poetry help a student develop stronger writing skills? To understand the *why* of student motivation for self-directed learning, we must first identify the four key characteristics of Free Agent Learning and explore what truly differentiates Free Agent Learnership from school- or classroom-based learning.

The Four Key Attributes of Free Agent Learning

Using research conducted by Project Tomorrow since 2014 on self-directed learning preferences and activities of students in grades 6–12, I have identified four key attributes or characteristics that define Free Agent Learning. Those attributes are:

1. **Place Independence.** While traditional learning is situated typically in a physical classroom or similar formalized learning environment, Free Agent Learning activities typically take place outside of school, beyond the classroom or a traditional learning environment. Free Agent Learning is not place dependent as the traditional learning environments of school or even afterschool or summer learning programs. Free Agent Learning is quite often facilitated through online tools and resources that enable the types of untethered learning experiences valued in the Student Vision for Learning. As would be expected, students are certainly self-directing learning at home, but they are also leveraging access to technology to engage with Free Agent Learning on a city bus or subway or

at their local Starbucks or sporting event. Technology access enables the physical independence of Free Agent Learning.

Education institutions continue to prioritize place-dependent learning in physical classrooms over virtual learning, despite evidence that the online learning experience is beneficial for some students. This preoccupation with the physical confines of learning environments blinds many educators to the value associated with Free Agent Learning that is not bound by the same institutional structures or boundaries. Though students have always self-directed learning within the traditional school confines (whether that was known by their teachers or not), most Free Agent Learning takes place outside of school when the student has maximum control over when, where, and how they learn without bell schedules or assigned class periods getting in the way.

2. **Power Ownership.** The Free Agent Learning activities are wholly self-directed by the student and are not driven or sponsored by a teacher or another adult in the student's learning life. The student is in the power pole position within the learning experience. This differs significantly from a traditional classroom setting. Traditional learning environments such as classrooms are steeped in an imbalance of power. Teachers are viewed as the experts in content, students as the empty vessels to be filled or completed by that knowledge. Teachers direct the time and place of learning experiences. Students are traditionally provided with only minimal voice or choice in the what/why/who/when of their learning activities. The assessment of the value or outcome of the learning experience is managed by the teacher or school administration based on their perceptions of what is meaningful achievement or the curriculum standards driving the learning process.

With Free Agent Learning, the table is flipped and students have the essential power or capacity to define all aspects of the learning experience, from the impetus for the learning to the assessment of the value of that experience. The students' use of their own personal technology tools further supports the power ownership shift in Free Agent Learning.

3. **Purposeful Technology Usage.** The use of digital tools, content, and resources to support Free Agent Learning is highly purposeful to effectively support the personalized learning goals of the student. Many researchers have documented how students and youth are using online and social media tools to engage with others, cultivate friendships, or seek identity. While those are meaningful uses of technology, the Free Agent Learning experience is focused on how technology supports self-directed learning specifically. Additionally, while many educators continue to leverage technology as a tool to promote student engagement in classroom learning, the Free Agent Learner is not employing digital tools for mere engagement within their learning experiences. Rather, the selection of the digital tools is artfully matched to the intended learning goals. For example, students say that the best tool for communication with their classmates and their teachers is their personal smartphone, most notably through text messaging. The convenience factor and the natural two-way communications support the utility aspect of the technology usage. Students' deep familiarity and appreciation for the best-use cases for technology support the purposeful usage attribute as well with Free Agent Learning.

4. **Passionate Motivations.** The fourth defining attribute of a Free Agent Learner is the intrinsic passion, drive, or motivation that is propelling students to tap into a wide range of digital tools to support their learning goals beyond the sponsorship

of their teachers. Despite the cynical views of some, most students are very interested in learning, and they are passionate about exploring the world around them and preparing themselves for future success. Too often those goals, however, are not met in their traditional school environments. Nonetheless, the pull for learning is strong enough that it is motivating students to seek out learning experiences on their own to meet their personally curated set of academic aspirations.

Unlike the passivity of many school-based experiences with the typical overdependence on telling rather than doing within instruction, the Free Agent Learning experience requires students to be actively driving their own learning destiny, seeking out the right online tools, websites, social media forums, and resources to meet their own needs. Driven by their passions, students are serving as their own personal librarian or information sherpa vetting and curating a collection of resources to meet their particular learning needs. The time and effort involved in that work demonstrates the powerful pull of the motivations.

Based on the research, four primary motivating factors drive the Free Agent Learning activities for most students:

- Self-remediation: Students are interested in improving their academic performance in class and have identified areas for self-remediation.

- Skill development: Students want to develop skills to support their current learning processes or to prepare them effectively for the future.

- Curiosity: Students have an innate inquisitiveness about a topic and want to learn more for the simple joy of learning.

- Career exploration and preparation: Students are driven to explore careers or investigate what they need to know to be well prepared for a future career.

The Free Agent Learner, therefore, is a student who is driven by a passion to learn and has the ability and agency to tap into a variety of digital tools, content, and resources purposely to self-direct independent learning outside of school on their own terms to accomplish specific learning goals. Free Agent Learnership is defined by place independence, a new power dynamic that prioritizes the student, and a more enlightened use of technology that is highly purposeful, and it is driven by strong motivations or passions for learning.

Humans are naturally curious beings, interested in learning more about the world around them. Thus, it should not be surprising to education leaders that students are involved with a fluid set of learning experiences throughout every day. For today's students, learning is a 24/7 enterprise with the depth and breadth of that enterprise being powered by technology. Learning in school is only a small part of that ubiquitous learning environment for most students. Additionally, students may flow in and out of Free Agent Learning activities depending on their needs, their physical locations, and the amount of agency they have at any given time to self-direct learning. In that sense, the frequency of Free Agent Learnership is less important than the reasons why students value these types of experiences over traditional classroom practices.

Understanding the *why* of Free Agent Learnership can help school and district leaders think about new ways to improve or enhance the value of classroom learning for all of their students. By understanding that learning and curiosity are inherent characteristics in children (and, in fact, all human beings) and core to their emotional and academic development, education leaders can gain a new appreciation for how all students have the potential to become Free Agent Learners, and why those self-directed, interest-driven learning experiences may be highly valuable learning experiences for all students.

Education Frameworks for Understanding the Motivations of Free Agent Learnership

In contrast to the use of technology in adult-sponsored learning spaces, within Free Agent Learnership both learning content and modality are inherently student initiated and directed. The increasingly ubiquitous availability and access of new online digital media tools for students is the fuel that is enabling this new learning paradigm, but the motivation behind these self-directed learning behaviors is more complicated. While many researchers have examined the *what*, *where*, and *how* of student use of technology outside of school, few before now have tackled students' motivations (the *why*) for using digital tools to support their interest-driven learning experiences outside of school settings.

I have identified several educational frameworks or theories that can provide a beginning point for understanding the motivations of Free Agent Learners. Most notable within this collection of frameworks and theories is self-determination theory, which provides a foundation for understanding how Free Agent Learning may help students address the basic human psychological needs of autonomy, competence, and relatedness through their self-directed learning behaviors. A brief review of the literature supporting these frameworks or theories is helpful for the context of the discussion. To set the environment for discussing those frameworks, a review of the differences between extrinsic and intrinsic motivations in education is valuable first.

Common wisdom says that students should always be intrinsically motivated to engage with learning activities. In other words, they should participate in learning activities or perform an academic task because it is personally rewarding to them, and they appreciate the value of that experience for themselves. Think about the student you know who goes far and beyond expectations with a particular assignment because they are so personally invested in learning more about that topic or subject area. Their motivation is not dependent on getting a good grade or passing a test. They are deeply engaged in that learning activity because the process of learning matters to them personally. That student is demonstrating intrinsic (from within) motivation for the particular learning activity.

However, too often, what we aspire to with our students is not aligned with actual classroom practices. Many aspects of our traditional learning processes and everyday classroom management practices are grounded in extrinsic motivations that connect completing an academic task or exhibiting certain appropriate behaviors with rewards or punishments. Grades, bonus points for early work completion, and student of the week recognitions are positive extrinsic motivations; detention, loss of classroom privileges, or public embarrassment are examples of negative extrinsic motivations. Intrinsic motivations come from within—extrinsic motivations come from outside.

Researchers have hypothesized that the sustainability of student engagement and motivation in learning is more dependent on intrinsic motivations.[2] Helping students develop a love of reading as a lifelong learning skill by providing students with a classroom library of diverse books and literature to meet individual students' interests (supporting intrinsic motivation development) may, therefore, be more valuable than publicly reporting and rewarding the students that read the most book pages per week (public praise or shame as the extrinsic motivation). Parents and district administrators report on the Speak Up surveys that students learning how to self-direct their learning and having the motivation to do that effectively are important skills for future success. But teaching those skills explicitly can be challenging. It may be that the pathway to better supporting students' development of an internal motivation for self-directed learning is to balance the use of intrinsic and extrinsic motivations in classroom-based learning. And to appreciate that when students are engaged in self-directed, interest-driven learning outside of school such as through Free Agent Learning, they are exercising the muscles that support and nurture intrinsic motivation.

As discussed in Chapter 1, student self-directed, interest-driven learning is propelled by an intrinsic desire by students to have greater control over their learning processes. As published by Richard Ryan and Edward Deci in 1985, the theoretical framework of self-determination theory (SDT) establishes a context for understanding student motivation and the importance of motivation and engagement in the learning process. The goal of the original SDT framework was to displace the dominant belief of the time that reinforcing behaviors with rewards was the best way to motivate human behavior. Rather, Ryan and Deci hypothesized that establishing intrinsic goals is directly linked to the satisfaction of three basic psychological human needs: autonomy, competence, and relatedness.[3] Consequently, the original framework has been expanded to include other aspects and mini-theories around intrinsic/extrinsic motivations with applications across a broad spectrum of human conditions and environments, including education. The three basic psychological human needs are defined as follows:[4]

- **Autonomy: A Sense of Choice and Endorsement in a Task**—Autonomy is based on the understanding that people are empowered when they feel a sense of choice and endorsement in a task—their actions are volitional. Deci and Ryan distinguish between autonomy and independence, whereby individuals act volitionally with a sense of choice, whereas those who are independent prefer to work alone. Autonomous individuals can choose to work alone or can rely on others yet still gain a sense of intrinsic motivation from engaging in tasks.

- **Competence: The Experience of Mastery Over a Task or Particular Domain** —The concept of competence originates from the idea that individuals seek to control outcomes, and this control allows them to experience mastery over a task or particular domain. In one of Deci's studies, he examined the importance of competence and feedback. When individuals were given positive feedback that was unexpected, this increased their intrinsic motivation to complete the task.

- **Relatedness: Social Connections and a High Concern for Others**—Individuals are social animals and have a need to interact with other human beings. This sense of relatedness is demonstrated through social connections and a high concern for others through caring. SDT posits that relatedness is important for individuals and is linked to intrinsic motivation. A study by Wendy Grolnick and Richard Ryan discovered that children who found their teachers to be cold and uncaring were less intrinsically motivated because the teachers did not fulfill their needs of relatedness.[5]

Additionally, the work of Daniel Pink and Tony Wagner has strong resonance as they reposition elements of SDT within the specific context of motivation, student learning, and preparation for post-school success. Discussions around the relationships between motivation, student learning, and preparation for post-school success are of high interest among education and policy leaders today as the implementations of Common Core State Standards and other state standards that put an emphasis on college and career readiness mature and evolve.

Self-Determination Theory Extensions into Education

While not ostensibly designed to explain educational outcomes, many researchers have adapted SDT to support theories and discussions around the relationship between academic achievement, motivation, engagement, and different types of learning environments, including informal spaces.

SDT and the key components of autonomy, relatedness, and competency provide a plausible starting point for understanding the benefits of motivating students with intrinsic rather than extrinsic goals. However, it can also be applied to exploring the role of technology in supporting students' intrinsic goals for academic success. The potential for digital tools and resources to support students' abilities to self-direct their own learning based upon personal interest choices (*autonomy*), to enable social learning environments that support connections and relationships (*relatedness*), and to establish personalized strategies that drive self-efficacy and agency as a learner (*competence*) are important considerations for education leaders today.

Autonomy

Monique Boekaerts and Alexander Minnaert, in their research on formal and informal learning environments, point out that in most school environments, the learning process for students is in service to teacher goals, not student self-initiated motivations.[6] The *autonomy* component of SDT relies heavily on students having a choice in how, when, and where they learn. Researchers acknowledge that many students set different goals for themselves in informal settings compared to the traditional, formal school environment. This is very interesting in light of the recent experiments with remote and virtual learning precipitated in schools. Some students appeared to flourish

41

Defining Free Agent Learnership

Table 2.1 Students' views on the benefits of virtual learning (2020–2021 school year).

Benefits of virtual learning	Grade 6–12 students in fully virtual learning environments	Grade 6–12 students in fully face-to-face learning environments
	% of students who agreed with these benefits	
Can learn at your own pace	63	64
Less school drama	63	63
Can develop technology skills	57	53
Learn to be responsible for your own learning	49	54
Easier to review class materials whenever you wanted	40	37

© Project Tomorrow 2021.

with the greater autonomy in virtual learning, while others did not. When asked about the positives of virtual learning, nearly two-thirds of students in grades 6–12 said a key benefit was being able to learn at their own pace (see Table 2.1). This was true even for students not engaged in virtual learning during the 2020–2021 school year. Approximately 50% of the students from both classroom models reported that they had to learn to be more responsible for their own learning as a result of the virtual school format.

However, it is also well documented that virtual learning is not a positive learning experience for all students. In fact, education leaders involved with the establishment and management of virtual schools have long realized that reality. Unfortunately, in the quest to provide continuity of learning at any cost during the COVID pandemic, districts had to leap into virtual learning even though many did not have a solid foundation either on the types of students best served in that environment, how to acclimate their students to a virtual learning environment, or even best practices for effective online teaching and learning. For those schools and districts that had embraced virtual learning as an alternative for students before the pandemic, they had a leg up in terms of strategies and practices to support effective implementation. For example, school district leaders in the upper Midwest and Northern Rocky Mountain states shared with me that due to the prevalence of inclement weather in the winter months, they had policies and procedures in place to switch quickly to virtual learning when it became impossible for their students to get to physical school buildings. They relied on those preexisting practices when it became necessary for them to close their school buildings due to the pandemic. For the majority of districts, however, virtual learning was a thoroughly new experiment. It is, therefore, shortsighted to assume that the implementations of fully online learning during the pandemic in most districts represents the best-of-breed cases. School and district leaders are realizing that now as they implement new virtual academies for students who did flourish in that environment and want to continue learning using that modality.

An emerging outcome from the virtual learning experiment was that in many cases our schools are not effectively preparing students to be self-directed, independent learners. The pandemic-induced shift to remote learning exposed that reality also. The shift was more than just moving from the physical classroom to a Zoom meeting platform. Additionally, many teachers who may have been highly effective in classroom engagement and inquiry-based teaching practices adopted new practices that focused more on independent student work. Unfortunately, many students were not prepared for that shift either and did not have the skills necessary to self-motivate and engage in that high degree of independent learning. The change in the structure of the learning process also resulted in a decline in the types of extrinsic motivations that many students relied upon, including positive teacher feedback, grades that counted, and social interactions with classmates. The impact was the development of a cohort of students in our schools that were functionally rudderless, lacking skills and motivation for this new learning environment. As one high school student told me in spring 2021, "I don't know how to learn without my teacher telling me what to do."

While it may be easy to villainize remote learning as the culprit, a key takeaway should be that we need to rethink how we are preparing our students to be self-directed learners and how educators can help students develop those essential college and workforce skills as well. Certainly, more research is needed to understand what types of different environments are best for individualized students, which environments inherently support SDT and the development of intrinsic motivations, and what teachers and schools need to do to help students develop the skills of self-learning. Our examination of how some students are optimizing autonomy as a motivation for their self-directed, interest-driven learning without the explicit direction of teachers, or the extrinsic motivators of traditional school, is a valuable input into this discussion.

Relatedness

Andrew J. Martin and Martin Dowson study the role of interpersonal relationships in students' academic motivation, engagement, and achievement. Their work helps us understand how relatedness, another foundation block of SDT, is a fundamental ingredient of student motivation in learning. Martin and Dowson postulate that when students feel a connection or sense of *relatedness* to peers and teachers, they are more likely to take on tougher academic challenges, set positive goals for their achievement, and establish high expectations for themselves, thus extending the learning beyond the initial goals.[7] Again, the impact of the COVID pandemic on student learning over the past few years provides new insights for understanding the importance of relatedness in education. In particular, many educators are concerned about the mental, social, and emotional health of their students and what that health profile means for student learning today and tomorrow. When asked during the 2020–2021 school year to identify the top issues that were "waking them up in the middle of the night," 58% of school principals identified mental health supports and the social and emotional well-being of their students as a top concern. To address that concern, two-thirds of principals also report that they have implemented a formal social-emotional learning program at their schools and they are seeing positive results from that program implementation.

Relatedness as a student motivator is inherent in the Student Vision for Learning component of social-based learning. Students have long valued the idea of peer-to-peer learning and collaborative learning with other students, their teachers, and experts on a grander scale than their classroom. They emphasize that while many collaborative projects in schools are not necessarily well designed, they do provide the students with opportunities to learn new skills around shared problem-solving and decision-making. Interestingly, students also say that their teachers are not assessing collaborative projects effectively or appropriately. The students believe that the assessment of the value of the project should be based on how the students interact with each other, the ways they distribute the project tasks among themselves, and the strategies used to create consensus around project deliverables. However, the students note that most teachers assign a grade to the project based on their analysis of the final project deliverable, not the process of creating that deliverable. Reflecting a keen understanding of the value of relatedness as a motivator, the students would like project assessment to be based on the interrelationships within the project group and the decisions that were derived from that relatedness, not just if the final project met the rubric in terms of number of pages, slides, or primary sources. This

Defining Free Agent Learnership

focus on how people work together is also evident in the competitive multiplayer game play that is increasingly being popularized as esports (electronic sports, a form of competition using video games), a long standing Free Agent Learning activity.

Competence

Eric Toshalis and Michael J. Nakkula built on the findings of their colleagues and introduced self-regulation theory into the discussion by examining how students sustain their engagement in learning beyond the initial goals.[8] For this research team, a student's ability to identify and implement specific strategies that support their academic learning process is the key to successful self-regulation. With an explicit recognition that students are the primary agents of their own learning, they surmise that self-regulation (the ability to sustain the motivation and engagement) is best served when students feel a sense of *competency* (another building block of SDT) in a specific domain, field of study, or task endeavor.

Throughout the nearly 20 years of research through the Speak Up Project, a reoccurring theme has been the value that students place on developing technological competency through the effective use of digital tools and resources, both in the classroom and on their own through their self-directed learning. As noted in Table 2.1, students identified stronger technology skills as a side benefit of their virtual learning experience. In my focus groups and interviews with students during school closures, many noted that they were developing important technology skills that would help them be more successful in college and their future workplace. And they noted that without this virtual learning experience, they may not have developed those essential skills.

The competency component of SDT also relates to students' developing a greater sense of confidence and self-efficacy as a learner. In 2018, the Speak Up Research Project polled students about their use of YouTube in their personal lives. Contrary to the popular perceptions, students' use of YouTube far extends beyond simply watching videos. Our research shows that many students are actively engaged with creating their own interest-driven YouTube content, curating the content, and then remixing and repurposing that content for specific audiences. A quarter of high school students at that time had their own YouTube channel; 6% were running a for-profit business through that channel.

All of these activities represent Free Agent Learning pursuits that meet the four key attributes or characteristics discussed earlier in this chapter. As a by-product of these activities, the students are developing skills and competencies they believe are essential for their future success. In fact, the students actually prioritize the skills they are developing through their interactions on YouTube as more valuable than what they are learning in school. While 41% of high school students say that the skills they are learning in school are important for their future, 51% say that the skills and competencies they are developing through their YouTube interactions are valuable for their future success. Students' feelings of competency, a key component of SDT, is well-represented in their Free Agent Learning activities. The question is how to ensure that our students are developing similar feelings of competence in what they are engaged with in school.

Connections to Free Agent Learning: Other Theories on Motivation

The application of Daniel Pink's theories on motivation helps us understand why students may be interested or motivated to pursue Free Agent Learning outside of school. It is human nature to be curious. Acting upon that curiosity requires a level of self-directedness and individual initiative in most cases. A student may learn in class that emergency medicine, for example, was a by-product of how medical professionals learned to deal with trauma during the Civil War. However, if that student is curious about the types of traumatic injuries experienced in the battlefield or the products that were invented to support surgery under battlefield conditions, they may need to explore those topics on their own if they are beyond the scope of the class curriculum. The ability of the student to find appropriate and accurate information, resources, and experts on this topic requires self-directed learning that is individually sponsored. The learner in this case is satisfying a desire for autonomy in the learning process.

Taken to the next step, Pink also proffers that engagement in an activity such as learning is part of the process of developing mastery or competence, an important component of self-efficacy.[9] Like Carol Dweck's work on growth mindset, Pink sees mastery as a specific mindset or way of thinking about one's abilities to learn. While autonomy and mastery are important components of motivation, the fuel that drives the engine for personal motivation is purpose. Similarly, Tony Wagner also identifies purpose or the identification of intrinsic goals as a key component to understand how today's students are motivated differently, especially as it relates to school-centric learning and pursuing self-directed learning beyond the classroom.

Wagner's work on the ineffectiveness of traditional education to support the development of creative problem-solving and innovative thinking skills is helpful to set additional context around self-directed learning, and potentially, the role of digital tools in that pursuit. At the heart of his argument is that traditional school environments are not focused on the skills that students need to be successful in the future, his "seven survival skills."[10] The traditional classroom rewards individual achievement rather than the success of collaborative efforts, is organized around communicating specific subject content rather than exploratory learning skills, and relies upon extrinsic motivations such as grades and test scores rather than the intrinsic motivators such as play, passion, and purpose. This environment stands in stark contrast to how today's students, whom Wagner calls the Innovation Generation, want to experience learning.[11] Reminiscent of the results from earlier studies, Wagner says that students want to learn through connections with others, self-directed discoveries, and creation of content or different ways to display their knowledge or skills.

Wagner's interpretation of what students want from their learning experiences is aligned with the four components of the Student Vision for Learning as described in Chapter 1—socially based learning experiences, learning that is untethered from traditionally limited resources, contextually rich experiences, and opportunities to self-direct the learning process. Wagner believes these types of learning experiences allow students to become not just self-directed learners but effective innovators armed with the requisite skills to be successful in a global, information-intensive society. Whereas Pink provides the context for understanding how SDT drives personal motivation, Wagner establishes the importance of the development of these self-directed skills for future success. Both are critical inputs for our further discussions on Free Agent Learnership and its connections to in-school learning.

Clayton Christensen, Michael B. Horn, and Curtis W. Johnson in their second edition of *Disrupting Class: How Disruptive Innovation Will Change the Way the World Learns* provide valuable insights on how the structure of school itself maybe de-motivating for some students.[12] Their approach is to examine the student motivation for learning through the lens of the "job to be done" in education. I have long noted in my reports, articles, and conference presentations that today's students like learning but do not necessarily like what they are learning in school. There is an important distinction here. Christensen, Horn, and Johnson make a similar point in that "teachers and parents offer education, but many students are not buying what is offered." It really comes down to understanding the job of education and how students and educators approach that job very differently. For example, Christensen et al. note that for many teachers they see the delivery of education as their objective or final product; in other words, their job is the delivery process. Students, however, see their job as twofold: feeling successful and having fun with their friends. Not only is there little synergy between the students' jobs and the teachers' job, but the students also have many other external opportunities to accomplish their job going to school or being engaged in classroom learning.

The aspect of school as the social hub of students' lives today is a myth that many educators are holding onto but is no longer true. When asked to identify the downsides or challenges with virtual learning during the pandemic, 90% of school principals cited that their students missed the social aspects of school. And yet, while two-thirds of high school students (69%) also noted that they missed their school-based social life during remote learning, 31% did not. As one high school student explained to me, "I don't need to go to school to have a social life. I am interacting with my friends all of the time online." The days of needing to meet up at your locker to make plans for Friday night are truly in the past.

Besides not having the monopoly on students' social planning, schools are not necessarily helping students feel accomplished or successful, the other job that motivates students to be engaged with school. The extrinsic motivations of grades, report cards, and academic recognitions only work for the highest achieving students in terms of sustaining their preexisting feelings of personal success. And the types of extracurricular activities that other students point to as motivators are not always available or convenient for all students. For too many students, school is not helping them develop the intrinsic motivations for feeling successful as identified with SDT, namely autonomy, relatedness, and competency. School as it exists today is simply not helping many students do the job they need to do. Rather, many students are "hiring" Free Agent Learning as a viable vehicle not only for feeling successful and engaging with friends but also to develop greater self-efficacy as a learner through the motivating factors of autonomy, relatedness, and competency.

Our understanding of Free Agent Learnership starts with appreciating that students want learning experiences that support the satisfaction of three basic psychological needs—autonomy, competence, and relatedness—and that in too many ways, the traditional school environment is not meeting their needs in terms of helping them develop intrinsic motivations for learning. But by understanding what motivates students today and how Free Agent Learning experiences are satisfying that motivation urge, school and district leaders have the opportunity to not only rethink and reimagine the job of school but find new ways to engage students in meaningful learning experiences that address the Student Vision for Learning components.

Connecting the Dots

- Free Agent Learnership is the process by which students self-direct highly personalized learning experiences outside of school around topics and subjects of strong interest or academic passion for them as independent learners and owners of their own educational destiny.

- Free Agent Learning by students is distinguished by four key characteristics:

  - Place independence;

  - Power ownership;

  - Purposeful technology use; and

  - Passionate motivations.

- Based on research findings about students' Free Agent Learning activities, the following four motivations are the most popular: self-remediation, skill development, curiosity, and career exploration and preparation.

- Several educational theories and frameworks support the valuation of Free Agent Learning as a positive experience for students. Those theories and frameworks include the following:
  - SDT, which prioritizes autonomy, competence, and relatedness as critical for self-efficacy;
  - Daniel Pink's insights on intrinsic and extrinsic motivations;
  - Tony Wagner's work on how self-directed learning is a positive response to the lack of career or skill preparation in traditional learning settings; and
  - The Christensen Institute's "job to be done" philosophy and how the job of school is different depending on the point of view of the educator or the student.

Now, Think about This!

1. How are students in your school, district, or community practicing Free Agent Learnership?

2. Are your teachers and administrators aware of the Free Agent Learning activities of their students? If not, why not? If yes, then how are they valuing those experiences?

3. What will be the potential pushback from educators and other adults about the value of understanding students' Free Agent Learning experiences outside of school?

4. What is one thing that you can do today or tomorrow to increase your colleagues' awareness level and valuation of students' Free Agent Learning experiences?

Notes

1. For more information about the Speak Up Research, please visit https://tomorrow.org/Speakup/speakup_data_findings.html.
2. https://www.verywellmind.com/differences-between-extrinsic-and-intrinsic-motivation-2795384.
3. https://selfdeterminationtheory.org/SDT/documents/2000_RyanDeci_SDT.pdf.
4. Extracted from https://www.ckju.net/en/dossier/why-basic-psychological-needs-autonomy-competence-and-relatedness-matter-management-and-beyond.
5. https://psycnet.apa.org/record/1989-34682-001.
6. https://www.researchgate.net/publication/222933832_Self-regulation_with_respect_to_informal_learning.
7. https://journals.sagepub.com/doi/10.3102/0034654308325583.
8. https://www.howyouthlearn.org/pdf/Motivation%20Engagement%20Student%20Voice_0.pdf.
9. https://www.danpink.com/books/drive.
10. https://www.tonywagner.com/the-global-achievement-gap.
11. https://www.tonywagner.com/creating-innovators.
12. https://claytonchristensen.com/books/disrupting-class.

Chapter 3

Motivations for Free Agent Learner Behaviors

It would be easy to assume that students' motivations for Free Agent Learning are all about the technology usage. And it would be easy even to think that this phenomenon of how students are self-directing learning beyond school sponsorship is merely a justification and/or validation for the value of digital tools and resources used by students. However, a deeper analysis of the motivations of Free Agent Learners provides evidence that the defining characteristic of who qualifies as a Free Agent Learner is not based on frequency or regularity of the behavior, or the sophistication of the digital tools used, but rather that the self-directed, interest-driven learning is purposeful and serves to satisfy students' needs for realizing autonomy, competence, and relatedness in their out-of-school learning lives.

In my description of who is a Free Agent Learner in Chapter 2, I identified four key attributes or characteristics that distinguish the types of self-directed, interest-driven learning that students are engaging with outside of school. Those four attributes or characteristics include: place independence, power ownership, purposeful technology usage, and passionate motivations. This chapter will focus on the fourth of these characteristics, the intrinsic passions, drives, or motivations that are propelling students to tap into a wide range of digital tools to support their learning goals on their own beyond the sponsorship of their teachers.

Gaining Insight into Four Primary Motivating Factors

Based on a comprehensive analysis of both the quantitative and qualitative data results from Project Tomorrow's Speak Up Research Project, four primary motivating factors have emerged to explain the passions that drive Free Agent Learning activities for most students:

- **Self-remediation:** Students are interested in improving their academic performance in school and identify specific areas for self-remediation;

- **Skill development:** Students want to develop skills to support their current learning processes or to prepare them effectively for the future;

- **Curiosity:** Students have an innate inquisitiveness about a topic and want to learn more for the simple joy of learning and acquiring knowledge; and

- **Career exploration and preparation:** Students are driven to explore careers or investigate what they need to know to be well-prepared for a future job or post-graduation pursuit, including college and the military.

The most effective way to understand how students are translating these motivations into self-directed learning actions is to listen directly to the voices of students about their Free Agent Learning behaviors. In addition to the quantitative questions that ask students about the frequency of their Free Agent Learning activities, the Speak Up surveys also periodically ask students to share their personal Free Agent Learner story in an open-ended narrative response. Here is the open-ended question that was asked on the Speak Up surveys during the 2020–2021 school year:

We want to learn more about how you are self-directing your learning using digital, online, or social media tools. Your insights are important to us—thanks for sharing!

- *What topics or subjects are you learning about outside of school using technology?*
- *Why is that topic or subject interesting for you?*
- *How do these technology tools help you develop new skills or acquire new knowledge?*

The students' narrative text responses, sometimes a sentence or two, other times a paragraph or more, provide rich insights into not only what students are doing outside of school to support self-directed learning but also their motivations for those activities and behaviors. And those narrative responses provide school and district leaders with an unprecedented glimpse into the out-of-school lived experiences of their students. As will be further discussed, the self-directed learning experiences that students are having beyond the classroom, especially those using digital tools and resources, influence students' impressions and expectations for the type of learning experiences they want to have in school.

While it may be customary for some adults to assume that students' technology use, especially with social media, may be trivial and noneducational, they are missing the bigger picture with that erroneous assumption. Students are taking control of their educational destiny through these Free Agent Learning activities both because school in its traditional sense is not meeting their learning needs or goals and because those learning needs and goals may be best served through the students' own self-directed learning paths. The students' first-person narrative responses provide a unique opportunity for school and district leaders to gain a greater comprehension of Free Agent Learning and understand how these lived experiences could be a valuable input into school improvement planning. But to fully grasp the depth and breadth of the student experience requires leaders to suspend long-held assumptions about the purposes of school or reserve judgment about the tools students are using to pursue knowledge and skill development on their own.

To help support that mindset change, each of the four primary Free Agent Learning passionate motivations (self-remediation, skill development, curiosity, and career exploration) are more fully explained in this chapter. Each dedicated section includes a description of the passionate motivation, a dissection of a particular sample quote, and a representative collection of additional sample student responses. The dissection analysis examines a variety of aspects of the Free Agent Learning behavior: motivation, digital tool employed, frequency of experience, and the element of self-determination theory (SDT; see Chapter 2) that is being amplified through the students' activities (competence, relatedness, autonomy). The representative collection of student quotes were taken from the hundreds of thousands of narrative responses provided by students since 2014 to the survey prompt about their Free Agent Learning activities. The purpose behind providing this curated collection is to help education leaders realize the multitude of different ways that students are leveraging their access to digital tools outside of school to support self-directed, interest-driven learning and to further substantiate that this learning modality is not a one-size-fits-all. Nor does it easily fit into a typical learning framework. Rather, the high degree of personalization of this learning process that students are leading for themselves is again an actuation of the Student Vision for Learning covered in Chapter 1. The collection of quotes is meant to enlighten and educate school and district leaders about the reasons students are purposefully self-directing their own learning.

But the quotes are also meant to inspire you to go beyond this chapter and this book and ask your students directly to share their lived experiences with you as well. New ideas on how to engage with your students to learn about their Free Agent Learning activities is provided in Chapter 10. To provide additional context to the quotes, I have included some metadata with each student response: self-identification of gender (girl, boy, non-binary, decline to state), grade level, community type (urban, rural, or suburban), and state location. The quotes are also provided here exactly as they were input by the students without any corrections for grammar, spelling, or clarity.

Passionate Motivation: Self-Remediation

My physics teacher this year didn't do a great job explaining half of our units, so to help me understand I watched hours of Khan Academy videos. Khan Academy videos for physics and calculus were extremely helpful in allowing me to understand the topic at hand. I would take hand written notes when watching the Khan academy videos so I can review the information later.

Boy/Grade 12/Suburban Community/California

The self-remediation category represents students' attempts outside of school to address what they perceive as weaknesses or deficiencies in what or how they are learning in school or to provide themselves with additional support in an academic topic where they would like to be more proficient. Recognizing this personal need propels the students to utilize a variety of digital tools to which they have access to self-remediate their perceived academic deficiency or weakness. The types of activities included within this category of self-remediation included specific references to needs for greater competence where students feel either a lack of understanding or a need to be taught in a different manner than their school experiences. For example, student responses frequently reference a need to improve their math knowledge or skills, a need to improve their grades in math, and a need to experience a different teaching and learning modality to gain greater competence, again quite often in math, specifically.

When I am confused on something we did in math I usually use youtube to search a video on how to solve that math problem, which actually really helps.

Girl/Grade 8/Rural Community/North Carolina

In most cases, the responses indicate how a self-directed approach to gaining this greater competence is preferred, or the student believes that this approach will yield a more successful outcome than traditional classroom learning. While the students describe using a variety of digital tools to support self-remediation, the most frequently noted tools are videos and websites, quite often in combination with each other. In my analysis of the students' qualitative responses (coded for specific motivations), the self-remediation motivation was the most frequently cited driver by both middle school and high school students for propelling their Free Agent Learning behaviors. This is not surprising given that 81% of middle and high school students say that school is important for their future. Students want to be successful in school. And they often have a better grasp of their own academic weaknesses than their teachers. Armed with a plethora of readily accessible online resources and tools to support their personal brand of just-in-time tutoring, the students feel compelled to take matters into their own hands and develop self-initiated learning paths to support their own learning needs. The self-remediation motivation is also a reflection of the student belief that they need to be responsible for their own learning destiny, that leaving their education outcomes to the variances of the school structure is too risky. The following example provides additional insight into not only the motivating factors behind the self-remediation activity but also the tools used and the rationale as to why the Free Agent Learning modality is more significant for this student, including how the activity supports the components of SDT.

Free Agent Learning Experiences to Support Self-Remediation

I often use khan academy when I don't understand my algebra 1-2 class. Doing the questions instead of just writing notes verbatim helps me in ways that a traditional classroom could not.

Girl/Grade 7/Urban Community/Arizona

As articulated by this 7th grade student from an urban community, the purpose of her self-directed learning is to address her lack of understanding of content in her algebra class. In my interpretation of the purposes identified by students, this one qualifies as an example of self-remediation. To address the need that she has to gain a better understanding of some algebra concepts, she says that she often (*the indicator of frequency*) uses Khan Academy (*the digital tool, an online repository of videos demonstrating different ways to solve math problems*) to acquire that needed understanding. Additionally, she points out that the learning experience acquired through the watching of the videos (*the learning behavior*) helps her learn in a different way from her classroom experience (*satisfies need for competence*). The impetus for her self-directed learning behavior, the choice of the digital tool, the frequency of the behavior, and the resulting satisfaction of a basic psychological need is all driven by her central purpose to gain a better understanding of algebra.

The following collection of additional student responses illustrate how middle school and high school students are both articulating the need for competence and addressing it through self-directed, self-remediating approaches that leverage the identified digital tools.

I'm very interested in chemistry and physics and instead of learning the same lesson that has been taught since the 90's, I've been teaching myself by reading papers I find online, watching videos, going on free online textbooks, and having online discussions with other students and experts.

Boy/Grade 7/Urban Community/Arizona

I use YouTube to see how stuff is done such as point slope form and distribution of property for fractions. I usually check like 5 videos to make sure the contents of that video is correct.

Girl/Grade 7/Suburban Community/Texas

Well, I often have troubles in my Spanish class so I used this app called, 'Rosetta Stone' where you are being taught different other languages while having fun. This is an excellent app for me because I love having fun while learning something new.

Boy/Grade 7/Suburban Community/Maryland

When I am outside of school, I sometimes look up topics that I do not fully understand. By doing this, I can learn about this topic more than the teacher explained it making it easier to understand. For example, if my science teacher explained to us the difference between what a chemical and physical change was and I did not fully understand it, I could go online after school and research it.

Girl/Grade 7/Urban Community/Arizona

I am learning outside of school using new web sites that could help me with math skills. Also I learned more about power point while messing around with it after school.

Boy/Grade 7/Rural Community/Indiana

I am using Study Island to practice different concepts so when I am in math or english it is easy for me to understand the concept.

Girl/Grade 8/Urban Community/Arizona

I use YouTube a lot to watch videos on how to do math because I am really struggling in that subject.

Girl/Grade 6/Rural Community/North Carolina

Our teachers teach us one way to solve things when there are lots of ways to do things but when we think outside the box our ideas are shut down. I go online after school to help myself better understand how something because in school they did not help me understand it in a way that would better help me.

Girl/Grade 8/Suburban Community/Maryland

When I'm outside of school, I often partake in writing my own stories. Because of that, I do research about certain time periods and fictional creatures. I think this stuff is interesting because it allows me to be more creative and escape into a world of my own. I think that by doing this, I'm helping myself succeed better in school as well. I'm prepared for writing assignments as well as certain history topics.

Decline to state/Grade 7/Rural Community/Alabama

I always research different math topics to understand them more because in Advanced Math we are just told to do assignments, we do not get any learning experiences. I also read and research interesting reading topics daily after school to learn more about a subject. math, writing, and reading are interesting to me because I am very good at these subjects, and I excel at them in school. Some of the technology tools I use to understand subjects more are YouTube, educational websites, researching, and online programs to help me better my understanding of certain topics and subjects.

Boy/Grade 6/Suburban Community/Arizona

Outside of school, I have many interests that I partake in. For example, I may use social media to access political ideas such as theory recommendations, creators in leftist politics, and organizations that I can support. Leftist politics, specifically Marxism, interests me because I am a part of multiple minority groups and am concerned about the well being of the future. In addition to this, I will be a part of AP Seminar next year, and learning more about this subject will advance my performance in that class.

Non-binary/Grade 9/Urban Community/Florida

Writing is one of my main hobbies so I have been using online writing tools and asking more qualified individuals to improve my writing skills. I mostly do fictional writing because I find it both interesting and an escape from other parts of my life. These tools (both technology and people) give me more insight into advice and how my writing can be better, so I'm very grateful for that.

Girl/Grade 10/Suburban Community/California

I often use the internet to search up homework questions or questions in general that I find intriguing. I often search up tutorials on my work or in my own matters. Sometimes it will just be a guide on a new game that I would play or it could be the critical point when I am writing an essay. The internet is vast in its capability and it allows us to freely search our interests and what we have questions on.

Boy/Grade 9/Suburban Community/ Florida

Im mostly learning calculus and physics topics to prepare me for the AP tests, but I also have a strong interest in physics outside of typical school learning. These skills can help me elevate my academic performance to a level I'm satisfied with.

Boy/Grade 11/Urban Community/Florida

Passionate Motivation: Skill Development

Outside of school using technology, I am learning about stocks and investing. It is interesting because people could earn money based off of trends and statistics and is determined by projection. I utilize apps that demonstrate stocks itself and research on websites like the Motley Fool to determine what to invest in. Think or Swim enables one to use "Paper money" or fake money to practice investing and grants tools to analyze the patterns of stocks, such as supports and candlesticks. Because one could orchestrate these tools to better investments, they help me develop new skills I will need in the future and acquire new knowledge.

Boy/Grade 10/Suburban Community/California

The skill development motivation includes ways that students are using digital tools to support the acquisition and refinement of a wide variety of tangible proficiencies or competencies. The origin for these learning behaviors is different from the impetus for self-remediation. Whereas self-remediation starts with a need for improvement in some academic area, the starting place for skill development is with the student's personal interest or curiosity and their understanding of the skills they will need to be successful in a future context. The outcome is an increased competency in a particular skill or talent. The interest areas that drive the skill development learning behavior are not limited to academics but rather include sports, personal grooming, and a laundry list of the types of workplace- and college-ready skills that students believe are important for them to acquire for their future success. Again, educators will need to suspend assumptions or beliefs about what constitutes learning and the value of different types of skills. Another key component of the skill development behaviors is a belief that the skill or aptitude not only can be acquired outside of formal education, but potentially that informal approach may be a better learning modality for that experience and that student. An additional differentiator for the skill development category is a focus on *learning to do something*, rather than *learning about ideas or concepts*. Students have long reported on the Speak Up surveys a penchant for learning how to build or make things and learning how to do things, both of which echo the contextually based learning component of the Student Vision for Learning.

I am learning how to play the guitar I know it's not educational for school but its something I've always wanted to do so thanks to the school for letting us use iPads. I can search what I need to search. Mostly they are videos on YouTube that teach me how to play guitar.

Girl/Grade 7/Urban Community/Nevada

Students report using a variety of digital tools to enable their skill development. As was noted in the self-remediation activities, there is a heavy emphasis on the value of video to support self-directed learning activities for skill development as well. The sample student narrative responses around skill development demonstrate how the students are tapping into digital tools to develop new skills and in many cases, the rationale as to why that skill development is important or valuable for them. More so than was evident with the student responses to support self-remediation, the students' perspectives on the skills they need to acquire provide new insights into the types of skills students value and how the development of those skills contributes to their future plans. The following example connects the skill development motivation to the SDT components of both competence and autonomy.

Free Agent Learning Experiences to Support Skill Development

Outside of school I do my own art work and post to Instagram. Many people on the site give useful tips on how to improve my art which is very helpful. I plan to make my art a potential business so the internet has been more useful compared to my teachers.

Boy/Grade 8/Suburban Community/Florida

For this 8th grader, their self-directed learning activity is highly purposeful: to develop better skills with their artwork so that they can ultimately be good enough to establish an art business. In this narrative response, the student notes that they are leveraging a particular social media vehicle, Instagram. The student is posting their artwork on Instagram *(the digital tool, the learning behavior)* and getting feedback from a public audience *(relatedness)*. The student acknowledges the helpfulness of the feedback as a way to support the improvement of their art skills. In this way, the student is taking an active role in the development of their new skills, thus satisfying a need for *competence* in the skill development process, *autonomy* as they are driving this effort independent of school, and also *relatedness*, as they are finding an audience and informal mentors through social media. It is also noteworthy that in this example, the student notes that they believe that this type of a learning experience, self-directed and highly purposeful, is more useful than what could be provided by their teachers in school. The impetus for this student's Free Agent Learning behavior, the choice of social media as both a vehicle for finding audience and gaining skill development feedback, and the resulting value and satisfaction of the basic psychological needs is all driven by their central purpose to develop an improved set of skills that they personally have determined as vital for their future.

The following collection of additional student responses illustrate how middle school and high school students are leveraging a wide variety of digital tools to support a multitude of different skill development and improvement processes. Central to many of these Free Agent Learning activities are the key elements of SDT, competence, autonomy, and relatedness.

I just use things like, Instagram and Twitter and other popular apps to learn about things and I think the apps are actually teaching more important things for life than what I'm learning in school. They teach me the easiest ways to get jobs. The easiest ways to get money. How to act around people and, so on.

Girl/Grade 8/Rural Community/North Carolina

I use YouTube to learn how to work on trucks. I use google to learn how to do stuff on our farm.

Boy/Grade 8/Rural Community/Indiana

I am learning to code outside of school because I have an interest in it and there are jobs for people who can code. I am using khan academy to learn coding and I'm using cs101 which is another online coding class.

Girl/Grade 8/Urban Community/Arizona

I learn German through video chat and language apps like duolingo.

Girl/Grade 8/Suburban Community/Maryland

I use YouTube to look of videos about topics that interest me. I also use online story sharing websites to write stories and books to share with other young authors and get criticism on them, and also use forums to learn how to be a better writer.

Boy/Grade 7/Urban Community/Arizona

I have learned more about how to paint and secrets to make my paintings look better. I find this interesting because I am learning about something I never knew about painting and the videos are giving me good advice. They help me improve my painting skills by teaching me new things.

Girl/Grade 8/Rural Community/Alabama

I use online tools often outside of school to get recipes. I often make meals for my family when I am home. I also love to bake, ever since my grandmother dies it seems like I slightly took her spot, she is not here to do it or help anymore so I love to keep her traditions going.

Girl/Grade 8/Rural Community/Pennsylvania

I am learning how to create and edit my own YouTube videos outside of school. I have my own YouTube channel that I run from my phone. I currently have about 250 subscribers.

Girl/Grade 7/Rural Community/Alabama

I use Duolingo to learn Japanese, so that i can be an exchange student and even eventually move to Japan. Duolingo is an app you can get from the app store, and it teaches you the language you chose.

Girl/Grade 7/Suburban Community/Colorado

Some topics that I am learning about outside of school is entertainment and editing skills. These topics interest me because I like to create things with my own creativity and I find it generally entertaining. They help me develop skills in confidence, speaking, and general editing.

Non-binary/Grade 8/Suburban Community/California

I like to learn how to do nails and hair i watch videos to tech myself how to do it.

Girl/Grade 8/Rural Community/Alabama

Engine repair, It intrests me because there is so much that you can customize when it comes to engines. We have four wheelers and cars that I work on and I learn by watching youtube videos.

Boy/Grade 10/Rural Community/North Carolina

One subject I've been enjoying is animation and writing. Its interesting because its able to bring my thoughts into a visual version instead of just my head. Technology can help me learn animation and writing because it makes more information and tutorials available to me.

Boy/Grade 8/Suburban Community/California

You can learn just about anything from the internet. Everything is basically a click away and social media helps you connect to people that share those interests. I use technology to help with my art skills and social media has helped to connect me to other people that are also pursing art skills and we can share information we learned together.

Girl/Grade 12/Rural Community/Alabama

I'm learning how to learn ASL on apps, it interested me because it could become useful in the future. The apps help because there aren't many other options to learn.

Girl/Grade 9/Suburban Community/Wisconsin

I have been learning the Korean language for a few years using my phone and I personally think it's pretty cool how someone can learn a whole new language using their phone.

Girl/Grade 10/Suburban Community/Florida

A topic I somewhat interested in is mechanics I love cars and I always try to learn how people restore cars. There is a Netflix show that is based on restoring cars that i watch. I also watch YouTube videos of people restoring cars that I like because I find the process of it interesting.

Boy/Grade 9/Suburban Community/California

I am learning how to use Adobe Photoshop and Illustrator outside of school. This is interesting to me because I get lost in graphic design and it's a lot of fun for me. This helps me learn new tools within editing/designing projects.

Girl/Grade 11/Suburban Community/Wisconsin

I'm learning how to make conversation with people. It's interesting for me because I'm shy yet I really want to talk about my interests.

Girl/Grade 9/Suburban Community/California

I've learned how to record music with a digital software called Focusrite Protools. Music is my passion so learning this was very interesting to me and should honestly maybe be made in a class like "music recording." I'm sure this would be interesting for many students even if they don't play an instrument or have a musical background.

Boy/Grade 9/Suburban Community/Florida

I use mainly youtube to learn more about physical training such as, weight lifting, plyometrics, agility, and cardio workouts. I am very interested in physical training because I am a student athlete who plays basketball.

Girl/Grade 10/Rural Community/California

Passionate Motivation: Curiosity

There is information all over the internet, even if no one realizes. Every day, and I mean EVERY, I go on things like Instagram and Tumblr. There is information about current events, facts, and more that you can learn. I learn more on social media then in school sometimes.

Girl/Grade 8/Rural Community/North Carolina

Daniel Pink, in his seminal book *Drive*, provides the grounding for this category of purpose, curiosity. As previously discussed, Pink maintains that people are innately curious and often pursue interests and learning to satisfy that curiosity or to solve a problem. The student responses substantiate that premise. The students' curiosities or interests in learning things that are beyond the scope of traditional schoolwork content are often precipitated by a range of different stimuli. In their responses, many of the students mention that the spark for their self-directed learning activity was a discussion in their classroom or a topic that was being studied in school. In some cases, the teacher may have moved on with their curriculum or lesson plans to another unit of study. But the interest to learn more lingers with the student. The result is a self-initiated, self-directed initiative to learn more, to explore that topic to a deeper level, and to make connections between that new information and other aspects of their life, both their school life and their personal interests. This is reminiscent of Chad's Free Agent Learning experience described in Chapter 1. Chad's out-of-school learning was propelled by an innate and personal curiosity to learn more about quantum mechanics.

The ubiquitous connectivity of today's students to the Internet also means that their awareness of global situations and happenings is very high as well. Many students note that their familiarity with current events and societal movements and changes leads them to the pursuit of more information, and it makes sense to use the same online tools that sparked that interest in the first place. This is particularly true for students who are interested in social justice issues today.

By using social media and reading articles, I have been able to learn more about political awareness and the BLM movement. Most of my feed and the news were filled with stories, so I was able to become more active in supporting the movement.

Girl/Grade 12/Suburban Community/Wisconsin

The students again demonstrate a proclivity for using a wide range of digital tools to satiate their curiosities about the world around them and specific topics of interest. The role of social media tools is particularly noteworthy as it presents a unique way for the students to learn about people's ideas and how those ideas translate into other ideas and actions. Videos and websites still figure

73

predominantly in the landscape of self-directed interest for these purposeful actions, as was noted for the self-remediation and skill development activities. The analysis of the students' responses in this category, however, was distinctly different from the responses for self-remediation and skill development in one significant way. While the students' actions in those two motivation categories seemed both purposeful and planned, many of the students' statements about self-directed learning in pursuit of curiosities is distinctly more sporadic, spontaneous, or impulsive in nature. As students increasingly have a connection to the world in the palm of their hand, the ability to act on a curiosity is more realistic today than ever before by posing a question to Siri or Alexa, doing a quick Google search, or scanning a Twitter deck.

Free Agent Learning Experiences to Support Curiosity

The way I use technology to learn new things outside of school is that sometimes when I learn about a new person or thing, I like to learn more about it. So sometimes during passing or after school I look up the person or thing and read a couple articles about it. The websites I usually use are old news stories or bios about the thing or person. For example, in social studies when I learned about the Marbury vs Madison trial, I was very interested about it. And I ended up learning more about it.

Girl/Grade 8/Urban Community/Arizona

The purpose of this student's self-directed learning activity is to learn more about something that they learned about in school. Their purpose is therefore driven by a curiosity for learning. To address the need the student has to learn more about a person or thing, they sometimes (*the indicator of frequency*) use websites, old news stories, or online articles (*the digital tools*) to satisfy that curiosity. The *learning behavior* includes a variety of activities such as looking up information and reading articles or stories. Ultimately, the student notes that they learn more from that experience (*satisfaction of a need for competence*). In this case the impetus for their self-directed learning behavior seems to have originated in a school-based learning environment. This is similar to the experience of Chad with quantum mechanics (see Chapter 1). This student also extends their learning experience from the classroom to their own environment by using a variety of easily accessibly online tools to satisfy their curiosity for learning more. While doing so, they are satisfying the need to develop competency but also exercising their right for autonomy in the learning process. The central purpose for their actions is a very simple curiosity to acquire new knowledge.

The following examples of student responses about how they are self-directing learning outside of school, beyond teacher sponsorship or direction, include several different representations of students using digital tools to satisfy a curiosity or to pursue information in an area of high personal interest.

I usually use Instagram to discover other people in the world that like and want to do the same things as me. I personally believe it is easier for people to express who they are and what they want n life through technology and pictures. I find it easier to use social media and videos to learn things.

Boy/Grade 8/Urban Community/Arizona

After I come back from school, I like to go on YouTube and watch Scishow, Vsauce, AsapSCIENCE, MinutePhysics, and TedED. I learn a variety of things that seem interesting to me, from why rain smells to what if the Earth was flat.

Boy/Grade 8/Suburban Community/Maryland

Sometimes i watch videos about space and videos i see that are interesting. this one time i watched a video about supernovas and black holes.

Boy/Grade 6/Rural Community/North Carolina

I use technology outside of school to learn new things fairly often, and I learn something new at least once a week. I am learning about different things in science using Youtube.

Boy/Grade 7/Urban Community/Arizona

I use stuff like google to look stuff up that i had questions about or just want to look up. I use youtube to watch videos about simple things that everyone wonders about daily.

Girl/Grade 8/Rural Community/North Carolina

I use technology outside of school to learn new things or skills by researching something to know about it better. I go on a lot of websites circled around the topic that I want to learn more about and usually that topic leads me to another topic that I want to learn more about. (Example: learning about space led me to wanting to know more about a certain planet like Neptune.) I often like learning about new things or current/past events happening around the world and I like using Google to research more about this. I also just like reading from the news website.

Girl/Grade 8/Urban Community/Arizona

I'm very interested in chemistry and physics and instead of learning the same lesson that has been taught since the 90's, I've been teaching myself by reading papers I find online, watching videos, going on free online textbooks, and having online discussions.

Boy/Grade 7/Urban Community/Arizona

I have several lists. But I think I'll stick for one. Astronomy. I absolutely ADORE Astronomy. I want a career in it. I love astronomy because I love the night sky-stars, black holes, space – it's all so interesting! I love the string-universe theory, etc. I often watch videos, research websites, etc.

Non-binary/Grade 8/Rural Community/Alabama

I like to learn about fishing, historical events like Pearl Harbor, and welding and blacksmithing. I like welding and blacksmithing because I get to learn how make different objects with metal. I like to learn about Pearl Harbor and other historic events that happened in our nation. I like to learn about all the different types of fish and lures that I can use to catch fish. Technology helps me learn about these things because there are so many sources online.

Boy/Grade 6/Rural Community/Alabama

I enjoy learning about anime and Japanese culture, I just love the art style of anime and i find it interesting, I sometimes watch documentaries.

Non-binary/Grade 6/Suburban Community/Florida

I sometimes go on Google and ask questions that have popped up in my head about what we learned in school that day or the day before.

Girl/Grade 8/Rural Community/North Carolina

Motivations for Free Agent Learner Behaviors

In my own time, I am do lots of studying on politics and injustices in our society and ways to fix them. These topics are important to me because people should not be exploiting working class citizens and there is no reason to hate people different from yourself. I also just feel obligated to research this topic so I can help people less fortunate than me. I use google scholar a ton because it has reliable resources such as official documents and popular books on these topics. I also use many YouTube channels that cover different topics.

Decline to state/Grade 7/Suburban Community/California

Well, since I started using technology more often, I got to know more about history and the Napoleonic Wars which I am very interested in. I get to acquire new knowledge from Youtube videos, and online friends who have similar interests like me. I've learn more about military tactics, uniforms, organization, and etc just from online sources from friends and experts. I get to know more about how Russia's government work and it's corruption and all sorts of stuff.

Boy/Grade 7/Suburban Community/California

WW2 and I use the Call of Duty WW2 campaign because it is accurate and still entertaining so you learn things without even knowing it because you are playing a fun game.

Boy/Grade 10/Suburban Community/Wisconsin

I am learning more about American Political standpoints. This topic is interesting because it is where I reside. Technology helps me by seeing both sides of each argument rather than some more biased news.

Girl/Grade 12/Rural Community/Alabama

Outside of school I am always learning about the world and what is going on all around the world. Like what is going on in politics, what is going on in social media, and just big news from around the world. I think it is interesting because I like learning about different parts of the world and how they are effected and how they are living everyday.

Girl/Grade 10/Suburban Community/California

I am learning about politics, economics, and social justice through online articles and online books. Sometimes I hear opinions on certain topics on tik tok that allow me to use that and take it as a jumping off point to learn more. This is interesting with me because it is important to me that the world improves and becomes a place that is equal for everyone and free of bias.

Girl/Grade 11/Suburban Community/California

In general I like science and technology. I will sometimes go on Google News and look at some headlines to see if any are interesting to me. Occasionally they are and I click on the link and read the article. Often these articles will include scientific concepts or terms that I am not familiar with so I look those up and read other, reputable, articles about them I recently learned a lot about antimatter and how it's not just science fiction. With my new knowledge, I then think deeply about the implications of such things existing and what they mean in regards to how the universe functions. I even did not know that the Big Bang wasn't a conventional explosion that we think of. It did not occur from a single point. It happened everywhere all at once.

Boy/Grade 12/Suburban Community/California

Literary analysis, with topics such as symbolism, tropes, art (film, paintings, performance, literature, etc.) history, culture, and much more. I also enjoy commentary and news channels, as well as independent artists. I find these subjects very interesting because I love seeing the way people create and express themselves, as well as

79

what informs and shapes those creations. Without technology, I wouldn't any access at all to the videos and papers I primarily learn from, so tools like my phone and laptop are crucial to me.

Girl/Grade 11/Suburban Community/California

I'm learning about philosophy, mythology, religion, and meditation. These topics are interesting to me because I believe they can lead me to personal growth and a better life, as well as continual questioning of my place as it is. I regularly watch videos or read books about these subjects, but overall i find that I don't have nearly as much time or energy to actually learn about these subjects as I'd like to, because of school.

Boy/Grade 11/Suburban Community/California

I'm very interested in politics so I read a lot of articles about the current political climate and the problems facing our nation. This research and further education is important because I love politics, and I truly believe I can make the world a better place. Also, I take an online cybersecurity course which is more to satisfy my curiosity about computers.

Girl/Grade 9/Suburban Community/Florida

I've taken a course on Managing Emotions and I started a course on Conflict Transformation both on Coursera. I've been struggling with my mental health lately, especially now that I'm back in school, and I've found some valuable information in these lessons. They help me lead the life I want to lead by teaching me the tools I need to identify and regulate my emotions. Self regulation is important everyday, whether I'm at school, home, or elsewhere. Having these courses and technologies available to learn coping mechanisms, especially now that therapy or counseling isn't much of a possibility, helps me lead a more healthy life.

Girl/Grade 11/Urban Community/Florida

A subject I learn more when Im not doing school is Conceptual Physics, its interesting to me because I learn a lot of different things in that class. It kinda just makes me think about things more when I learn about it.

Girl/Grade 10/Rural Community/California

I use my laptop and phone to learn about art-related topics, such as painting techniques and origami tutorials (lame, I know). They're interesting to me simply because I like doing them (creating stuff is fun) and they look pretty. Using technology gives me free access to tutorials and lessons/advice about these topics, also I'm able to access these things whenever I want/can and can pace myself in learning about them. One downside, however, is that it's sort of difficult to get some constructive criticism or direct assistance from an instructor.

Girl/Grade 11/Rural Community/California

Outside of school I spend a lot of time researching and learning about both business and real estate investing. This is important to me as I have found that there is ton of information available online for free and that anything can be learned with a little bit of self discipline.

Boy/Grade 11/Suburban Community/Wisconsin

I learn more about politics and worldwide problems, because it is important for teens to kow what going on and how they can help. I use online articles, statistics, and social media in order ot gain accurate information.

Girl/Grade 9/Rural Community/Florida

Personally I love baseball, so I look up information about it online. Watching games is fun for me, so I ill often look up information about baseball online to better understand what is happening. Using this technology gives me more practice, which is good as even though baseball itself is not important, using technology is. As using social media is critical in the world today, I just started using it in order to try and understand what exactly it is. Using this is not that interesting to me, although I follow things that I like, but is helpful as understanding social media is important.

Boy/Grade 9/Suburban Community/Arizona

I like to learn about the real world and real world problems other than the curriculum. I often look how taxes and mortgages and colleges even though i tend to be too young to do so. I find that it is crucial for me to learn this things and i figured that it would be better to learn now so that i dont have to cram information about world history and i can figure out how to write a resume because that is more important. Social media allows me to look up these sort of things so that i am aware and i know what to do.

Girl/Grade 7/Suburban Community/Florida

Passionate Motivation: Career Exploration and Preparation

I go to website called space.com and it teaches me the things that are going on in space and how it can affect earth because I want to be an astronomer when I grow up and I want to study space.

Girl/Grade 6/Suburban Community/Maryland

With this motivation area of career exploration and preparation, the students connect their use of digital tools to specific goals that support their aspirations for the future. The students seek highly targeted information about specific career fields and jobs and research information about higher education attainment and preparation. Students report using digital tools to research colleges that meet their specific interest areas and exploring admission requirements and financial information.

Quantitatively based on the coding of the student responses, this motivation category is the smallest of the four general motivation categories with the fewest number of students reporting this type of Free Agent Learning. The student responses, however, provide valuable insights for education leaders about how students are thinking about their future and how they are using the digital tools available to them outside of school to explore their options after high school. Curriculum standards today place a high emphasis on supporting the development of college- and career-ready skills within everyday instruction and instructional practices. This new attention on defining and articulating the types of skills that students need for future success is not lost on the students.

I want to be a writer so I use Pinterest for my creative writing. I also use google and I have a tablet so therefore I can access these things. If I had these things in school I could be more creative and be more inspired by fellow writers.

Girl/Grade 7/Rural Community/Indiana

While the assumption would be that high school students are the most likely age group to be exhibiting self-directed learning behaviors to support career preparation, it may be surprising to some education leaders to learn that middle school students are actively pursuing the same types of activities already. As noted in some of the earlier student responses coded for self-remediation and skill development, the students' frustrations with what they perceive as the lack of relevancy in their school-based education is often quoted as the basis for why the students need to pursue their own exploration of information about future careers or jobs. The following examples of student responses demonstrate the variety of tools that students are using to self-direct learning for career preparation and the variety of motivations that are driving those exploration behaviors.

Free Agent Learning Experiences to Support Career Exploration and Preparation

Outside of school, I enjoy learning online about psychology and mental illnesses. This subject is interesting to be because I want to become a therapist and understand myself better. Technology helps me acquire new knowledge because I'm not limited to a few sources unlike a physical library.

Decline to state/Grade 12/Suburban Community/California

For this student, their use of technology outside of school is in service of learning about a future career field. To address this learning motivation, the student researches online information *(digital tool of choice)* about psychology and mental illnesses. They note that this self-directed learning activity benefits from technology access since it provides more informational resources than what would be available in a physical library. The searching for the information is the self-directed *learning behavior*. The key components of the Free Agent Learner profile, self-directedness and interest-driven, is evident in this activity. The self-directedness of the activity supports both competence and autonomy for the student. And the student specifically talks about the personal interest and enjoyment of the activity, validating the value they place on this type of learning experience. The purposefulness of their actions, scaffolded by the technology access, is evident by the attention to career preparation. In addition, that purposefulness drives the choice of the digital tool, the frequency of the behavior, and the resulting satisfaction of the basic psychological need.

The following representative responses from the students provide valuable insights into both what types of career interest development and preparation students are doing on their own and the value they place on those self-directed experiences.

Sometimes I go on Google and search about my future job and what it takes to succeed in that career. Also, I look up colleges that have my profession that I want to major in.

Girl/Grade 8/Rural Community/North Carolina

Well I want to become a firefighter, police officer, be in the army, or be in the CIA/FBI . . . with a degree of being an E.M.T. I use technology outside of school to help prepare me for my future like going to medical school, and researching whats on the firefighter and police test, and all of the important things that take place to getting my job and getting me to the right college.

Boy/Grade 7/Urban Community/Arizona

I use my devices that I borrow at home like a laptop, kindle, or smartphone to look up my dream college, Stanford. I search what it takes to be accepted and what programs it has to offer, I also sometimes search what different jobs pay the best or what career would best fit me.

Girl/Grade 7/Suburban Community/Texas

I am using engineering software on my laptop. Also, since I want to be an engineer/design cars or houses, I use Minecraft to design lots of things. This type of technology helps me out a lot.

Boy/Grade 8/Rural Community/North Carolina

i am learning about mechanics & engineering. i am using websites that help me understand the basics of building, fixing, & putting back together a car. i am also using toy cars, by taking them apart & putting them back together (while timing myself).

Girl/Grade 8/Rural Community/North Carolina

I am learning by researching about what I want to do as a career, because in school, the math and science and english and history I am learning is in no way helping me as my career. I search online about horseback riding and horse trainers, and how they teach, because Algebra, and learning about World War 2 is not helping me learn about horseback riding. I think we should be able to take classes around what we want to do as a person, not what the district wants us to learn.

Boy/Grade 8/Urban Community/Arizona

How to work on mechanical things (trucks, cars, bikes). It interests me because I want to become a machinist when I grow up.

Girl/Grade 7/Rural Community/Alabama

I am learning Elementary School education because I want to be a teacher. This topic is interesting because I am learning the skills needed to become an elementary teacher.

Boy/Grade 8/Rural Community/Pennsylvania

I am really interested in becoming a dermatologist, so I watch videos on different things dermatologists deal with on a day to day basis sometimes.

Girl/Grade 10/Suburban Community/Wisconsin

Outside of school, I am learning about computer aided design, coding, prototype building, computer science related stuff. I find computers and machine code interesting. I feel that these activities will help me learn things that will be beneficial in my career path.

Boy/Grade 9/Suburban Community/Wisconsin

I'm learning how to start manufacturing video games in Roblox. This subject interests me since I want to become a video game designer in the future.

Girl/Grade 9/Suburban Community/California

Criminal Justice has been a topic that I been intrested scince I was 7 years old. This topic intrested me becuase I eaither want to be a Lawyer or SWAT member. These technologies help me develop my skill becuase I could reasearch more about and see what going on.

Boy/Grade 9/Suburban Community/California

I'm currently studying up in medical illnesses, such as encephalitis. I think I'll fill a notebook up with medical conditions I find fascinating. This subject is interesting to me because I plan to go into the medical career in the future. Technology aids in this research because the information is more readily available.

Girl/Grade 12/Suburban Community/California

I am learning how to improve my field hockey game through you tubers who go over certain skills and watching collegiate level hockey games. That subject is interesting to me because I am trying to get recruited and it matters for my future.

Girl/Grade 10/Suburban Community/California

I want to be in the armed forces at one point in my life and the technology now can help me watch videos about the expectations about the job.

Boy/Grade 9/Suburban Community/California

I learn about baking and engineering outside of school using technology. I like baking because it's my hobby and I like engineering because I plan to be a civil engineer. Youtube videos help a lot with understanding these things.

Girl/Grade 11/Rural Community/California

I am learning how to create a website and sell art online. This helps me acquire the knowledge of how to run a business online.

Girl/Grade 11/Suburban Community/California

I learn about topics in ministry because that is an area I am interested in going in online allows me to watch others in that field

Girl/Grade 9/Suburban Community/Alabama

Outside of school, I am looking into colleges that interest me. This is interesting to me because there are so many options. The technology tools help with developing knowledge because they provide all of the information I could want about a specific thing in a second.

Boy/Grade 11/Suburban Community/California

I am learning about how to start my own business and work to become a business owner as well as investing in stocks, bonds, and buying into real estate so I will have multiple streams of income when I am older. For this, I watch millionaire mentors, the news on stocks, and people's financial experiences.

Girl/Grade 10/Urban Community/Florida

I taught myself how to build a PC by watching YouTube videos and reading websites. During this summer, I am going to teach myself how to code with Java. I am looking at becoming a CS major, so these skills should come in handy.

Boy/Grade 11/Rural Community/California

A Free Agent Learning Experience: Anna

One of the key components of the Student Vision for Learning is a strong desire for learning experiences to be untethered. As described in Chapter 1, students want to be able to access learning resources from anywhere and not be artificially limited in their learning to only local resources or knowledge. For Anna, a high school student in Wisconsin, this meant being able to use online and digital tools to help learn more about her desired career field, naval architecture, the building of ships. As Anna explained, geography (living in Wisconsin) was in many ways restricting her abilities to learn about naval architecture as a career and the types of college programs that would be the most helpful for her. Anna was also very interested in learning more about oceans and oceanography, and there simply were not that many resources, knowledge-based or human, that could help her in her small central Wisconsin town.

To satisfy this passionate motivation for college and career preparation, Anna watches online documentaries and researches scientific articles. She also has reached out to people she found online who are in the field of naval architecture to learn more about college programs. Through those efforts, Anna learned about a summer program at the Naval Surface Warfare Center (https://www.navsea .navy.mil/Home/Warfare-Centers) where she could be an intern in the Science and Engineering Apprenticeship Program (SEAP). The SEAP internships provide ways for students to do research alongside professional Navy personnel at a Department of Navy laboratory. The program is designed to support students' interest development in science or engineering fields and also to provide mentors to help students plan for potentially a career with the Navy. Anna was selected to participate in this competitive program in summer 2021. Due to continuing pandemic concerns, the internship was a virtual experience, which in many ways followed the pattern of Anna's career preparation activities anyway, using online and digital tools to support her self-directed learning.

Anna's personal career exploration experiences are reflective of her broader thinking about school and learning. As I have heard from so many students over the past few years, Anna believes that it is important for students to be able to do independent research on their interests and that those interests could support a future job or career. She believes this is especially important for students in small towns who may only have visibility into the jobs or careers of their parents or other family members. Through access to technology, students can informally explore a wide range of different interests before committing to a career path or college major. The self-directedness of the career exploration may also be a more comfortable process for some students than the formalized structure of meetings with guidance counselors or even visiting colleges. For Anna, this career exploration path was certainly representative of the untethered learning aspects of the Student Vision for Learning. Anna is a Free Agent Learner. Following her high school graduation this year, Anna will be attending a university that specializes in naval architecture.

The centrality of purpose within students' self-directed learning activities outside of school is supported by Daniel Pink's premise that what motivates people toward competence or mastery is purpose. My Free Agent Learning grounded theory focuses on the centrality of purpose within students' digital behaviors. This new theory has its roots in Tony Wagner's identification of intrinsic goals as driving students' motivations to learn differently from the way they are learning in school. My theory extends the current research that acknowledges that purpose plays a role in students' digital lives and stands on the shoulders of SDT and the work of Pink and Wagner.

Additionally, the focus on purpose as the driving force behind students' self-directed learning supports the quantitative and qualitative results from the Speak Up Research Project. Students exhibit the characteristics and behaviors of Free Agent Learners when they use digital tools, resources, and content outside of school to self-direct learning to support remediation, skill development, curiosity, and career preparation objectives. The students' actions are driven by purpose. Understanding purpose has a double benefit in this discussion. First, it is the key to a greater appreciation of how, when, where, and why today's students are pursing self-directed digital learning outside of school, and second, it provides a sustainable construct for examining how tomorrow's students may use the next generation of digital tools to self-direct their learning as well.

Connecting the Dots

- Based on a comprehensive analysis of both the quantitative and qualitative data results from Project Tomorrow's Speak Up research, four primary motivating factors have emerged to explain the passionate motivations that drive Free Agent Learning activities for most students:

  - Self-remediation: Students are interested in improving their academic performance in school and identify specific areas for self-remediation;

  - Skill development: Students want to develop skills to support their current learning processes or to prepare them effectively for the future;

- Curiosity: Students have an innate inquisitiveness about a topic and want to learn more for the simple joy of learning and acquiring knowledge;

- Career exploration and preparation: Students are driven to explore careers or investigate what they need to know to be well-prepared for a future job or post-graduation pursuit including college and the military.

- Students are taking control of their educational destiny through these Free Agent Learning activities both because school in its traditional sense is not meeting their learning needs or goals and because those learning needs and goals may be best served through the students' own self-directed learning paths.

- Free Agent Learnership is not based on frequency or regularity of the behavior or the sophistication of the digital tools used but rather that the self-directed, interest-driven learning is purposeful and serves to satisfy students' needs for realizing autonomy, competence, and relatedness in their out-of-school learning lives.

Now, Think about This!

1. What passionate motivations are propelling your students to be Free Agent Learners? Are some more prevalent than others, and if so, why might that be the case for your community?

2. How can understanding the motivations of students for Free Agent Learning help you think differently about in-school learning?

3. How well are your schools incorporating ways for students to develop autonomy, competence, and relatedness within everyday classroom learning?

4. What is one thing that you can do today or tomorrow to evaluate if your schools are effectively addressing student needs for remediation and skill development or if there are more effective strategies that can be employed to help students pursue their academic curiosities or career preparation interests?

Motivations for Free Agent Learner Behaviors

Chapter 4

Meet the Free Agent Learner

M y identification of the types of learning behaviors and attitudes that I would ultimately categorize as Free Agent Learnership began in Rosedale, Mississippi, in spring 2003. Rosedale is a small city in the Mississippi Delta (population under 2000) with a proud, well-deserved heritage as a designated site on the Mississippi Blues Trail. But it has been challenged by many of the same economic and societal trials that have plagued other predominantly agricultural communities along the Mississippi River for the past hundred years. A history of chronic unemployment and home poverty levels at least twice the statewide average has negatively affected local educational opportunities for over 20 years. This included the ability of the local school district to fully embrace and adopt new technologies to support learning. Project Tomorrow (then called NetDay) identified Rosedale's school district, the West Bolivar Consolidated School District, to be a project site for a federally funded technology intervention grant program implemented from 1999 to 2005. At the time, the school district included just three schools, an elementary school, a middle school, and a high school, and served approximately 1360 students (94% qualifying for the federally funded free lunch program; 100% of the student population was Black/African American).

The goal of this strategic project was to both improve educational opportunities within this community and build a replicable model of effective technology integration in schools in the Mississippi Delta. As part of the project, Project Tomorrow brought hundreds of computers into local classrooms and trained over 100 teachers using an innovative approach to teacher training. Using forward-thinking in-classroom coaching and mentoring strategies, our focus was to build sustainable capacity for teacher adoption and adaptation of technology resources to improve student outcomes and teacher effectiveness. This type of an approach, novel at the time, has now proven to be effective and is now a new standard for efficacy in teacher training. Alongside our partners in the Rosedale community and West Bolivar School District, I was very proud to welcome then Secretary of Education Richard Riley in August 2000 to the Rosedale schools as part of his "Success Express" bus trip to schools across the southeast.

As part of my ongoing research about technology use in schools, I visited West Bolivar High School in spring 2003 to conduct a student focus group. My trip was precipitated by a report published by the American Institutes for Research (AIR) in January 2003 titled "The Digital Disconnect: The Widening Gap between Internet-Savvy Students and Their Schools."[1] The report findings piqued my interest since they closely paralleled what Project Tomorrow had been seeing in our project schools, namely that students were using technology in different ways than adults assumed to support both academic and personal interest tasks. However, the AIR research had only collected feedback from students in suburban communities, and I was curious about the views of the students in the schools where our projects were situated, all of which were in low-income, primarily Black and Brown communities. Would the findings be the same in our project schools, or were the experiences of students in our communities different than those in better resourced schools?

I launched a series of face-to-face focus groups with students, starting in West Bolivar High School in Rosedale, Mississippi, to answer that big question. In spring 2003, I would ultimately meet with over 60 middle and high school students in five distinct communities,

Rosedale, Mississippi, Detroit, Michigan, Mercedes, Texas in the Rio Grande Valley, Oakland, California, and Santa Ana, California, to collect firsthand insights from the students directly. An appreciation of student voice, particularly around technology use, was not a mature concept in 2003. The prevailing wisdom (some of which may still exist today) was that students' views and ideas about their education was not consequential to school planning or even classroom instruction. Correspondingly, for many educators, their personal learning curve on technology was so challenging that it seemed inconceivable and maybe even dangerous to consult with students about their preferences for using technology within learning. The focus groups with the students in Mississippi, Michigan, Texas, and California brought home for me that idea that students not only needed a seat at the table in terms of education and technology use planning but that their insights based on their experiences, both in school and at home, were important assets for school and district leaders interested in improving their educational enterprises. The rationale for launching the Speak Up Research Project to collect and report on the authentic, firsthand views of K–12 students on digital learning (and subsequently expanded to include parents and educators) was born from those focus groups with students in spring 2003.

Identifying the First Free Agent Learners

Armed with a long list of questions drawn from our research and the findings from the AIR report, and with some realistic trepidation about whether the students would be forthcoming with me, an outsider to their community, I met my first group of students in West Bolivar High School's historic school theater on a sunny spring afternoon in 2003. The events of that afternoon with those 11 students are as vivid today as then. The conversation started off slowly as I asked questions about the students' access to technology in school and the ways their teachers were using digital resources within lessons and classroom activities. Their responses mirrored what I knew about teacher usage of technology at the time. The students felt that their teachers were not fully taking advantage of the potential of the digital tools to transform the learning process. Some teachers used technology; some did not use any technology at all. When it was used, that usage was sporadic and seemed to the students to be more gratuitous, lacking connection to the lesson or unit of study. Some students were participating in a distance learning class providing access to a teacher in another school district via closed circuit television. Most of the regular classroom usage was primarily to support classroom management efficiency rather than student learning. All of this aligned to what I had been hearing and seeing in most other classrooms around the country.

Certainly, some teachers in 2003 were using technology effectively to support student learning, but they were still the early adopters with most teachers still feeling very tentative and fearful about what technology use would mean for their own classroom practices. The students had a very real sense of resignation relative to their teachers' lack of enthusiasm for improving educational processes through the effective use of technology. I continue to hear similar feelings from students even today. One of the 12th grade students summed up her peers' perspective succinctly when she asked me, "Why is it that our teachers do not realize that when they hold back on using technology in class, they are holding back our future?"

The conversation with the Rosedale students changed dramatically, however, when I asked the students about their ideas for improving school technology use. The students became quite animated about the potential of digital tools to improve learning and provided me with a wealth of examples of how technology should be used in their classes. Many of the students based their recommendations on their own experiences using technology outside of school to support learning activities as well as relationship development. Little did I know at this point that my own personal belief system and set of assumptions about these students and their personal technology access beyond school would be tested.

Being aware of the home poverty levels in Rosedale, I assumed that the students did not have Internet connectivity at home, and thus, their familiarity with potential uses of technology for learning would be limited primarily to their school experiences. My assumption was only 50% correct. When I asked the students whether they had a computer and Internet access at their homes, the students literally laughed at me. No, they did not have access to technology in their homes. But despite that, each student verified that they had multiple email addresses, were active on the social media sites of the day, and regularly used technology and the Internet outside of school, just not necessarily when they were at home. This revelation flew in the face of the way most researchers were approaching discussions about the digital divide at the time. The common practice was to ask students whether they had a computer at home and whether they had Internet access at home. If they said no to either question, the researcher would not do any follow-up questioning about their use of technology outside of school. The assumption was that home technology access was the exclusive gateway to personal usage and personal familiarity with technology use. Without that home access (specifically an Internet-connected computer), the prevailing belief was that there was no way that the students would be fluent in digital use outside of their in-school usage. And that students without home connectivity were on the wrong side of the digital divide, and that deficit belief set prevented those students from having any meaningful input into how technology could support their learning.

But that was not the reality here in Rosedale, and it would prove to not be the reality in Detroit, Mercedes, Oakland, or Santa Ana either. At that point, I realized that my carefully crafted focus group questions were based on a false hypothesis. I folded up my list and put it away. I suspended all of my previous assumptions and ventured into a new series of questions that ultimately would reveal how these students way back in 2003 were already exhibiting Free Agent Learning behaviors even before I had identified that as an important trend to watch.

The Role of Technology Within Free Agent Learning

The Rosedale students' articulation of the ways that technology could be better used in their school to support student learning and prepare them effectively for future success was in fact based on their experiences using technology outside of school. The students were very savvy about the potential of technology to transform teaching and learning in school because they were using technology in their personal lives to support their own self-directed learning all the time. The high school sophomores, juniors, and seniors explained to me that out-of-school access to technology and the Internet was absolutely critical for their own education. They understood the resource limitations of their own community and even of their school and teachers. The students knew that the world beyond Rosedale, particularly in terms of acquiring knowledge and expertise, could be accessible to them if they could use the Internet. Thus, these highly resourceful students had developed their own asset map (my words, not theirs) of community locations and people who could help them get online. The asset map included myriad opportunities for access though it was sporadic and not always easy or convenient.

The students had negotiated with the local bank manager to use the bank's Internet-connected computers on Saturdays to research websites about topics and subjects they were interested in learning more about. They tapped into the laptops of older family members who came home to Rosedale on the weekends to gain access to their email and social media accounts. And the students had figured out that if they could get a ride 19 miles down the road to the bigger city of Cleveland, Mississippi, the librarian at the Delta State University library would sometimes allow them to get online there. The students shared that this was simply the way of life for their generation in Rosedale, Mississippi, in 2003. This DIY approach to getting online was not just a niche experience for them but a regular part of the learning environment for their peers as well. The types of online activities that these students spoke about to me that spring afternoon and the tools they were using to connect with others and become informed about the world beyond the Mississippi Delta were consistent with what I subsequently heard from all of the other focus groups I facilitated. It was also in alignment with what the AIR report and other research noted were the experiences of students in better resourced suburban communities where students generally had an Internet-connected computer at home.[2]

Despite not having a computer or Internet access at home, these ingenious teenagers from this small rural community had found a way to be connected to a world of learning beyond their school. They used that hard-fought connectivity to support their extended learning outside of school, focusing on exploring personal interests and developing skills they believed were essential for their future success. And thus, their views of how technology could be better leveraged during the school day were highly informed because of their authentic experiences using these digital tools in their personal learning lives. Though I did not realize it at the time, those 11 students in Roseville, Mississippi, were the first identified Free Agent

Learners. Their actions and attitudes were consistent with what I have framed as the four key characteristics of Free Agent Learners (introduced in Chapter 2):

- **Place Independence.** While traditional learning is situated typically in a physical classroom or similar formalized learning environment, Free Agent Learning activities typically take place outside of school, beyond the classroom or a traditional learning environment.

- **Power Ownership.** The Free Agent Learning activities are wholly self-directed by the student and are not driven or sponsored by a teacher or another adult in the student's learning life.

- **Purposeful Technology Usage.** The use of digital tools, content, and resources to support Free Agent Learning is highly purposeful to effectively support the personalized learning goals of the student.

- **Passionate Motivations.** Free Agent Learning is directed by the students' intrinsic passion, drive, or motivation to tap into a wide range of digital tools to support their learning goals beyond the sponsorship of their teachers.

Assumptions and Myths

During the nearly 20 years of researching students' use of technology for learning purposes, both in school and out of school, I am frequently asked this question by education leaders, policymakers, and media representatives: What are the biggest differences you see between students in their use of technology? Sometimes I am prompted by the questioner to specifically delineate differences by gender, community type, or racial/ethnic/cultural identifiers. This question is laden with many assumptions, most of which are incorrect.

Adults make assumptions about how and why students use technology for learning purposes based on their own view of the value of technology and their own experiences in using various digital tools to support their own productivity.

To illustrate the problem with adult assumptions, I am reminded of the middle school students who told me that in their technology applications class in school, their teacher spent an entire week of instructional time teaching the class about each of the disparate functions under the "File" tab in Microsoft Word. The teacher explained that this was the way they were taught to use Word, going through each component of the navigation bar and thus the best way to teach students about all of the functions of the product. For the students, most of whom were already using Word to create schoolwork documents, this teaching strategy seemed irrelevant, unnecessary, and a waste of time. But without the realization of how students interact with technology and how they have learned on their own to use various products, the teacher relied upon the approach that worked for them personally. They overlaid their learning modalities on to their students without a more thorough understanding of what their students actually needed.

Similarly, a focus group of high school students shared with me a story about how their English teacher sought to resolve a concern that they had about student plagiarism. In this class, the students were instructed that for an upcoming essay on the novel they were currently reading, they needed to write that essay in long hand on notebook paper. They were required to turn in a physical, hand-written document, not a printed or uploaded digital document. The teacher's belief was that this approach would stem any inclinations some students might have to plagiarize or lift sections from existing online documents or CliffsNotes about the novel's theme. The students were baffled by this assignment requirement but dutifully handed in their essays, written in long hand on notebook paper.

What the teacher did not realize was that universally the students had actually written their essays the way they always do—using Google docs or Microsoft Word on their laptop or Chromebook, tapping into the online thesaurus or dictionary to check on word choices, moving paragraphs and sentences around to create a more coherent flow for their essay, and then using spell check and Grammarly to fix errors. The students took those digital outputs and rewrote them by hand on notebook paper before handing in the assignment. The teacher may have felt that they resolved a perceived plagiarism problem. But in reality, they created a much larger relevancy and respect problem in their class due to their failure to understand the ways that digital tools support efficiency and effectiveness in the learning process. Too often the assumptions that adults make about students' use of technology are based on blind spots they have that are actually manifestations of their own values and usage behaviors, not the real world of the students.

The question that I get repeatedly about the differences between students in terms of their technology usage comes from this same place of blindness. Belief systems and assumptions that adults, including educators, make about student technology access and usage is more a reflection of their own experiences, not necessarily what we actually know about students and digital learning. Adults assume, for example, that students who may not have broadband at home are not part of the digital society. Or they assume that certain profiles of students don't like using technology since they themselves don't enjoy those experiences. The realization of the near antiquity of these perspectives is critical to appreciate the broader range of student technology use in general and specifically with Free Agent Learners. For example, education mythology says that boys are more eager to use technology than girls, and subsequently, boys are more interested in STEM (science, technology, engineering, and math) fields and careers than girls. Another myth is that students in low-income homes do not have access to the Internet and thus are not digitally savvy. That same "date expired" conventional wisdom assumes that students use technology more in better resourced suburban communities compared to rural or urban communities. These assumptions often stand as inaccurate proxies for beliefs about the experiences of Brown and Black children with technology.

The Real Headline: Universal Experiences

Based upon my research with K–12 students nationwide each year, I believe it is long overdue to retire these myths and for new frameworks of understanding to emerge that can inform and guide better decisions and policies in schools and communities. While the Speak Up data shows some differences between students' attitudes, activities, and aspirations around technology usage, the similarities between students and the universality of their experiences using technology for learning, especially outside of school, is the actual headline story. What I heard from the students in Roseville, Mississippi, about the websites they visited, their use of email, and their expectations for more effective in-school usage of technology proved to be very similar to what I heard from students in Michigan, Texas, and California in subsequent focus groups in those communities also. And those values and insights closely align with the national Speak Up data as well. Contrary to what many continue to believe, the Internet has created common experiences for students that transcend the typical barriers of community, gender, poverty, or race and ethnicity. In many ways the traditional research organizations and administrator preparation programs have not caught up with this reality. They continue to be "sight challenged" about the real ways that students are using technology to support learning, both in school and out of school.

In the intervening years since that prescient discussion with the high school students from Rosedale, Mississippi, on that spring afternoon in 2003, I have conducted hundreds of interviews, focus groups, and panel discussions with elementary, middle, and high school students about not only their use of technology in school but their experiences using digital tools to support self-directed, interest-driven learning and how those activities have influenced their expectations for in-school learning. Those conversations have taken place all across the country in classrooms and libraries, after-school recreation centers, and hearing rooms in the United States Capitol Building, and even occasionally in high school theaters, though none as historic as the original West Bolivar High School building. In each conversation, the students speak passionately about the value of self-directed digital learning in their lives, echoing beliefs and aspirations that are remarkably similar to the insights first expressed by the Free Agent Learners in Roseville, even though it has been almost 20 years since that meeting.

While the qualitative data collected through the interviews, focus groups, and panel discussions with students nationwide presents an interesting sketch of Free Agent Learning, the national Speak Up research provides the quantitative data to substantiate how students are using digital tools to support self-directed learning, and the implications of those learning activities on in-school learning expectations. Since fall 2003, the Speak Up Research Project has provided relevant quantitative data to validate and shine a national spotlight on the ideas and views of students about their learning experiences, both in school and out of school. Starting in 2009, the Speak Up surveys have collected data on the extent to which students exhibit Free Agent Learning behaviors and use technology tools to support their self-directed learning outside of school. In 2014, the research was further refined to capture the frequency of these Free Agent Learning behaviors. The Speak Up research therefore not only documents the existence of Free Agent Learnership but provides valuable insights into the profile of Free Agent Learners, their self-directed, interest-driven learning, and the implications of these learning behaviors on students' perceptions around school-based learning. Specifically in this discussion, my analysis of the Speak Up data focuses on the feedback from nearly 1.2 million middle and high school students during the period from fall 2014 through spring 2021, comprising a representative sampling of schools and communities throughout all 50 states plus the District of Columbia.

The following sections therefore discuss the types of self-directed learning activities that students engage with as well as the regularity of those interest-driven learning experiences outside of school. Additionally, new information is provided to help school and district leaders understand the relationship between students' attitudes about school and learning and their Free Agent Learning behaviors.

A Free Agent Learning Experience

Inherent in the definition of Free Agent Learning is a heavy orientation to the value of student choice in their learning path, pace, and place. Consequently, there is not a single template or profile of learning activities or behaviors that is universal among all students. Rather, students in their interest-driven learning are regularly picking and choosing from a diverse toolkit of digital resources to support specific learning goals in a highly purposeful way. On Monday that may mean researching the latest hairstyles on your favorite influencer's YouTube channel. On Wednesday, it could include posing a question on a Reddit forum about restorative justice policies and legislative gains over the past year. And then on Saturday the learning activity might involve participating in a video game stream with people from around the world discussing in the chat the critical decisions being made by the players. Starting with a curiosity or a desire to learn something, the digitally savvy students create their own unique learning recipe identifying the right tools, content, and processes to satisfy their learning goals. Every recipe is different and unique because every student starts with their own highly specific learning purpose. No cookie-cutter recipe to follow with Free Agent Learning.

Contrary to some conventional wisdom about students' out-of-school technology usage, the starting point is not the technology. The digital tools and resources play a supporting role as ingredients in the recipe, but the true driver is the students' passion for learning something. As discussed in Chapters 2 and 3, that "something" most usually is to satisfy a need for self-remediation in an academic content area, to learn new skills, to follow a path of curiosity about a topic they are interested in, or to explore a future career field.

The following example presents an illustration of a string of interrelated Free Agent Learning behaviors. In this illustration, four key points are representative: the intentionality of the student's actions, the fluidity of the learning process and how it fits into the student's daily life, the cumulative effect of the learning experience and how each action leads to another action, and how a variety of digital tools support the Free Agent Learner's behaviors. While this particular example will feel very "academic" to many school and district leaders, students' interests in learning span a wide spectrum. The key representative points illustrated in this example are the same whether the student is learning about climate change or how to replicate the latest snowboard trick.

- As part of their environmental science class in school, a student learned that climate change could potentially have an irreversible impact on the ability of many sea animal species to survive. Curious to see if this was true, the student searched for YouTube videos on the subject and found a short YouTube video from CBS News about the impact of climate change on manatees in the Florida Keys.[3] The student has always wondered about a potential future career in marine biology, and so they were naturally interested in learning more about this connection between the impact of climate change on our oceans and sea life. After more searching online, the student discovered a learning site called ASAPScience (https://www.asapscience.com), which has YouTube videos on different science topics including about oceans.[4] The ASAPScience videos appealed to the student because they included easy-to-understand illustrations and the educator hosts were personable and approachable, providing a high degree of relatedness to this student. For 38% of high school students, watching a video is a more meaningful learning experience than reading a book.

- Understanding that discussions about the impact of climate change on oceans are happening all the time with new information becoming available, the student taps into their existing social media accounts to identify different experts in this space to follow and to find out what others are doing to change this climate trajectory. Searching on Twitter specifically, the student sees a posting on the @NOAA (National Oceanic and Atmospheric Administration) account that alerts them to new information on the Global Climate Dashboard about changes in sea level around the world.[5] The student follows the @NOAA account and favorites the Global Climate Dashboard for more follow-up later.

- After school the next day, the student decides to check out this Global Climate Dashboard on the NOAA website (https://www .climate.gov/climatedashboard) to see if it might provide valuable information to their personal journey to learn more about climate change and oceans. The Dashboard information was very informative with lots of interesting indicators, including about ocean temperature in addition to sea level changes. The student adds the Dashboard to the home page on their smartphone for quick access.

- As time permits, the student spends time searching through the different sections of the Dashboard and other resources provided by NOAA. They learn about something called the Coastal Ocean Observing System, and that piques their interest for a particular reason. The student likes the self-directed learning process accessing websites and social media posts, but they now also want to take their passion to the next level and get involved with solving the ocean climate change problem. Their research skills ultimately take them to the Center for Climate Change Impacts and Adaptation (CCCIA), which is housed at Scripps Institute of Oceanography at the University of California San Diego.[6] While the research activities of this organization appear to be more oriented to undergraduate and graduate students, our Free Agent Learner is excited to be able to connect with people who share their passion and interests. The student sends an email to the center director inquiring whether they have any opportunities for high school students to be involved in their work or whether they know of other organizations that might provide those kinds of firsthand learning experiences.

This example illustrates how students can use a variety of different digital tools to support their self-initiated learning pursuits and to satisfy a variety of goals. In this example, the Free Agent Learner watched online videos, conducted research on a website, picked up new information via a social media post, and contacted an expert to get answers to their personalized questions, all of which in this case was focused on climate change, environmental sustainability, and a particular interest in oceans. The tools employed may be different to meet different learning goals. In this case, this unique mix or recipe of learning ingredients not only helped this student meet their learning goals but also directed them to additional resources, both human capital and digital resources, to continue the learning process. The student's personalized goals for this self-directed learning path may have included acquiring new information as well as building a community or a personal learning network for ongoing support of their interest-driven learning. It may also have been initiated by their interest in exploring a career field or giving back to the larger community through volunteer efforts on climate change. Each learning activity propelled the student to a follow-on exploration or curiosity. The digital tools provided the means for efficient and effective exploration, but the driver every step of the way was the student's self-directed purpose.

The learning behaviors exhibited by this student align with the four key components of Free Agent Learning as follows (the components were introduced in Chapter 2):

- **Place Independence.** While the student's initial interest in climate change and oceans may have been aroused by a unit of study in class or a teacher discussion, the learning activities undertaken by this student were independent of the traditional school environment. In this example, the students' Free Agent Learning took place outside of school using their own digital devices and was not dependent on school resources.

- **Power Ownership.** The student in this example owned the power relationship of the learning activity from the beginning. Each step in the learning process was student initiated and managed, including the exploration of how to get more involved in a real-world setting to support climate research. A common feature of most Free Agent Learning experiences is that the student's teacher is not aware of the types of self-directed learning that is happening outside of school even though that knowledge may help to inform in-classroom discussions and experiences. When asked whether they have told their teacher about their self-directed learning activities outside of school, most students tell me that it never occurred to them to tell their teacher. This lack of awareness of the value to the teacher of this knowledge further validates the student power ownership of the learning process.

- **Purposeful Technology Usage.** Students have at their disposal today a wide variety of digital tools, content, and resources to support Free Agent Learning. Their ability to select the tools that are most appropriate for their learning purposes is on its own a valuable college- and career-ready skill that few education leaders value today. In this example, the student leveraged online and digital tools, some that were fairly traditional (online search, email) and some that may still qualify as emerging (Twitter, YouTube). The novelty of the tool is not as important to students as the utility of that tool to help them achieve their desired purpose.

- **Passionate Motivations.** At the heart of Free Agent Learning is a student's intrinsic passion, drive, or motivation to learn something, and to take the steps to actuate that learning process. In our example, the student was curious about the impact of climate change on oceans, and that passion to learn about that topic propelled them into self-directed learning along some highly personalized pathways. In contrast to many school-based learnings, a hallmark of Free Agent Learning is active learning. By virtue of self-directing the learning process and having that learning activity focused on a topic of high personal interest, the student is an active learner with a high degree of personal engagement. That is evidenced throughout our example by the way that student continues to come back to the learning activity and build on each bit of knowledge gained to extend the learning experience further.

Connecting the Dots

- Too often, educators' personal assumptions and beliefs about students, learning, and technology get in the way of seeing potential opportunities for new student outcomes. Given the experiences during the COVID pandemic with the disruptions in school operations and shifts to digital learning, it is time to retire many of these outdated assumptions and myths.

- Technology plays an important role in understanding Free Agent Learning and the Free Agent Learning activities undertaken by students. Digital tools, content, and resources are the fuel that empowers students with the abilities and capacities to self-direct highly personalized and meaningful learning experiences outside of school.

- But there is no one Free Agent Learner profile or standard set of activities. By its very nature, Free Agent Learning is individualized to each student by type of activity, use of various digital tools, and frequency or regularity of the self-directed learning experience.

- Students are broadening their Free Agent Learning experiences with the help of a plethora of digital tools and resources that they independently source, vet, and curate.

Now, Think about This!

1. What myths, conventional wisdom, or assumptions are you or your colleagues holding on to about students, learning, and technology that should be retired now? Why have you been holding on to them past their expiration date?

2. Why do students' learning lives outside of school look so different than their experiences in the traditional classroom?

3. Why are the learning outcomes from self-directed learning not as highly valued as the in-school learning experiences, especially when students seem to be more engaged with their own academic pursuits than classroom instruction?

4. What is one thing that you can do today or tomorrow to expose the hypocrisy of these outdated beliefs and encourage your colleagues to think differently about how students are leveraging technology to support personalized learning outcomes?

Notes

1. https://eric.ed.gov/?id=ed471133.
2. https://nepc.colorado.edu/sites/default/files/EPRU-0208-36-OWI%5B1%5D.pdf.
3. https://www.youtube.com/watch?v=tRkUW6BuOxk.
4. https://www.youtube.com/watch?v=0yywWKtKheQ&t=42s.
5. https://www.climate.gov/news-features/understanding-climate/about-global-climate-dashboard.
6. https://climateadapt.ucsd.edu.

Chapter 5

Free Agent Learning Activities and Behaviors

By its very nature, Free Agent Learning is highly personalized to the passions and purposes of each individualized student. There is no standard playlist of learning activities that all Free Agent Learners subscribe to or follow religiously. Nor is there a uniform set of digital tools that every student uses to support their self-directed, interest-driven learning activities. And while some students may engage in Free Agent Learning every day, for others it may be more of an occasional pursuit, driven by a timely curiosity or exposure to a new idea. A key challenge for educators is that the inherently amorphous nature of Free Agent Learnership runs dramatically counter to most of the logistical and procedural aspects of school-based education. Free Agent Learnership simply does not fit neatly into the prescribed views of how learning should take place in many ways, especially given the often rigid constructs that underpin school-based learning.

School-based education has long placed a premium on an elaborate set of structures, standards, and policies that define everyday educational processes as well as intended outcomes for both students and teachers. The stubborn resiliency of that infrastructure, even as needs have changed in communities and new theories of learning have emerged, creates a universality of the experience of school for students, teachers, administrators, and parents. The middle school that I visit on Tuesday in Jacksonville, North Carolina, may outwardly look differently than the middle school in San Marcos, California, I visit on Thursday in terms of student population demographics, physical plant, and/or resources available for learning, but the cadence of the systems underpinning the day-to-day operations and classroom processes are mirror images. Schools run on policies and rules that define the nature of teaching and learning in the classroom and the expected behaviors and attitudes of students and educators. And these tenets of what school is and how it should function are generally the same today as they were when the parents of our current students were in school and maybe even their grandparents. Examples include the following:

- Students are assigned to classrooms and teachers and attend school during a set number of hours per day over a 10-month calendar;
- Teachers deliver lessons that follow curriculum standards using instructional materials prescribed by higher authorities;
- Grades and test scores are used to document student outcomes and serve as metrics for understanding teacher effectiveness;
- Parents are expected to monitor student progress and homework but not necessarily to have a large say in what happens in the school-based learning process or content; and
- Communities applaud objective metrics of local school performance such as graduation rates or percentage of students attending college but are most often not aware or informed about the alignment of tangible student skills with local workforce needs.

Many schools and districts have definitely been nibbling at the edges of this strong adherence to rules and requirements for many years. But they have generally been nibbles, not large bites of whole-sale transformation.

The Pull of Tradition Even in Innovative Schools

By virtue of focusing on schools that are implementing digital tools to support new learning models, I tend to visit schools where leaders are actively working to support innovation as much as that can be, given the inherent inertia of traditional education norms. Quite often my visits take me to schools that have adopted a new vision around personalization. The school leaders and staff talk eloquently and enthusiastically about how they have implemented a one-to-one program where every student has a digital learning device that facilitates more individualized instruction or that they have restructured the learning day to support blended learning where students drive the pace and path of instruction with a mix of online and in-classroom activities. Many note that they have embraced project-based learning, competency-based learning, and other new learning modalities that are meant to enhance or improve educational outcomes for all students, creating new opportunities for learning to be customized to the student instead of the other way around. The classrooms are abuzz with active learning, and I often find it difficult to locate the front of the classroom when these new models are employed, a litmus test of sorts for how deeply teachers have adapted their practices in this new environment.

Yet, despite these outward signs of innovation in the daily practices, the pull of the status quo of the traditional education infrastructure is often still too strong even in these exemplar schools. The intractable pull toward prioritizing system expediency and adult efficiency over student learning needs reveals itself when I ask a seemingly innocuous question: How are students assigned to guidance counselors in your school?

Free Agent Learning Activities and Behaviors

Most school guidance offices are structured with students assigned to counselors based on the first letter of their last name. For example, in a high school, Counselor Smith is assigned students whose last names begin with A to G, Counselor Jones has the students with last names from H to O, and Counselor Davis is responsible for the students from P to Z. The portfolio of students assigned to each counselor inevitably includes a broad range of different types of students with different learning needs and career or college aspirations. In most schools, the selection of classes in high school and navigating the gateways to certain programs, including Advanced Placement, honors, thematic academies, or trade programs, is facilitated with support and guidance from the counselors.

And yet, too often, the counselor's portfolio of students whom they are responsible for guiding or advising is a mixed bag of students with highly varied needs and expectations. Within each portfolio, there may be students on an honors or Advanced Placement track with personal or parental expectations for a highly competitive college or university and students who want to attend community college with a goal or not to transfer to a four-year institution later. Some students within the portfolios may have a military or public service goal in mind. Other students may be more interested in entering the workforce or attending a trade or professional school to develop skills. And increasingly, some students may want to take a gap year to travel or decide on a career path. Each portfolio most likely also includes students who need more handholding than others because they lack family resources or support to help make decisions about high school classes or post-graduation plans. Conceivably, Counselors Smith, Jones, and Davis would need to be an expert in the needs of each type of student in their portfolio, understanding what opportunities exist and how to best address both every individual student strength as well as improvement area to serve each student effectively.

With so many options available to students today, it is increasingly difficult for them on their own, even with family support, to pick the right classes, take the right tests, and select the right path for their future success. The importance of effective and personalized counseling in high school is more important than ever, especially as post–high school education becomes increasingly more expensive and students have more needs for remediation or additional support as a result of the COVID pandemic. But the reality is that there are still not enough counselors in our schools today, and schools lack vision as to how to create more personalized advisement experiences for students. School district investments in guidance staff and processes are highly sensitive to district budgets, and that certainly is an important factor. However, while so many other aspects of our society have endorsed expertise segmentation as a way to personalize the customer experience, that market-proven approach has not made it yet to most school guidance offices. I rarely see guidance offices where counselors have developed expertise in supporting certain student needs and their student assignments follow those expertise areas. The result is that for most students their guidance office experience too often follows a "one-size-fits-none" approach even in schools where the vision and instructional practices in the classroom have changed to emphasize a more personalized learning experience. The pull of traditional school structures and policies is simply too much to overcome even in our most innovative schools.

It is understandable, therefore, that the concept of Free Agent Learnership and its potential to help transform K–12 education may have some challenges gaining traction with school and district leaders, both because of the amorphous nature of those learning experiences and the inherent resistance within the education ecosystems to ideas that do not fit within the traditional structures. As with technology use by students in general, adults need to suspend long-held assumptions and beliefs about what constitutes real learning and be open to new

119

realities about this student-driven ecosystem particularly because of the connection to helping students develop lifelong learning skills.

To support this education process, I have developed a Free Agent Learning activity and behavior typology to identify the most common self-directed, interest-driven learning activities that students are engaging with. As noted earlier, to catalog every type of activity would be a fool's errand akin to documenting every snowflake or butterfly wing pattern. The Free Agent Learning Activity Typology, however, provides a level of structure to the learning activities so that education leaders can gain a tangible understanding of not only the variety of learning behaviors but the frequency of those experiences and the types of digital tools that are being employed to support the learning.

Free Agent Learning Activity Typology

The Speak Up Research Project has documented 15 different Free Agent Learning activities that constitute this typology. Feedback on these learning activities has been collected since 2014 for 12 of the behaviors; three are new since 2018 and represent activities that utilize more recent technologies. The Free Agent Learning Activity Typology representing the self-directed, interest-driven learning activities that are most common with middle and high school students is depicted in Table 5.1. Each learning activity on the Typology also includes an authentic example from middle and high school students about how they are actuating their Free Agent Learnership through the use of digital tools or resources to support their learning interest.

Frequency of the Free Agent Learning Behaviors

Free Agent Learners represent a diverse set of learners in terms of the types of behaviors they are engaged with and the frequency or regularity of that behavior in their out-of-school life. There is not a single Free Agent Learner profile. Rather, the students' behaviors

Table 5.1 Free Agent Learning activity typology.

The most common self-directed, interest-driven learning activities and behaviors undertaken by students in grades 6–12	
Free Agent Learning activity	**Examples from students**
• Ask a voice-enabled virtual assistant a question.	Alexa, what is a blue moon?
• Create, edit, and post videos on social media sites to show what you know or to develop video production skills.	Create and post a 2-min video about the origins of public education.
• Find experts online to answer questions.	Emailing a scientist at the Scripps Institute for Oceanography.
• Play an online game or augmented reality / virtual simulation activity.	Learning about World War II by playing Call of Duty WW2.
• Post a question on a discussion board or forum.	Learning about pinball machine tech by asking questions on online pinball forums.
• Read or watch an online news story or report about a topic of interest.	Watching news reports about hate crimes against Asian Americans.
• Research information on a website to answer a question.	Search for answers to sports questions on ESPN.
• Research information on a website to learn more about a topic.	Learning about stocks and investing through research on websites such as the Motley Fool to determine what to invest in.
• Take a self-paced tutorial or online class.	Taking a course on managing emotions and now starting a new course on conflict transformation on Coursera.
• Use online writing tools to improve writing skills.	Learning how to write fiction by taking part in an online challenge called NaNo WriMo. Website forums give advice, encouragement, and examples of other people going through problems in writing.
• Use social media to identify people who share interests.	Participation in a video editing community on Instagram and a writing community on other platforms.
• Use social media to learn what others are doing or thinking about relative to an interested topic.	Learning about what others are thinking about the Black Lives Matter movement.

(Continued)

Table 5.1 (Continued)

The most common self-directed, interest-driven learning activities and behaviors undertaken by students in grades 6–12	
Free Agent Learning activity	**Examples from students**
• Watch a TED Talk or similar short video about someone's ideas.	For time management and motivational topics, watch TED Talks online and dive into the wise words of speakers on that stage.
• Watch a video to learn how to do something.	Learned how to play the guitar by watching YouTube videos.
• Watch other people play online games.	Watching Twitch streams on Dream SMP to learn about real history that the streamers make fun by using Minecraft to act it all out.

Source: © Project Tomorrow 2021.

and their motivations are as diverse as the students themselves. The commonality is how all of these self-directed, interest-driven actions support the students' own personal actuation of the Student Vision for Learning (see Chapter 1).

Just as to satisfy their personal entertainment and friendship development goals, some students use some types of digital tools more frequently than others to satisfy those needs. The differences in how students are using these technologies and the frequency of those learning engagements by students when they are outside of the classroom should be an important consideration for school and district leaders. While some educators continue to be too quick to dismiss students' use of technology outside of school as trivial or non-consequential, the reality is that these self-directed experiences are shaping not only the expectation that students have for technology use in school but also their aspirations for more meaningful learning experiences in the classroom. Given the heightened concern emerging from the COVID pandemic about student engagement in school and learning, providing a way to mirror the high engagement learning experiences students are having outside of school may be a good strategy. The first step to implementing such a novel approach, however, would be to understand the Free Agent Learning behaviors at a deeper level.

In terms of the frequency of regularity of the Free Agent Learning activities or behaviors and the use of digital tools and resources to specifically support the students' learning goals, my analysis indicates that the more common practices (as described in Table 5.1) can be segmented into three usage tiers. I have identified these three tiers based on the seven-year average percentage of middle and high school students who say they use these tools to support their self-directed, interest-driven learning when they are outside of school. The students who indicated that they never or rarely engage with these tools for those purposes were excluded from this analysis. The three tiers are described as follows:

- The **Tier 1 Prevalent Free Agent Learning Activities** are identified as such since over 50% of high school students are engaging with these learning behaviors on a regular basis to support their personal learning interests outside of school. Using data collected from the 2014–2015 school year through the 2020–2021 school year, the following Free Agent Learning activities are representative of the Tier 1 Prevalent behaviors:
  - Watch a video to learn how to do something (78% of high school students);
  - Research information on a website to learn more about a topic (75%);
  - Read or watch an online news story or report (62%);
  - Use social media to learn what others are doing or thinking about relative to a topic that interests me (56%); and
  - Use social media to identify people who share my interests (53%).

123

- The percentage of students who are engaging with the **Tier 2 Emerging Free Agent Learning Activities** is generally between 40% and 50% of high school students according to Speak Up Research findings. Those types of self-directed learning activities using digital tools and resources include:
  - Ask a voice-enabled virtual assistant a question (49% of high school students);
  - Watch other people play games (49%);
  - Play an online game or augmented reality / virtual simulation activity (47%);
  - Find experts online to answer questions (41%);
  - Use online writing tools to improve my writing skills (41%); and
  - Watch a TED Talk or similar short video about someone's ideas (40%).

- The **Tier 3 Distinctive Free Agent Learning Activities** are undertaken, at least currently, by a smaller percentage of high school students on a regular basis. According to the seven-year average of Speak Up data findings, between one-fifth and one-third of high school students are engaging with various technologies to support these learning behaviors. The distinctive activities include:
  - Take a self-paced tutorial or online class (32% of high school students);
  - Post a question on a discussion board or forum (27%); and
  - Create, edit, and post videos on social media sites (20%).

The tiers for middle school students vary slightly from their older peers. Middle school students place playing games, watching others play games, and using a virtual assistant to answer questions in their list of the Tier 1 Prevalent Free Agent Learning Activities. Middle school students, at least currently, report that they are less likely to use social media tools on a regular basis to support their Free Agent Learning activities, thus resulting in those activities being cataloged as Tier 2 Emergent for students in grades 6–8. As younger students become more engaged with social media tools including TikTok, we may see the regularity of the use of such tools change over time.

The same will be true as new technologies become more readily available to students, particularly outside of school. For example, it will be interesting to see over the next few years whether students report using augmented or virtual reality as a Free Agent Learning modality. Students are already reporting some interest in these types of technologies for in-school learning. From the 2020–2021 Speak Up results, for example, 24% of students in grades 6–8 say that virtual reality experiences and hardware (headsets and devices) would be valuable for helping students improve academically. The longitudinal Speak Up data from 2014 to 2021 on students' use of various technologies to support Free Agent Learning provides a potential glimpse into the future of how students are adopting certain digital tools as vehicles for self-directed learning.

Free Agent Learning Experiences: 2014–2021

We all have a plethora of digital tools, content, and resources that we can tap into today to help us be more productive, save time, and engage with others more easily. The pervasiveness of many of these technologies in our everyday life may also cloud the reality that these tools are still relatively new players in our world. Chromebooks, iPads, Alexa, Snapchat, Instagram, Apple watches, Fortnite, and Oculus virtual reality sets were all examples of technologies that have been introduced to the world since 2010. Putting that in the perspective of a student's learning life, when our class of 2022 high school seniors started kindergarten, none of these digital, online, or social media tools had even been invented, let alone served as standard bearers for current technology usage.

It therefore goes without saying that the study of Free Agent Learning and how technology enables and empowers students to take control of their learning destiny outside of school is an incomplete science. As new technologies emerge, students will adopt and adapt those tools to support their academic interests. The constant is the passion for self-directed learning; the variable is the selection of which digital tools available are the most effective for supporting that learning pursuit.

The analysis of the longitudinal usage patterns of Tier 1 Prevalent, Tier 2 Emerging, and Tier 3 Distinctive Free Agent Learning Activities is helpful to understand the consistency of the students' pursuit of self-directed learning. It also provides a starting point for thinking about the impact of external and environmental factors such as the COVID pandemic on students' learning experiences. Figures 5.1–5.3 depict the trend lines associated with all three tiers of the Free Agent Learning experiences as collected from high school students in the 2014–2015 school year through the 2020–2021 school year.

Note: The data on students' use of virtual assistants and watching others play online games as modes of self-directed learning was only collected starting in the Speak Up surveys during the 2019–2020 school year.

Three insights are particularly noteworthy from this longitudinal analysis of the Free Agent Learning activities of high school students from 2014 to 2021.

1. **Growth in five specific Free Agent Learning activities.**
   From 2014 to 2021, an increased number of high school students (and also middle school students) reported using various

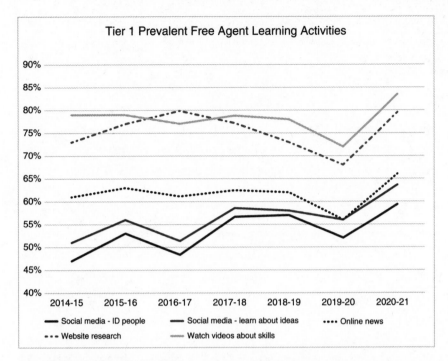

Figure 5.1 Percentage of high school students engaged with Tier 1 Free Agent Learning behaviors **(2014–2021).**
Source: © *Project Tomorrow 2021.*

digital tools to support their out-of-school, self-directed learning pursuits. Among the high school students, the largest increases over that seven-year time period are noted in these five use cases:

a. Use of social media to identify people with shared interests (26% increase over that time, or 12 percentage points);

b. Use of social media to learn what others are doing or thinking about a topic of interest (25% increase over that time, or 13 percentage points);

c. Use of online writing tools to improve personal writing skills (25% increase over that time, or 9 percentage points);

Free Agent Learning Activities and Behaviors

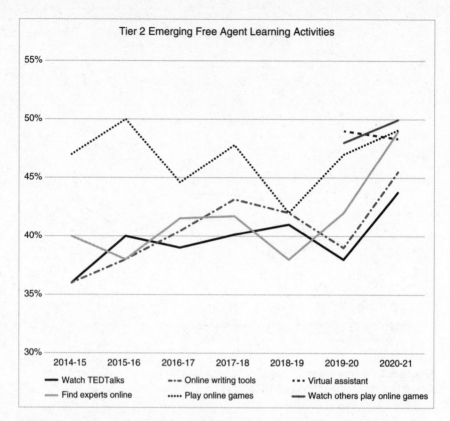

Figure 5.2 Percentage of high school students engaged with Tier 2 Free Agent Learning behaviors **(2014–2021)**.
Source: © Project Tomorrow 2021.

    d. Find experts online to answer questions (23% increase over that time, or 9 percentage points); and

    e. Watching TED Talks or other short videos about people's ideas (22% increase over that time, or 8 percentage points).

2. **Minimal impact of pandemic and school closures on Free Agent Learning.** In addition to those significant growth areas, other use cases had slight year-to-year up-and-down fluctuations in the number of students reporting various Free Agent Learning behaviors. Those fluctuations in the student reporting

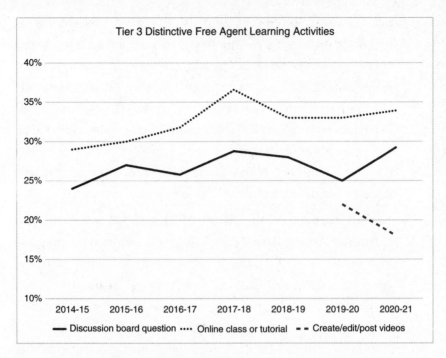

Figure 5.3 Percentage of high school students engaged with Tier 3 Free Agent Learning behaviors **(2014–2021)**.
Source: © Project Tomorrow 2021

can be attributed to multiple factors including the makeup of the sampling each year. For the most part, these small differences year to year are not statistically significant or noteworthy (example: 48% of students reported playing online games as a self-directed learning behavior in 2017–2018; 42% reported the same in the 2018–2019 school year). However, the 2019–2020 school year data from the Speak Up Research Project is particularly interesting since it was in spring 2020 when most school buildings were closed and students were learning remotely, mostly through virtual means. Despite the move from the classroom to the kitchen table for school-oriented, teacher-facilitated learning, students did not give up their self-directed, interest-driven learn-

Free Agent Learning Activities and Behaviors

ing. Even with the heavier emphasis on screen time during virtual learning to satisfy schoolwork requirements, students still continued to tap into their digital tools on their own to support personalized learning goals, beyond the virtual classroom. Fluctuations in the percentage of students' reporting those behaviors were all within a 6% point swing, some higher than the year before and some lower. Notably, the data does not reveal that students relinquished their digitally enhanced self-directed learning because of online school.

3. **School format in the 2020–2021 school year did not influence Free Agent Learning.** In examining the increases in the number of students reporting Free Agent Learning behaviors in the 2020–2021 school year specifically (compared to the previous two years), some may make a wrong assumption about the reasons for those increases. One incorrect assumption would be to believe that students who were still engaged in virtual learning in the 2020–2021 school year may be more likely to pursue self-directed learning. The school format employed in the 2020–2021 does not, however, appear to influence students' likelihood for Free Agent Learning. High school students who continued in remote learning for most of the school year were just as likely to say that they watched a video to learn something (84% of those students) as students who were in fully face-to-face classrooms (83% of those students). Any differences noted based on school format were negligible or not statistically significant.

Others may also conjecture that the uptick in Free Agent Learnership behaviors may be the result of more students being provided with a personally assigned, school-owned laptop or Chromebook to support schoolwork at home and at school. There is an element of veracity to this belief, but the conclusion is incorrect. Indeed, high school teachers report in 2021 that their students have much greater access to school-provided devices (primarily laptops and Chromebooks) than they did just five years previously. While only 24% of teachers in 2016 said their students were assigned a digital learning device to use at school and at home for school-based learning activities, 79% say that is the case in 2021. It is conceivable to think that the students are taking advantage of these school-owned devices to support their self-directed, interest-driven learning at home. However, when asked which devices they were using at home to support schoolwork-related activities, 72% of high school students said they were using their personally owned devices anyway. For both schoolwork and self-directed learning, students prefer their own devices.

As we are already seeing in many education topics, the impact of the COVID pandemic and how schools addressed learning continuity during the health crisis will have a long tail. The same is true here with Free Agent Learners. I believe that the increasing number of students exhibiting the Free Agent Learner behaviors in the 2020–2021 school year is a result of the increased agency and self-efficacy as learners that students developed during the past two school years. When asked on the Speak Up surveys to identify the pros and cons and benefits and challenges of virtual learning, 67% of students in grades 6–12 said that the top benefit was being able to learn at their own pace. This was true even for students who were not engaged in virtual learning in the 2020–2021 school year but had that experience in 2019–2020. The second top benefit identified by the students was the development of skills including technology skills and being responsible for their own learning. Students valued these attributes before the pandemic. This is evident by the longitudinal review of the Free Agent Learner behaviors. The difference here is the acknowledgment, or dare we say, permission, provided by educators that students can self-direct learning, even in a school setting.

A high school student from California summed it up this way in October 2020: "It has become aboundingly clear during the pandemic that students are in charge of their own learning. It always has been actually, but now everyone just knows it."

Analysis of Free Agent Learning Activities Using Demographic Variables

A common theme throughout the discussion about the Free Agent Learning activities and behaviors is the need for adults to suspend their preconceived assumptions about students' use of technology and how those tools support self-directed learning outside of school. That same need to put away out-of-date myths or conventional wisdom also applies to the impact of gender, race, home poverty, technology access, digital skills, and interest in certain career fields. Traditional belief systems around these variables that have long defined school policies, programs, and learning opportunities are not as applicable in the Free Agent Learner ecosystem where a passion for learning combined with even minimal technology access can supersede what many may view as intractable obstacles. The following two analyses of the Free Agent Learner data collected through the Speak Up Research Project provide valuable new insights to help school and district leaders understand the universality of self-directed learning by students. Both analyses examine data collected from middle school students about their learning experiences outside of school.

Free Agent Learning Activity Analysis by Student Demographics

For this analysis, I used a large data set of the authentic feedback from 133,212 middle school students collected through the Speak Up Research Project. The analysis endeavored to investigate differences

132

in middle school students' self-directed, interest-driven digital behavior based on three personal characteristics (gender, self-assessment of technology skills, and interest in a STEM career field) and one environmental asset (access to Internet connectivity at home).

The selection of gender, technology skill, and home Internet access as entry points for the investigation was precipitated by previous studies that followed traditional research norms by disaggregating their results using these demographic identifiers as potentially significant for a technology-related study. Home Internet access in particular has become a proxy identifier for family poverty. The inclusion of students' interest in a STEM field was suggested by several studies that focused on the use of digital tools in school to support science, math, and engineering learning. A common goal today of digital tool usage within the STEM curricular areas is to drive increased student interest in those fields for a career pathway.

The Speak Up surveys ask students several profiling questions that can be used to further explain or explore differences or similarities between students. The key additional items that are relevant to this discussion about the differences or similarities between Free Agent Learners are the following:

- What is your gender? (potential responses: girl, boy, non-binary, decline to respond)

- What kind of Internet access do you have at home? (potential responses: various options that can be used to identify the home connection as fast, slow, or nonexistent)

- How would you rate your technology skills compared to other students in your class? (potential responses: advanced, average, and beginner-level skills)

- Are you interested in a job or career in a STEM field? (potential responses: five-part Likert scale of interest)

For all of these data items, the statistical analysis included independent sample t-tests as well as effect size testing.

The results of the statistical testing indicate that there is not a defining profile of the Free Agent Learner that can be easily categorized by demographics or student characteristics. Rather, it appears that while gender, home Internet access, technology skills, and STEM interest play a role in students' self-directed learning behaviors, the effect of those differences between the subgroups is small. Thus, the practical significance of these factors in educational settings as consequential in defining what types of students are using digital tools to self-direct learning is small also.

For example, middle school girls were more likely to research a website to learn more on a topic, watch a video to learn how to do something, access social media tools to identify people with shared interests or to learn what others were doing or thinking about a topic, and use writing tools to improve writing skills than their male peers. The middle school boys were more likely to post questions on a discussion board or forum, find experts online to answer questions, and play an online game or virtual simulation activity than their female classmates. However, while the statistical significance may be present, the practical significance of the finding is inconsequential due to the small effect size.

What this means is that based on the statistical testing, the differences between the girls and boys in terms of their Free Agent Learning activities is unimportant and thus should not be used to predict or explain as being influenced by gender. This is noteworthy as it may refute some outdated conventional wisdom that girls are reluctant or disinterested in using technology in general. Rather, this finding further supports the idea that students' interest in using digital tools for self-directed learning is not a one-size-fits-all proposition and that traditional means of differentiating digital behaviors based on students' demographics such as gender may not be as relevant today as they once were in the past.

Similar patterns exist for the other studied student characteristics and assets. While differences in the frequency of the learning behaviors exist based on students' level of access to high speed or broadband Internet at home or their self-assessment of their technology prowess, the effect size of the differences and subsequently the practical significance of those differences makes it inappropriate to define those as true disparities, especially as it relates to policy or programs. As noted earlier, students' increasing access to Internet-enabled devices in their pockets and backpacks changes the connectivity equation when Wi-fi hot spots are prevalent within the community. The hard-wired, high-speed broadband connection at home is less relevant to the student who is using his smartphone on the school bus ride home to look up information about the intriguing historical figure discussed earlier in the day in class. This finding does not take away from the important work to ensure that all students have safe, consistent, and reliable Internet connectivity at home to support remote, virtual learning as demonstrated during pandemic-induced school closures. However, it does open up the conversation to appreciate that students' self-directed learning especially as facilitated through a smartphone is an important part of the overall learning ecosystem. The implications of this change in perspective on the type and quality of the Internet connection employed by students should be of high interest to policymakers, business leaders, and educators still exclusively focused on broadband connectivity at home.

The analysis of the learning behaviors of students with and without an interest in a STEM career field yielded an interesting finding that was subsequently echoed in other findings. For the supplemental analysis, students were categorized as "STEM-interested" or "STEM-disinterested" based upon their response to the Speak Up question about their level of interest in a STEM field as a career choice. While only small statistical and practical differences existed between these two subgroups of students on six of the Free Agent Learning behaviors, no difference was evident for the two social media-oriented activities: using social media to identify people with shared interests and to learn what others are doing or thinking about a topic of interest. Social media usage, therefore, appears to transcend students' curricular or career interests in STEM.

The analysis of the open-ended narrative responses from the middle school students about their self-directed learning behavior noted a complementary finding. While students researching websites and watching videos often mentioned math and science topics as the focus of their self-directed behaviors, the majority of the students' responses about their use of social media tools were devoid of references to curricular topics and more focused on general learning.

Free Agent Learning Activity Analysis by School Demographics

For this supplemental analysis, the Speak Up data from middle school students was examined to identify or evaluate differences based on home community type (urban, suburban, or rural) and also the racial/ethnic identity of the school population. As in the preceding analysis, this type of disaggregation of data follows research norms that typically look at community type and race in particular when discussing differences in technology access and usage. Data for this analysis was at the school level rather than the student level. For analysis like this, the Speak Up Research Project utilizes the US Department of Education's Common Core of Data (CCD) to gain additional insights into the types of schools participating in Speak Up and the analysis at the school level of the Speak Up data. CCD includes a broad spectrum of information on all public elementary and secondary schools in operation during a given school year. That information includes school location (community type), enrollment by grade, student characteristics and demographics, and the number of classroom teachers.[1]

As noted in the earlier analysis, the findings of this special analysis support differences in the percentage of students engaging in Free Agent Learner behaviors based on community type and school population, but those differences are small and inconsequential in terms of profiling the Free Agent Learner. Table 5.2 depicts the top five Prevalent Free Agent Learner behaviors of middle school students and the percentages of those students who report participating in those self-directed, interest-driven learning activities outside of school across different communities and schools. As illustrated, grade 6–8 students are just as likely in urban schools (75%) to watch videos to learn how to do something as their age-level peers in suburban communities (77%) or rural locations (76%). Similarly, students who attend schools where the majority of students are students of color are just as likely to report that they are self-directing their learning outside of school by researching websites (72%) as students who attend schools where the student population is primarily white (72%).

Education practitioners and researchers often look for discrete ways to categorize behaviors or attitudes, often relying on student demographics or characteristics to define a population or to explain a phenomenon. The existing body of research on students' self-directed, interest-driven use of digital tools outside of formalized education settings has favored small-scale case studies, observations, and limited qualitative or descriptive approaches to understanding this emerging trend. Additionally, some limited studies have focused on the logistics and interpretations of students' use of discrete types of digital media or tools (e.g. digital games, online communities,

Table 5.2 Free Agent Learner behaviors by community type and majority student populations (2020–2021).

Free Agent Learning behavior	Percentage of Grade 6–8 students who report these Free Agent Learning behaviors						
	Nationwide (%)	Urban communities (%)	Suburban communities (%)	Rural communities (%)	Schools where majority are students of color (%)	Schools where majority are white students (%)
Watch a video to learn how to do something	76	75	77	76	79	76
Research information on a website to answer a question	72	69	73	72	72	72
Play an online game or augmented/virtual simulation activity	61	65	60	60	56	61
Watch other people play online games	57	61	59	54	58	57
Use social media to learn what others are doing or thinking about relative to an interested topic	46	48	48	45	46	46

Source: © Project Tomorrow 2021.

mobile devices) rather than developing a learning ecology perspective on the interlaced media culture to explain how the technology is supporting students' motivations for learning.

The outcomes from this supplemental analysis of the large Speak Up data set have the potential to change existing perceptions and challenge longstanding mythology about students' digital learning experiences outside of school. The finding, therefore, that the participants in the Free Agent Learner Ecosystem defy easy or traditional categorization and represent girls *and* boys, tech savants *and* tech novices, students with access to high-speed Internet at home *and* those who may be accessing learning content through a Wi-Fi hot spot at McDonald's, students in urban, suburban, *and* rural communities, students in majority white *and* majority-minority schools, as well as students with varying levels of interest in STEM fields is an important outcome and valuable for education leaders who want to embrace the Free Agent Learner Ecosystem within their school or district.

Connecting the Dots

- Many aspects of Free Agent Learnership run counter to the traditional norms and cultural cornerstones of education. This makes it difficult for many educators to see how this new concept can fit within the typical school environment. But the question is really a different one. The real debate should be about how traditional education needs to change to embrace Free Agent Learning.

- The Speak Up Research Project has identified 15 of the most common or popular Free Agent Learning activities undertaken by students, with varying levels of frequency or regularity.

- Students across a broad spectrum of schools, communities, demographic groups, interest groups, and family backgrounds exhibit Free Agent Learning. While some differences exist around particular Free Agent Learning activities, those differences are small and insignificant statistically.

- Free Agent Learning is not an isolated trend nor is it a niche activity for only certain types of students. While some may want to put their heads in the sand and ignore the digitally enhanced, self-directed learning pursuits of our youth today, educators would be missing a valuable opportunity to support a new form of student learning that has potential to positively influence in-school learning also.

Now, Think about This!

1. What is needed to help you and your colleagues see Free Agent Learning as an asset for improving education for all students?

2. How many of your colleagues (teachers and administrators) ask students regularly about what they are learning outside of school or how they are pursuing academic passions or curiosities on their own? How could that information be used to support school transformation efforts?

3. How does a deeper understanding of the depth and breadth of students' Free Agent Learning alter our perceptions around how to address equity in education issues? Does this help us frame educational equity solutions?

4. What is one thing that you can do today or tomorrow to understand the lived experience of students with Free Agent Learning? Does it start with some new ideas about the value of social media or watching an esports competition to understand the skills being developed by those e-athletes?

Note

1. https://nces.ed.gov/ccd/.

Chapter 6

The Free Agent Learner's Perspective on School, Learning, and Technology

Too often in my conversations with policymakers or business leaders, and even the occasional school board member, I hear a common refrain: "The problem with today's students is that they are not interested in learning." The COVID pandemic and resulting sudden shift to remote learning for many students triggered an avalanche of more people, including parents, adopting a similar position about today's youth.

The problem with this adult-held belief is that for most students, it is simply not true. But the nuance is important. Students like learning, but many simply do not like school, or at least do not like the educational processes we define as school. For most students, learning and school are not synonymous or exclusive. As noted in earlier chapters, learning for today's students is not limited to what happens in the classroom. According to the Speak Up Research Project, nearly a majority of middle school and high school students are regularly leveraging a broad range of digital tools and resources to self-direct learning around topics and subjects they are interested in beyond their classrooms. These students are actively engaged in learning but on their own terms.

But the reality is that for too many students, school is not an effective or particularly engaging learning experience. There are probably many different hypotheses to explain why traditional school-based learning does not work for all students. Based on the research that

I have done with students in a wide variety of communities and environments, it often comes down to the fact that most learning experiences in school do not encompass the essential elements of the Student Vision for Learning discussed in Chapter 1: learning that is socially based, untethered, contextually rich, and independently driven. The result is that we see schools overprioritizing the process of "learning stuff" to the detriment of empowering their students to become "learners."

Distinguishing School and Learning

In his writing and speaking about the connections between innovation and relationships in education, George Couros, a noted education author and thought leader, draws a stark distinction between school and learning that I think would resonate with many students. The four essential elements of the Student Vision for Learning are notably included in Couros's descriptions of learning. His defining properties of school may not apply to all in-school environments, of course. But the differences between school and learning as articulated on Couros's list may help to clarify for many adults this dilemma of why some students may not like school but still value learning.

- School promotes starting by looking for answers. Learning promotes starting with questions.
- School is about consuming. Learning is about creating.
- School is about finding information on something prescribed for you. Learning is about exploring your passions and interests.
- School teaches compliance. Learning is about challenging perceived norms.
- School is scheduled at certain times. Learning can happen any time, all of the time.
- School often isolates. Learning is often social.

- School is standardized. Learning is personal.
- School teaches us to obtain information from certain people. Learning promotes that everyone is a teacher, and everyone is a learner.
- School is about giving you information. Learning is about making your own connections.
- School is sequential. Learning is random and nonlinear.
- School promotes surface-level thinking. Learning is about deep exploration.[1]

Students in their valuations on school and learning underscore this same dichotomy. According to data collected from over 236 000 students in grades 6–12 over the past three school years (2018–2019, 2019–2020, and 2020–2021), students overwhelmingly believe that it is important for them to do well in school (see Figure 6.1). But

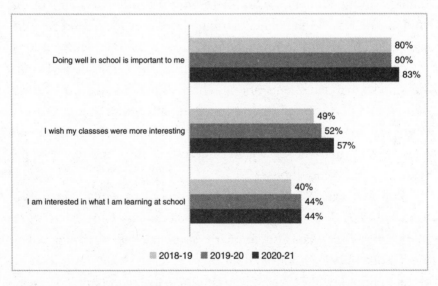

Figure 6.1 Grade 6–12 students' valuations on school and learning—three-year perspective.
Source: © Project Tomorrow 2021.

The Free Agent Learner's Perspective on School

students also wish that their classes were more interesting (57% in the 2020–2021 school year) and only 44% admit they are actually interested in what they are learning at school. For 56% of students, therefore, the education process that many deem as critical to their future success is simply boring. This reality should not be conflated, however, with the COVID pandemic and online learning. Contrary to some popular opinions, students value doing well in school as much today as they did before the implementation of remote learning. And students' level of interest in what they are learning in school is also relatively the same as well, both before and after school closures.

To counter the argument that students don't like learning, it is important to also further segment the ways students think about learning compared to their views about school. When asked about learning without the construct of school, 68% of middle and high school students said they like learning about how to do things, emphasizing the experiential aspect of an effective learning process inherent in the Student Vision for Learning. Nearly two-thirds of the students (62%) said they like learning about new ideas, and 51% expressed support for learning that includes building or making things.

At this point you may be asking yourself these questions: Do the students' belief statements about school and school-based learning versus out-of-school self-directed learning align with their actions or is this just an example of typical generational angst? Haven't students claimed that their classes weren't interesting since the dawn of the one-classroom schoolhouse?

Consider this: While 54% of high school students said during the 2020–2021 school year that they wished their classes were more interesting, 76% were also regularly sourcing and watching online videos outside of school, on their own, to learn about things that interest them, a key Free Agent Learning Activity (see Chapter 5). Nearly two-thirds of high school students also report using social media to learn about people's ideas and to identify people who share their learning interests, not just posting selfies and random comments about celebrities. And this may come as a surprise to some English teachers, 45% of students are regularly tapping into online writing sites to self-improve their writing skills, another documented Free Agent Learning behavior. The difference is all about purpose and passion. These types of self-directed learning are highly purposeful and most importantly are driven by the students themselves around what they perceive as specific learning needs or interests.

While access to technology has empowered students to pursue self-directed learning, the disconnect between students and school goes beyond a preference for digitally enhanced learning. Rather, students want learning experiences that are highly personalized to their interests. The plethora of digital tools, content, and resources available to students today (both in school and at home) provide an egalitarian way for a student to have meaningful personalized learning experiences more easily and efficiently than ever before. Too often, however, traditional school environments and even out-of-school extracurricular or supplemental academic programs still rely on outdated institutional structures including rigid bell schedules that can artificially stifle important learning moments or discussions, formalized curriculum that is not culturally responsive, and standardized achievement metrics that are blind to individual academic strengths or differences. A strict adherence to these structures, especially in light of the Student Vision for Learning, may inadvertently discount or devalue students' preferences for learning and misrepresent or misunderstand the value of using digital tools, content, and resources to support self-directed learning. For example, a common misunderstanding about technology use for learning, both in school and out of school, is an outsized emphasis on the connection between digital tools and student engagement. The students' view on the value of using technology within learning is dramatically different than the adult perspective.

Technology Use and Student Engagement in Learning

For many educators, student engagement in learning is a critical goal on the path to realizing student outcomes, especially with achievement measures. Researchers have long documented a connection between student engagement in the learning process and the potential for higher academic success. Highly valued and frequently cited education research notes that when students are engaged in the learning process in class, they not only demonstrate higher satisfaction with those types of learning experiences, but they are also more likely to have higher academic performance and better graduation results. This makes common sense given that researchers define engagement as the level of attention to a task or activity. Students on task in the classroom are perceived to be engaged with the learning activity.

But we also know that student engagement is influenced by several factors, some learner-centric and others that are dependent on the teacher. The learner's personal level of motivation, their focus aptitude, and cognitive ability affect their engagement levels in class. Additionally, how the teacher structures the lesson or learning activity and their implementation style also influence the level of engagement by their students. Given the pervasiveness of the research findings that increased student engagement affects academic performance, teachers increasingly feel a need to make their lessons more appealing, stimulating, and even entertaining to grasp students' attention. Many teachers talk about feeling like they have to compete with social media and other sources of compelling content that students access regularly to keep students' attention. The quest, therefore, to ensure students are cognitively and emotionally engaged in that math lesson on adding compound fractions or the literature debate on the dark themes in Nathaniel Hawthorne's short stories is often a paramount objective for teachers and one that can be very challenging. For every teacher like Dave Robles, who uses rap to engage his young students in learning grammar,[2] there are many more teachers who struggle to find the optimum recipe for engaging their students in today's lesson.

But what does engagement really look like today? How does a teacher know whether their students are really engaged in that fraction lesson? Linda Darling-Hammond and colleagues identify that learner engagement in a learning setting such as a classroom should address behavioral, cognitive, and emotional aspects of the learning process.[3] They further note that teachers should be able to know whether their students are engaged in learning if they exhibit the behaviors, thinking processes, and emotions that signal they are actively connecting with course materials as well as their teacher and with each other. For most teachers, this too often boils down to simply seeking smiling faces, twinkling eyes, and enthusiastic head nodding as the proof case that their lesson or lecture is engaging. Many educators continue to tell me that they know student engagement when they see it—but they cannot really explain how their actions or how the interest levels of their students result in those engagement signals. Or even if the nodding head and smiles really constitute meaningful engagement anymore.

Many acknowledge that it is increasingly difficult to stimulate or sustain student engagement in classroom learning due to the plethora of compelling content that is available to students beyond the textbook. Consequently, in many ways, the hunt to find new ways and strategies to engage students in learning served as an initial motivation behind the use of digital tools and content in the classroom. Rather than retire that tired lesson first used twenty years ago about the periodic table or about the differences between adverbs and adjectives, many teachers sought instead to infuse a technology component into their preexisting lessons with the hope that co-opting the technology would result in higher levels of student engagement. Simply overlaying technology onto lessons or units of study that are past their expiration date does not result in any sustainable boosts to student engagement. To take advantage of the potential of digital content, tools, and resources to support active learning by students requires teachers to throw out those lesson plans from the pre-technology era and create new learning experiences that are inherently constructed to leverage the unique features and capabilities of the digital resources available today. However, that work is not for the fainthearted and requires a significant change in mindset about the value of technology within learning. The perspective of students on that technology value proposition can be helpful to stimulate such a necessary mindset shift.

When asked about the value of using technology to support student learning, teachers, school principals, and district administrators continue to identify increased student engagement as a primary benefit, however. According to recent Speak Up Research:

- 83% of teachers say that using digital games within instruction increases student engagement in learning;

- 85% of school principals say assigning mobile devices to students (such as tablets, laptops, or Chromebooks) increases student engagement in learning;

- 64% of school principals attribute the same benefit to the use of digital content such as online textbooks and simulations;

- 56% of district administrators say the infusion of coding and computer programming within instruction increases student engagement in learning.

These valuations by educators are longstanding with few changes to the mindset that technology is all about increasing student engagement. In 2016, 74% of teachers credited the use of online games as engaging students in learning and 83% of principals said 1:1 programs where every student gets a mobile device promote student engagement in learning. Correspondingly, district leadership have so closely aligned technology use to student engagement that when asked how they would message a new digital initiative to their community, 88% said their messaging would emphasize that the new technology effort would increase student engagement in learning.

The point is not to say that student engagement is an incorrect goal or not a meaningful objective. As noted earlier, education research definitively links increased student engagement to improved student outcomes. The problem is that too often educators only see the value of technology through the lens of engagement. As I often tell my conference audiences, when discussing the benefits of digital learning, let's include engagement in our value proposition but put a comma after that word, not a period. There are other benefits that can be derived from the effective use of technology in the classroom and should be included in any sentences about the digital learning value proposition. In many ways, this is a noun-verb problem. In the quest to get technology in the classroom to address the student engagement challenge, many schools and districts focused almost exclusively on the nouns of digital learning—what devices to buy, what content to license, what skills teachers need. This was true before the COVID pandemic, though the sudden shift to remote learning to facilitate school continuity amplified that laser focus on the "stuff."

Too little emphasis has been spent on the verbs of digital learning that would describe the impact on student outcomes when technology is used effectively. Based on my experiences with helping school districts as well as education vendors quantify the benefits of technology use within learning, I believe that due to a lack of understanding how to know when technology is being used effectively to support student learning and ongoing confusion about the right metrics for measuring impact, many educators simply throw their hands in the air and say it is impossible to measure the value of technology. The default position is to focus on the smiley faces and shiny eyes as the only outcomes. Engagement is a meaningful but insufficient and incomplete way to assess the value of technology within learning. And our students know that intrinsically from their out-of-school usage in their self-directed learning experiences.

Students' Value Proposition on Technology Use in Learning

Students have a different perspective on the value and outcomes of using technology within learning. Leveraging how they use technology to support self-directed learning experiences, students articulate the advantages to using digital tools in class as the alignment with the four essential elements of the Student Vision for Learning: socially based learning, untethered learning, contextual learning, and self-directed learning. Students see the benefits of using technology within learning as having three primary outcomes: improved academics, development of skills they need for future success, and supporting the personalization of the learning process. As depicted in Table 6.1, the typical 6th grader based on the Speak Up Research findings from the 2020–2021 school year believes that when technology is used effectively in school, they acquire a stronger understanding of class content (55%), develop the future-ready skills of creativity (57%), critical thinking (48%), and collaboration (47%) so highly valued by colleges and employers, and are able to learn at their own pace (58%) just as they do in their Free Agent Learning activities now.

Increased engagement or motivation through the use of technology in class is noted by both high school and middle school students,

Table 6.1 Grade 6 students' identification of the outcomes of using technology within learning.

Benefits of using technology to support learning	Percentage of students in grade 6 who agree (%)
√ **Improved academic outcomes**	
Better grades and test scores	61
Stronger understanding of class content	55
More likely to complete homework assignments	51
√ **Future-ready skill development outcomes**	
Creativity skill development	57
Application of knowledge to practical problems	48
Critical thinking skill development	48
Collaboration skill development	47
√ **Personalized learning outcomes**	
Learning at one's own pace	58
In control of the learning process	50
Fits personal learning goals and style	50

Source: © Project Tomorrow 2021.

but it is simply not as important to students as educators give it credence. Among the high school students in the Speak Up poll, only 33% credited increased student engagement or motivation in learning to the use of technology. The results are similar for middle school students as well with only 4 in 10 students saying increased engagement was an outcome they realized from the technology use in their classroom. That is because the students, based on their out-of-school experiences using technology to address learning needs as well as to satisfy entertainment and social interactions goals, have a more fully formed appreciation for the true value of technology as a tool of learning, not just engagement. As noted earlier, the students see technology as a utility that helps them achieve specific, purposeful learning goals, not just as a way to keep them focused on a particular teacher-directed lesson or piece of content. Consequently, the lens they bring to this discussion about the value of technology within learning is fundamentally different than the way most adults view the situation.

This interpretation of the value of technology within education by our students should not be seen solely as an indictment on the way technology is being currently used in the classroom. But rather, it is a matter of perspective based on experience and context. Students simply have a different lens on the experience of using technology based on their out-of-school habits, and that creates a different context for their valuation on the experience in school. In my work evaluating the efficacy of mobile devices within instruction, I have visited more than 200 K–12 classrooms over the past 12 years to observe how students and teachers use digital learning devices (including smartphones, tablets, laptops, and Chromebooks) to support learning. Quite often, I see students taking notes in class on their assigned tablet or Chromebook while their teacher lectures on a curriculum topic or explains an abstract concept. The teachers often proudly tell me that they are so appreciative that their students have these digital learning devices. The teachers specifically mention to me that their students are more engaged in taking notes when they can use their device for that task versus the traditional method of writing down what the teacher is saying in a spiral notebook. But the reality is that taking notes while a teacher is lecturing is not an engaging or motivating learning experience for most students anyway. The novelty of using a device breaks up that monotony of note-taking, but it probably does not represent an effective or truly engaging use of technology within learning.

Unfortunately, sometimes our own blind spots about the value of technology within learning and a misunderstanding of what we are seeing when students use technology clouds our vision for appreciating why the Student Vision for Learning is important for the future of American education. Understanding the student perspective and the foundation for that perspective through Free Agent Learning is an underutilized asset in too many schools and districts interested in improving the efficacy of digital learning.

Making the Student Vision for Learning Real in School

The idea that students have their own vision for what constitutes effective learning may be a difficult concept for many educators to grasp. The traditional vision of learning in a school or district is often dictated by the state standards or local educational outcomes determined by the school board or district leadership. There is also sometimes a jaded view in education that students could not possibly articulate adequate goals for their learning since (i) they either had not had enough life experience to warrant an opinion, (ii) they don't know what colleges or employers are expecting in terms of outcomes from K–12 education, or (iii) kids are inherently lazy and just don't want to do the hard work of school. It is my long standing belief that the views and ideas of your K–12 students are an invaluable asset for a school or district to leverage to create a more informed vision for their educational enterprise. Too many schools and districts simply have not taken advantage of that asset yet.

Educators know the power of effective storytelling within learning, especially around new or complex topics. Students and adults alike respond positively to stories that can paint a picture of a new idea or clear away the clouds on a confusing or complicated concept that may run counter to conventional wisdom or long-held beliefs. The following research illustrates how the essential elements of the Student Vision for Learning, born out of the students' own

The Free Agent Learner's Perspective on School

self-directed learning experiences beyond the classroom, provide new insights into the different ways students think about various learning processes today and the purposes underpinning their use of digital tools to support that learning.

Students Differentiating Technology Tool Usage by Learning Task

Students realize that their ideal learning environment should not be bounded by the limitations of one device per student but rather that the ideal environment should support devices based on what features and functions are best to meet the needs of a particular task. Instead of trying to make one device be all things, they want to use the right tool for the right academic task. This awareness stems from their familiarity with using various devices in their personal lives and appreciating the pros and cons of differentiated usage. Through those experiences, students have developed their own highly personalized typology for device usage that is not dependent simply on the engagement level of the interaction per se but rather on the efficiency of the tool to meet the needs of a particular task. For example, a smartphone may be a highly convenient device to update your Instagram account with a photo of your lunch but is not the optimum tool for completing the application for that coveted summer internship at a local bio-technology company.

Contrary to conventional wisdom, today's students are highly savvy about the utility and efficiency of digital tools to support their interactions and activities. With increased access to mobile devices in class, students are now overlaying a similar typology on schoolwork activities. Similar to how students and adults view technology outcomes differently, students have a distinctive perspective on how mobile devices can help them address their learning goals. While many education leaders continue to hunt for the holy grail of mobile devices (the one perfect device to put in the hands of all their students to use for all learning tasks), today's students have transcended that question and approach the association of various devices with learning goals by emphasizing a differentiated model. When asked, for example, about the best device to accomplish typical academic tasks, middle and high school students demonstrate through their selections how the efficiency of the work supersedes the mere use of any particular device for engagement only. Through their experiences using these tools for learning, the students have gained a masterful set of knowledge about which types of activities or tasks are best served by various mobile functions or devices.

Within the students' typology of usage, for example, a laptop or Chromebook is the right tool to write that essay for class or take the state achievement test (see Table 6.2). Correspondingly, a smartphone is the optimal device for communication and collaboration with classmates and teachers. This acknowledgment of the value of a smartphone for timely, two-way communications was evidenced during the 2020–2021 school year when 54% of students in remote

Table 6.2 What is the best device to help you with these schoolwork tasks?

Academic task	Preferred mobile device for that task
Create multi-media presentation or content	Laptop or Chromebook
Take online tests	Laptop or Chromebook
Write reports or essays	Laptop or Chromebook
Read an e-book or online article	Digital reader or tablet with enhanced screen quality for reading
Take notes in class	Tablet
Create a video	Tablet or smartphone
Communicate with peers and classmates	Smartphone
Communicate with teachers	Smartphone

Source: © Project Tomorrow 2021.

The Free Agent Learner's Perspective on School

learning environments reported texting with their teachers on a regular basis. One-third of students in fully face-to-face learning environments also acknowledged the use of texting for their two-way communications as well. While many school districts prohibit or discourage student-teacher text messaging, students highly value the opportunity to engage with their teachers for quick, two-way communications, especially to solve a problem or answer a question in a timely manner. Additionally, this is learned behavior from their out-of-school learning lives that students see as highly efficient and effective. Why not be able to use this tool to support their in-school learning as well?

As evidenced by the differentiation in the use of mobile or digital learning devices by academic task, students view one-to-one programs where they are assigned a school-owned mobile device with skepticism. They value the opportunity to use the assigned device but are confused by their inability to use other devices including their own personal devices that might be better suited for particular learning tasks. The following example of how students differentiate learning tasks using a variety of devices, both school-owned and personal, illustrate a typical learning workflow and the efficacy of using the right device for the right task.

Workflow of Student Learning Activities using a Differentiated Set of Devices and Tools

Student assignment: As a group, create a slideshow to demonstrate what you learned from your science fair project about the toxicity of detergents that claim to be green products.

1. Upon receiving the assignment from their teacher, the five students in the science project group each use their own personal smartphones and a scheduling app to coordinate times to work together on the slideshow.

2. Later that night from home, the students use their school-provided Chromebooks and a virtual whiteboard to collaboratively design the storyboard for the slideshow. At the same time, one member of the group using their own tablet takes notes for the assignment on a Google doc that is shared across the group. From time to time, the students revisit the teacher's assignment rubric posted on Blackboard, the school's learning management system (LMS). Students can access the LMS from their phone, personal devices, or school Chromebook.

3. Based upon the storyboard skeleton, the students determine that they need some additional research to support key findings from the science experiment. Using their own personal digital reader, one student accesses their school library's Gale database of scientific journal articles to find the needed research. The journal articles are annotated, and the links are shared across the project group via the Google doc. The students each use the new research to separately annotate the storyboard when it is convenient for them. The journal article citations (already formatted by the Gale resource) are sent to a new Google doc.

4. Additional content for the project is available since one member of the group recorded their project being evaluated at the science fair by the judges. That student uploads that recording from their smartphone to the shared document drive for the project. Another student grabs that MP4 file and embeds it in the slideshow.

5. Assigned to seek out other images for the slideshow, students use a variety of devices to find images that have been tagged by Creative Commons for free and fair usage by students.

6. The students all contribute to the building of the slideshow using Google Slides. Most of the students use their school Chromebook. One of the group members is at their part-time

job, however, and so on their break they use a personal laptop to access the Google slides for their input.

7. The slideshow is almost complete, but the students worry if they have the right format for the citations. One student text messages their teacher to ask about the desired citation format. The teacher responds immediately with a reply text recommending the APA format. That was the selected format from the Gale database, and so the students breath a sigh of relief.

8. The students finish the slideshow with each being responsible for different content. The final product is uploaded to the class container on the LMS for teacher review.

The workflow of the students within this example illustrates how the use of various digital tools can work in concert with one another to support efficiency and effectiveness. Certainly, the project could have been completed even if the students only had access to their school-provided Chromebooks. But the integrated use of the various digital tools, each being implemented because of the specialty of the inherent features and functions of the tool (such as the video editing capabilities on a smartphone) and the convenient access to those tools, increased the overall efficiency of the process. This seemingly natural skill at differentiating tools to meet individual task needs is most likely a reflection of the types of experiences students have with self-directed learning outside of school. For today's students, technology is about utility first, engagement second. They see these devices as tools, not toys. The students' value proposition on why mobile devices are important in their learning life is about how they support the efficiency and effectiveness of the learning process, more so than the novelty of using the devices.

And yet, we continue to see that outsized focus on student engagement as the primary goal of 1:1 device programs. The students appreciate the inherently engaging and compelling nature of these devices, but because their primary focus is on the empowerment of their learning potential, they have unique sight lines to look beyond what they view as simplistic engagement to see the unrealized benefits that would enable more personalized, contextually relevant learning experiences. Their ongoing frustration is with the lack of visionary acuity by the adults who oversee their formalized educational lives. One size does not fit all in the students' prescription for effective digital learning.

Students Using Online Tools for Career Exploration

With so much emphasis nationwide on college and career readiness and preparation, students' use of various digital tools to support self-directed research on different career fields is particularly interesting. Traditional career exploration activities such as summer camps, after-school programs, skill competitions, or career technical education classes at school are not the only options for students who want to learn about different career fields or future jobs. New emerging use cases for digital tools, including social media and mobile-enabled experiences, are gaining and retaining student attention. Both the selection of the tools and the self-directed nature of these informal learning experiences are in alignment with the students' vision for optimal learning and how they want to acquire knowledge and skills to prepare themselves for future success.

Reflecting national attention on getting more students interested in the STEM fields, many school districts have established magnet schools or specialized academies to provide students with a deeper learning experience in these curricular areas. The theory of change is if we provide students with rich STEM learning experiences as part of their middle school or high school years, they will develop a greater interest in pursuing advanced education in STEM fields and will be better prepared to be successful in those educational and career pursuits. Research is indicating that this theory is valid. But what is missing from this equation is the understanding that students are also learning about STEM and future jobs or careers beyond exposure to school-directed curriculum or -sponsored activities. Increasingly, students are using the digital tools at their personal disposal to explore careers and prepare themselves for future success in those fields.

Career exploration is one of the explicit purposes of Free Agent Learnership that was discussed in Chapter 3. Speak Up research indicates that middle and high school students are interested in self-directed career investigation experiences that allow them to use already familiar personal tools and resources to support career interests and workforce preparation. These types of learning experiences share many of the same characteristics of the Student Vision for Learning. Interestingly, this interest in the use of social media and mobile-enabled online resources for career exploration is even higher among students who are attending a STEM magnet school or participating in a formalized STEM academy at their school. It would be assumed that those students are already having a rich STEM experience in their daily school life with a wider set of STEM-related classes to choose from as well as opportunities to learn from existing career professionals and participate in internships and job shadowing events. But these future engineers, scientists, technologists, and mathematicians also want to tap into social media, online videos, and game-based environments to direct more highly personalized learning experiences in their fields of interest.

For example, among middle school students attending a STEM-specific school or academy, 44% say that the best way for them to learn about careers is to watch self-discovered "day in the life"-type videos that document the real-world, day-to-day activities of an electrical engineer or computer scientist (see Table 6.3). The same

Table 6.3 Middle school students' interest in using digital tools to support career exploration.

Digital tools for career exploration	Percentage of students who want to use these tools for career exploration	
	Grade 6–8 students attending STEM magnet schools or in specialized STEM academies/programs at their school (%)	Grade 6–8 students attending non-STEM specific schools or programs (%)
Watch online videos about "day in the life" job experiences	44	44
Play a game or simulation activity about a job or career	43	37
Take an online class or self-paced online tutorial outside of school to learn more about a career or job field	42	35
Follow the social media posts of influencers/experts in my interested job and career fields	40	37
Research websites or use mobile apps about different jobs and careers	40	37

Source: © Project Tomorrow 2021.

percentage of students in non-STEM-focused schools have the same aspiration. An additional 42% of students would like to take a supplemental online course (in addition to their schoolwork) to learn more specifically about a future career. And 43% see playing an online game or simulation activity as an effective way for them to experience a future job, before needing to make a larger time and financial commitment to college or advanced technical training.

The fingerprints of the Student Vision of Learning are evident throughout this list of digitally enhanced career exploration experiences. The contextual relevancy of the learning experience is paramount with the "day in the life" videos. Games or simulation-based learning can either be solo pursuits or multiplayer experiences supporting the social-based essential element. The exposure to a wide field of experts through social media aligns with the students' desires for untethered learning experiences including about future jobs or careers. But the key characteristic in these emerging exploration methodologies is that the student is in charge of the experience and self-directing how they interact with and consume the online content in a highly personalized way.

The self-directed learning experiences that students are facilitating through their use of their smartphone as well as social media resources has another unintentional effect. Increasingly, through these experiences, students realize not only that they enjoy and benefit from the self-determination process, but their aspirations for better in-school experiences become clearer as well. It is through experiences such as these around career exploration that students are developing new expectations for their in-school learning practices. These new expectations should be of high interest to education leaders.

Students as Content Producers, Not Just Consumers

As noted by George Couros and others, the traditional school model is predicated on students as simple consumers of information. The teacher is the keeper of the information, providing selected and structured periodic opportunities for students to consume the precious content as part of the learning process. Yet today's students place a higher premium on the highly personalized learning experience of creating content and sharing their discoveries, masterpieces, and manuscripts with the world. Social media vehicles have provided an opportunity for everyone to become a media producer and to find an audience to reflect and comment on their self-created content, whether that is your Instagram collage of travel photos or replies to political commentary on Twitter. And while teachers may assign projects that require some level of multimedia manipulation or creation and enable new audiences for student work such as through literary journals or community showcases, these efforts do not fully address the Student Vision for Learning. Students have different expectations for school today and quite often, the heart of those expectations centers on how they can use digital tools and resources to self-direct and self-monitor their learning experiences.

And even with this realization, the battle over student use of their own online and digital tools continues to play out every day in classrooms. Many education leaders are valiantly trying to understand how to reconcile their traditional views with a new world order where students can with a few clicks on a mobile device have access to more information and expertise about any possible topic than by asking their teacher or going to the school library. And yet, 28% of high school students and 41% of middle school students in the 2020–2021 Speak Up surveys say their biggest obstacle to using technology for learning when they are at school is that they still cannot use their personal mobile devices, even after many of these students used their own devices to facilitate remote learning during school closures.

This pedagogical shift from thinking about students as primarily consumers in the learning process to reframing their role to include being authentic producers of content is challenging for many teachers and administrators. Only one-third of teachers (37%) say that they are regularly providing opportunities for their students create media projects. This represents a significant lost opportunity not only to help students develop key skills they need for future success but also to enable students to develop identity, agency, and efficacy as

The Free Agent Learner's Perspective on School

a learner and to bridge what students are already doing outside of school using these same tools to create and showcase their learning outputs to support more self-directed learning and more meaningful experiences in school. The out-of-school learning lives of students are rich with experiences where students have used the content creation process to build a community of shared learning and to establish new audiences for their content that can provide feedback for personal growth. Many education researchers have been documenting this shift with examples of how students are using the content development and audience creation process to actuate the Student Vision for Learning on their own terms.

- Students highly valued being able to use their smartphone to seek information that interests them, to have that information available at their fingertips, and to be able to then remix and repackage digital content in highly personalized ways. The researchers Kurt Squire and Seann Dikkers, in their extensive work on the role of educational technology in supporting self-directed learning, share an example of a student who was interested in music.[4] His personal smartphone enabled him to research songwriting techniques anywhere, anytime but also to use the device to assist with his writing process through audio recordings and playbacks in his family's basement where he would not disturb others. They labeled this heightened sense of empowerment and value as a self-directed learner as an *"amplification of self."*

- Michigan State University researcher Christine Greenhow also saw the impact of the empowered learner with her research on students' creation of content for a youth-initiated, current events–focused niche network within a social media site.[5] Documenting that two-thirds of the content on the niche site within one three-month period was contributed by students, Greenhow noted that the act of contributing that content resulted in the student-writers having an increased interest in the topics they were reporting on such as environmental science and climate change. Squire and Dikkers refer to this result of self-directed learning as an *"amplification of interest."* By acting on their own interests and creating content that supports and extends these interests, Mizuko Ito notes that students develop their own voice and agency as a learner and as a member of society.[6]

- According to danah boyd, Christine Greenhow, and Beth Robelia, social networking sites provide valuable opportunities for students to explore their own identity both within society and as a learner.[7] One of the most appealing aspects of the sites to youth is their ability to develop and showcase skills within a network of like-minded peers. Brigid Barron in her case study portraits of self-directed learners and Mizuko Ito in several of the studies she analyzed with her colleagues demonstrate the linkage between students' development of expertise in the use of various digital media such as gaming, web design, or video editing and their growing sense of self-identity and competence.[8] The arenas where students are developing these new identities, gaining prestige, and cultivating reputations as experts are very different than traditional academic performance-based settings. Student-sponsored arenas such as online communities for gamers and niche social networking sites have a solid foundation in peer learning, knowledge sharing, and a culture where failure is neither consequential nor has the high-stakes ramifications of traditional school achievement measures.

- By using digital tools to create content around interest areas and developing expertise within those areas of interest, the students are also acquiring or enhancing their technology skills. Two sets of renown researchers, John Furlong and Chris Davies, and Christine Greenhow and Beth Robelia, see the development of technology fluency as a key by-product of students' interest-driven digital learning.[9] Within all three genres of participation, *hanging out, messing around, and geeking out,* Mizuko Ito documents how students are not only developing new technical skills by using digital tools but many are also serving as "techne-mentors" to each other by sharing resources and knowledge and actively functioning as online peer coaches. Similar to what Greenhow and Robelia learned about how students are acquiring effective communications skills using a social networking site, boyd's research found that students' use of these sites also provided important digital citizenship lessons on how to manage public impressions and read social cues from both written content and imagery.

The Speak Up research findings also substantiate that the experiences that students are having with creating content and finding audience outside of school is already influencing their expectations for a school learning experience that more closely aligns with their vision for more effective learning. Nearly two-thirds of middle and high school students (63%) say that having access to digital media tools to support content creation is on their wish list for the ultimate school. How students are using YouTube specifically outside of school to support their own content creation provides another meaningful example of the Student Vision for Learning at work.

YouTube usage by students is highly pervasive, especially in terms of serving as a source for learning content. Nearly 78% of high school students and 84% of middle school students say they are regularly using online videos from YouTube on their own, not teacher directed to learn how to do something. In many ways, the experiences that

Table 6.4 How students are creating and curating content on YouTube disaggregated by gender.

YouTube activity	Percentage of students in grades 6–12 who agree	
	Girls (%)	Boys (%)
Recommend YouTube content to a friend	53	50
Use YouTube videos to learn more about a topic I am interested in	51	47
Post a comment on a video I found on YouTube	36	44
Have my own personal YouTube channel	20	33
Post a self-created video on YouTube	14	25

Source: © Project Tomorrow 2021.

students are having with YouTube is a microcosm of how students are tapping into online resources to support their self-directed learning, particularly around skill development (see Table 6.4). Students are using YouTube as a source for homework help (34%) as well as setting up their own YouTube channels (27%). But the YouTube usage is also about content creation and the students' role as content recommenders and curators. Over 50% of both girls and boys in grades 6–12 recommend YouTube content they find interesting or valuable on a regular basis to friends. One-third of girls say they have posted a comment on a YouTube video; 44% of boys in middle and high school say the same. And students are also creating their own YouTube content and posting that online for others to comment on, recommend, or utilize for their own self-directed learning. It is not surprising, therefore, that a majority of middle and high school students, most notably girls, believe that schools should allow access to YouTube during the school day. Not unlike the stated goals of many schools, YouTube functions for many students as a source of learning content, a place to develop important skills, and a public space for finding audience and community.

As educators think about the value proposition for technology within learning, it is important to appreciate that students view their out-of-school learning experiences, most notably on YouTube, as highly valuable skill development opportunities that will positively affect their future. While 40% of high school students say that they are learning important skills in their day-to-day classes at school to support their future success, a higher percentage of students (48%) say that the skills they are learning through their YouTube experiences are important for their future.

The Internet has forever changed the way we think about public spaces, and while some educators may not be comfortable with thinking about the online spaces of social media as learning environments, students view these places as opportunities to build community through self-expression. The process of creating content to represent what you have learned, even if that process is still evolving, is a critical component of the authenticity of the experience. And along the way, students say they are developing the types of workplace skills that will help them be successful in the future. Today's students are on the leading edge of understanding how to merge personal identities around topics that interest and engage them with the development of meaningful life and workplace-ready skills. For the most part, this critical learning process is happening outside of their formalized school environments, and the value of the learning experiences is still largely unknown and invisible to the adults in their learning lives.

A Free Agent Learner Experience

It was in middle school when Thomas realized that he really didn't like school. For Thomas, it was simple. The traditional school learning paradigm was no longer meeting his personal needs. Thomas liked learning; he simply did not feel that his classes in middle and then high school were supporting his learning goals and advancing him to future success. Way too often, he felt that his time sitting in class was unproductive and unrelated to his aspirations for his life.

Like lots of people of all ages, Thomas liked watching YouTube videos in his spare time. Beyond engaging with the entertaining content, however, Thomas developed a strong curiosity to learn more about how videos were made and promoted on YouTube. This curiosity evolved into a full-blown quest to develop a comprehensive set of workplace skills to support YouTube content creation and ultimately a business. To support this skill development process, Thomas in middle school set up his own YouTube channel and online store to buy and sell unique or high-end athletic shoes, an interest of his at the time. To be successful in this venture, however, Thomas needed to quickly develop a set of skills that were not part of standard school curriculum. For example, he had to learn how to create and edit videos, make video thumbnails to support his content, develop a brand identity for his channel and store, and learn how to effectively run a business online. Through a photography class in 7th grade, Thomas developed an entry-level understanding of Photoshop, but most of his learning on how to be a YouTube entrepreneur came from his own firsthand experiences with YouTube content development and seeking out others online to answer his questions. This is not something that Thomas could learn in school.

Through high school Thomas continued to pursue his curiosity about different YouTube business models and to develop new and more advanced skills to support a future career. He accomplished this through his own self-directed, interest-driven learning outside of school. His engagement in this individualized learning process propelled him to seek out new opportunities for growth and expertise development. Thomas graduated high school after transferring to a small alternative school that values students' independent study and empowers their students to follow personalized learning passions.

Today, at age 19, Thomas is a YouTube entrepreneur, managing a YouTube channel for a streamer who has over two million subscribers. Thomas also has his own online store where he sells video editing assets (tools used by online content creators to edit their videos) to other YouTubers. To support the work, he often hires 13- to 15-year-old students to do video editing for him now, similar to the work he did as a middle school student. This year Thomas's gross annual income will exceed that of his mother, a long time education leader in a county office of education. Thomas has big plans to build both his business and to further develop new skills that will allow him to take advantage of emerging opportunities in this marketplace. Thomas is a Free Agent Learner.

There are many more students like Thomas in our schools today than many educators would imagine or realize. There are students for whom learning traditional content areas without a connection to the real world is simply not engaging. There are students who have an identified passion for something, and a dream to build that passion into a future career, but that interest area or skill development process is not part of the standard curriculum or course catalog. Too often schools fail to realize that for every student who has no idea what they may study in college or want to do as professional work, there is another student who not only may have an interest area identified but who is eager to get started in that career preparation process, even in middle school.

Students tell me that the debates over whether schools should prioritize content knowledge acquisition or career skill development is silly. Why can't schools do both and meet students where they are in terms of their interests and goals? For students like Thomas, technology access, a school environment that valued self-directed learning, and very supportive parents provided the agency for him to explore his career passions on his own and develop proficiencies that he is leveraging right now for economic self-sufficiency.

The reality is that for too many students, school is not intrinsically motivating. Our overemphasis on artificial measurements such as grades and test scores and strict adherence to the traditional norms of school-based learning obscure in many ways that we are not really meeting the needs of all of our students. The resourceful ones such as Thomas are finding ways to supplant school learning with Free Agent Learning in pursuit of their personal goals. However, an opportunity exists today, through the realization of the value that students place on the Student Vision for Learning and their experiences with Free Agent Learnership, for school and district leaders to think differently about the purpose of school and what their students need today to be successful tomorrow. The question is whether our schools are ready to embrace this new thinking.

Connecting the Dots

- Students like learning, but many do not like school. However, meaningful learning is not dependent on being in school. This is evidenced by the students who are highly engaged in Free Agent Learning activities but are not engaged in school-based learning. This reality also points to why it is imperative for education leaders to understand the dynamics of Free Agent Learning and explore new ways to incorporate the key characteristics of these self-directed learning experiences within the school day.

- Students bring to the discussion of learning a different point of view on the value of technology use as well. While students focus on the outcomes or verbs of digital learning such as how technology changes their learning experience, adults in general are stuck on the tangible assets or nouns of technology, which include ongoing debates about device types, policies that

173

The Free Agent Learner's Perspective on School

prohibit usage, and structured time allocations for technology use in school. Students see technology as a utility, enabling a more efficient and effective way to address a need.

- Students' ideas about how to improve school are often reflective of their Free Agent Learning experiences. For example, identifying different digital devices as optimal for different learning tasks, incorporating career preparation activities in the school day, and providing more opportunities for students to develop creativity skills by becoming content creators, not just consumers, each have their roots in the experiences of students outside of school.

Now, Think about This!

1. What should be the types of appropriate outcomes or benefits from the effective use of technology that we measure and document? Are those the same ones that we are measuring or documenting today? Why or why not?

2. Are we so blinded by our own perceptions of the value of traditional school or even standardized curriculum that we cannot see where these structures may no longer be serving our desired end goals? How do we override those long-held perceptions to understand what our students really need from their educational guardians today?

3. How comfortable or ready are our teachers to internalize Free Agent Learning and the reasons why students may be more engaged in their self-directed learning pursuits than in classroom

instruction? How can we help them see their role in this new education ecosystem?

4. What is one thing that you can do today or tomorrow to help teachers in particular gain a new understanding of what is needed to help their students develop competency and capacity for self-sustaining future success?

Notes

1. https://georgecouros.ca/blog/archives/4974.
2. https://www.npr.org/2021/06/25/1010176528/new-york-teacher-drops-sick-beats-for-grammar-lessons.
3. https://www.tandfonline.com/doi/full/10.1080/10888691.2018.1537791.
4. https://www.researchgate.net/publication/258129784_Amplifications_of_learning.
5. https://www.researchgate.net/publication/49761164_Youth_as_content_producers_ in_a_niche_social_network_site.
6. https://mitpress.mit.edu/books/hanging-out-messing-around-and-geeking-out.
7. http://www.danah.org/papers/WhyYouthHeart.pdf; https://eric.ed.gov/?id=EJ856843.
8. http://life-slc.org/docs/barron-self-sustainedlearning.pdf.
9. https://www.researchgate.net/publication/233072742_Young_people_new_technologies_and_learning_at_home_Taking_context_seriously.

Chapter 7

Why Schools Are Not (Yet) Ready to Embrace Free Agent Learning

Structural, political, and cultural tensions often inhibit the adoption of innovations, especially in K–12 education. Such is the case with the lack of appreciation by educators regarding the value of students' self-directed, interest-driven digital learning taking place every day outside of school. As will be discussed in Chapters 8–10, embracing Free Agent Learnership as a valid and meaningful learning experience for students has the potential to help schools address three vexing challenges: increasing student engagement in learning, addressing the inequities in learning opportunities, and providing learning experiences that develop student self-efficacy and empowerment. The previous chapters have aimed to help education leaders gain a new understanding of the Free Agent Learner, their self-directed learning activities, and their motivations for valuing these out-of-school experiences. And while some leaders may be excited about seeking out the Free Agent Learners in their schools and examining new ways to incorporate the characteristics of self-directed, interest-driven learning within everyday instruction, others may already be making a list of all the obstacles that could stand in the way of embracing Free Agent Learning as a vehicle for improving education. That list will undoubtedly be a very long one.

For many seasoned school and district leaders there is an experiential understanding that the inherent structural inertia and longstanding cultural intractability within the education ecosystem can be a formidable enemy to all kinds of innovations. Driving innovation within a school or district, whether that new idea is about changing the start times for high school to meet teenagers' need for more sleep or embracing virtual learning for students who say that learning modality is best for them, is not for the fainthearted. The same will be true for thinking about how to transform school from the outside in by embracing Free Agent Learning. Specific to students' self-directed learning outside of school, there are three unique environmental factors or barriers that hinder greater appreciation of Free Agent Learnership as a potential leadership asset. Those barriers include: (i) a blindness to a broader definition of learning, (ii) a lack of foresight and sophistication regarding the real value and impact of using digital tools, content, and resources to support meaningful learning, and (iii) the ongoing battle in education for power, authority, and control. Each follow-on discussion in this chapter includes suggestions about how to embrace Free Agent Learning within the context of the barrier.

Barrier #1: Learning Happens Only in School

Most K–12 school and district leaders today say that their ultimate mission is to prepare their students with the knowledge and skills they need to be ready to tackle the challenges of college, career, and the workforce. But that was not necessarily the case a few years ago. This focus on skill development within the context of content learning was codified as a movement by the Partnership for 21st Century Skills (P21) in 2001.

Taking key concepts discussed by many educators at the time about the need to change the focus or purpose of American education to better address societal and economic needs, this public-private partnership developed new roadmaps for schools and communities to use to reframe their student learning goals. P21 models and graphical descriptions provided a new context for understanding the relationship between college and career skills and the traditional subject areas. And the organization helped to seed in the education ecosystem a new vocabulary for talking about these connections including an articulation of the 4Cs of critical thinking, communications, collaboration, and creativity as the new skills for learning and innovation. Rather than discussing these types of skills along with information, media, and technology skills as stand-alone silos, P21 provided a way for education leaders to think about how to integrate the development of those proficiencies in English, math, science, and history classes. Since the organization included business leaders as well as educators on their board of directors, the focus of ensuring that students were graduating with the skills needed to support economic self-sufficiency and participation in the increasingly global economy was baked into the organization's work.

Since P21, many other organizations and groups have taken up the mantle of supporting this new integrated approach that prioritizes the impact of school learning experiences on student outcomes and potential success beyond high school graduation. And while the terminology of twenty-first-century skills has evolved to include college and career preparation and future-ready skill development, this focus on including skills alongside content knowledge has prevailed. Today, P21 is part of the Battelle for Kids, a national, not-for-profit organization with a similar mission to ensure appropriate twenty-first-century learning for every student.[1] Future Ready Schools® (FRS) is a more recent initiative that helps "innovative educators ensure that each student graduates from high school with the agency, passion, and skills to be a productive, compassionate, and responsible citizen."[2] The group provides a very comprehensive set of professional learning experiences, resources, and toolkits to support school and district leaders in realigning their capacities to support students' preparations for future success. FRS is part of All4Ed (formerly known as the Alliance for Excellent Education), a national nonprofit advocacy organization committed to expanding equitable educational opportunities for all students.

Spurred by these movements and a greater emphasis by hiring companies on the tangible skills needed for their future workforce, an emphasis on the development of student skills for future-ready success, therefore, is now part of the nomenclature in most schools and communities. But what types of skills are school districts prioritizing as most important for students to develop to be successful after their K–12 education is completed? To answer that question, the Speak Up surveys periodically poll district administrators and parents about the types of skills or learning attributes that students need to be successful today. The skills identified by district administrators track closely with the ones noted by employers and parents. The list of skills and the rankings of those skills as recognized by the administrators have remained consistent year over year.

In the 2014–2015 school year, for example, district leaders identified critical thinking and problem-solving skills as the top future-ready attribute for students to develop. Administrators said the same in the 2019–2020 polling. Other top skills include the ability to work with diverse groups of people in different settings, teamwork and collaboration skills, and the capacity to learn independently. Seven in ten district administrators (70%) also identified technology skills as part of the top 10 list. The complete list of the top 10 skills identified by district leaders over the past six years is shown in Figure 7.1.

The Emergence of Graduate Profiles and Other Guiding Documents

The prioritization of these specific skills is important when thinking about how the instructional process has evolved over the past

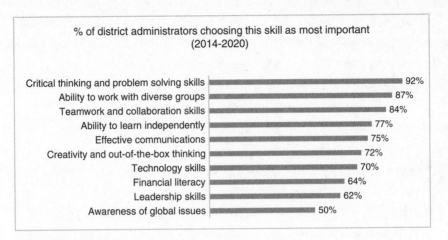

Figure 7.1 Top 10 skills students need to develop for future success.
Source: © *Project Tomorrow 2014–2020.*

20 years to put a greater focus on skill development. And the evidence is apparent not only in the development of new standards such as the Next Generation Science Standards but also in the explicit callout of these skills as school outcomes. School and district leaders share the importance of these skills with their community by codifying them in school or district mission and vision statements (example: "We develop leaders who shape the world through independence, creativity, and critical thinking."[3]).

An emerging trend in many districts today is the creation of additional guiding documents and statements that go beyond the 50,000-foot-level aspirations and articulate outcomes and competencies that will be the result of students attending their schools. These documents have various names and titles. Many districts with grades K–5 or K–8 are labeling them Learner Profiles or Student Promotion Profiles. Districts that include high school students tend to look at these outcomes through the lens of post-graduation proficiencies and thus have adopted names such as a Portrait of Our Graduate or a Graduate Profile. Former Superintendent Suzette Lovely's book

Why Schools Are Not (Yet) Ready to Embrace Free Agent Learning

Ready for Anything: Four Touchstones for Future-Focused Learning provides insights about the value of having Graduate Profile documents and provides a process for the development of a local version for your school district.[4] The El Segundo Unified School District in California provides a representative explanation of a Graduate Profile on their community website.[5] It reads as follows:

> *A graduate profile is a document that a school district develops with input from local stakeholders to specify the cognitive, personal, and interpersonal competencies that students should possess when they graduate from high school. A graduate profile outlines the necessary foundation for students' future success in college and career. The Graduate Profile serves as a True North, for which future district goals are formulated and aligned. Co-created with input from key stakeholders, this profile is a clear visualization of priority goals for teaching and learning that can be easily communicated to students, parents, faculty, and staff to align their collective efforts. A school district's adoption of a Graduate Profile is a nationwide movement to address the shift necessary in education to prepare students for the jobs of the future.*

Besides serving as a positioning document for both internal and external stakeholders about the purpose of education in their schools, many of these Graduate Profiles can also be used as assessment tools, to evaluate a school's or district's progress toward ensuring that their students are well prepared to meet the challenges of college, career, and work after graduation. It is also structured to allow for the assessment of an individual student with a scale of readiness or competency with the various skills. The Graduate Profile from the El Segundo district provides an example of how a district-developed document like this can be used to both guide policy and programs

182

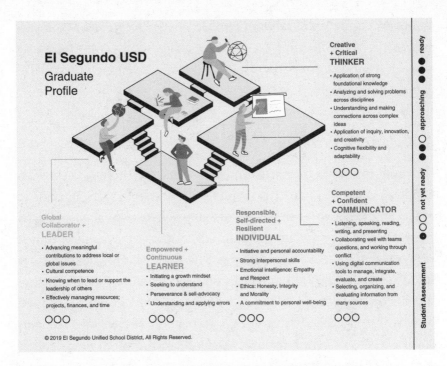

Figure 7.2 Graduate Profile from El Segundo Unified School District.

as well as assess progress. The skills identified in this example (see Figure 7.2) closely align with the top 10 skills and attributes identified by district administrators nationwide in Figure 7.1.

The development of a Graduate Profile (or similarly named documents) provides districts with many benefits. The process of creating such a guiding document usually involves the engagement of community members to ensure that the expectations are appropriate for the local area, including those of employers. That type of a community engagement process builds local support and buy-in. The resulting documents can serve as a roadmap, much like a business operating plan, to guide decisions and even investments within the district. They also signal to teachers and administrators the value of college and career skill development within their instructional practices and help them develop new mindsets and priorities around the

Why Schools Are Not (Yet) Ready to Embrace Free Agent Learning

Graduate Profile expectations. The Graduate Profile is a significant step in the right direction to not only changing the way we speak about learner outcomes but also quantifying those new outcomes as aligned to future-ready skills.

A Missed Opportunity

However, too often the focus of these plans and profiles is on what happens exclusively in the typical school day from 8:30 a.m. to 3:00 p.m., and how those school-based experiences almost singularly affect students' preparation for future success. This school-centric view obscures the value of the self-directed learning experiences students are having outside or beyond school and of teacher sponsorship or facilitation. This seems like a missed opportunity. Given what we have learned in earlier chapters about the reasons students engage in Free Agent Learning activities and the types of outcomes they are realizing through those experiences, guiding documents such as a Graduate Profile should consider the self-directed learning experiences that students are having as well as the teacher-led, in-classroom experiences. Additionally, if schools embraced Free Agent Learning by not only valuing the experience but encouraging it and integrating those student-led knowledge and skill development activities within a more holistic approach to learning, the Graduate Profile would represent the totality of a student's learning outcomes, not just what was in the narrow purview of the in-class experience.

Takes for example, the story from Chapter 1 about the Free Agent Learner Chad who wanted to learn more about quantum mechanics than what was part of his high school class curriculum. Chad went online to seek additional learning resources to satisfy his own curiosity for knowledge and in the pursuit ended up reading a college-level textbook on this branch of physics. That knowledge acquisition process, the content acquired, and the skills developed all contributed to Chad's overall learning experience. Those experiences should be recognized as important contributors to Chad's future-ready status. And yet, for the most part, these types of self-directed learning outside of school remain hidden to educators. While Chad's story is illustrative of the paths of many Free Agent Learners, an important element of the story is that Chad's teacher had no knowledge of how his student was supplementing his physics education on his own. And Chad did not ever think that his self-directed learning experiences in physics might be valuable information for his teacher. What if this situation was different and that high school physics teacher was not only aware of Chad's out-of-school learning but also encouraged that type of learning experience?

First, it is reasonable to expect that Chad's self-directed learning on quantum mechanics may have augmented Chad's overall physics knowledge and quite possibly enhanced his performance in the high school class. Teachers find professional satisfaction in the success of their students, and thus, this physics teacher may have attributed Chad's academic performance in their class exclusively to their own teaching capabilities. That could be the wrong assumption to make. I have seen a similar situation with 8th grade algebra teachers who marvel at their students' academic progress and their easy grasp of new math concepts, only to find out at the end of the school year that many of their students' parents had enrolled their children in a self-paced, online course in algebra as an insurance policy. Given the gateway nature of algebra for high school honors and AP math and science classes, it is understandable that the parents want to ensure that their children pass algebra in 8th grade. If teachers knew that students were supplementing their instruction outside of school, either as Free Agent Learners or through parent sponsorship of such learning, the in-classroom learning experience might look very different. And rather than simply patting themselves on the back as doing a good job as evidenced by standardized test scores or class pass rates, teachers could use this knowledge to explore ways to personalize the learning process, to meet each individual student where they were on the learning continuum, providing remediation for students who are struggling with polynomials or providing more enrichment activities such as in the case of Chad with physics.

However, too many teachers continue to think about the learning process as an exclusively in-school event and that learning that takes place beyond teacher direction or sponsorship is second rate. In many ways, this mindset was crystallized by the process of teacher assimilation of technology use in their classroom over the past 20 years. The COVID pandemic and sudden shift to remote learning had the potential to dramatically alter that mindset. However, as will be explained, the intensive emphasis on continuity of learning at all costs limited the true adoption of new learning practices, including how to explicitly empower student self-directed learning. Understanding the value of Free Agent Learnership demands a more comprehensive appreciation of how and why students use technology for self-directed learning and what that means for the efficacy of technology use in the classroom to support deeper learning. But first, teachers, principals, and district administrators need to know and appreciate that their students are in fact supplementing learning outside of school.

The second concept to unpack about a deeper understanding of the lived experiences of Free Agent Learners focuses on Chad's response to the question about whether he told his teacher about researching and reading the quantum mechanics college textbook. It never occurred to Chad to tell his teacher about his self-directed learning, even though Chad highly respected his teacher and valued the learning experience in the class. This reality may be representative of how learning has been defined, both by teacher and student. Educators most often see learning as a place-, time-, and expertise-dependent activity. Learning happens in a classroom during a set period of time. For the learning experience to take place, it must be directed or facilitated by a trained professional who understands the content area, the desired outcomes, and the learning science pedagogy. Before the increased access that students have today to learning content online, this narrow definition made sense.

However, the increased availability of learning content and subject experts online opens up that definition significantly. For today's student, learning is a 24/7 enterprise, one in which they are increasingly directing around their own areas of interest and passion for highly purposeful outcomes. And since we cannot put that genie back in the bottle, it is time to think with a broader perspective on the multitude of learning experiences that students have available to them and how they are using that access to develop the same types of outcomes noted on most Graduate Profiles. Just as we have widened the aperture to see the development of future-ready skills as important outcomes from our schools, we should also adjust our definition of learning to include students' self-directed, interest-driven pursuits. This has the potential to have a significant impact on student outcomes as well.

Many educators acknowledge that the list of student outcomes as typified on a Graduate Profile may be more aspirational than realistic to attain. The inclusion of students' self-directed learning experiences may help to address that challenge. Students themselves already identify the problem-solving skills they are acquiring, for example, through competitive online gaming experiences. In some cases, those problem-solving skills may be more fine-tuned and developed through those out-of-school activities than the inquiry-based activities in fourth-period biology. If the infusion of skills alongside subject content knowledge was step one in the process of helping students be prepared for future success, then appreciating that school is not the only place where learning happens may be the next important mindset shift.

Barrier #2: Incomplete Valuation of the Role of Technology within Learning

Despite the proliferation in the use of various technology tools and resources in our everyday personal lives, many educators and researchers believe that the impact of the use of such technologies to transform teaching and learning in most K–12 schools has been limited. This situation has not been lost on the students who increasingly feel that their schools do not "look like the world in which they live." The students' rich and varied out-of-school use of digital tools to support personal networks, communications, information collection, and social interactions stands in stark contrast to how technology is typically used in their classrooms. Some thought leaders position students' informal digital activities as central to their success in the twenty-first-century global economy and contend that their out-of-school, technology-enabled learning experiences are often more meaningful educationally than what happens during their standard school day. Paradoxically, these informal experiences of students are often discounted or excluded from school conversations about how to effectively leverage emerging technologies within learning environments to prepare students for future college or workplace success despite extensive recent research on the familiarity of today's students with these digital tools.

Fueled by media stories and limited anecdotal vignettes, many educators (and parents) continue to see students' technology usage outside of school only as a series of unguided, passive, and frivolous activities. If school-based learning is the nutritious breakfast or lunch including all the FDA-recommended food groups, many adults see students' personal technology use as the unhealthy mid-afternoon snack, filled with empty calories and just enough of a jolt of addictive additives to keep the students engaged in the short term and coming back for more. Unfortunately, this narrow perspective limits them from seeing the potential of technology in the hands of students to address some of the deficits in the school-based learning model. Too many adults, including teachers, lack the foresight to see beneath the surface and realize that in creating that TikTok video about applying eyeliner, the student is developing a set of future-ready skills through the process of creating, editing, publishing, and promoting their own original content. The same is true for online and video-based game playing by students. Teachers continue to be blind to the potential of the game play experience to help students develop self-efficacy as a learner and exercise many of the skill muscles highly valued in the workplace, including collaborative decision-making, communications, and critical thinking, muscles that it is often difficult to develop in traditional learning paradigms. Rather, they focus only on what they can see on the surface (the noise, the rapid-fire action, the nonstop streamers' commentary, the violence in some cases) without taking the time to discover the motivations of students for the game play or the outcomes of those experiences.

But it is not just about valuing what students are doing outside of school. Researchers postulate that teachers do not appreciate or understand how the types of Free Agent Learning experiences that students are engaging with outside of school have the potential to complement and support the standards-based instruction that is happening in their classrooms. These do not need to be two totally separate worlds anymore—in school versus out of school—but rather the potential exists to utilize how students are using technology to support their Free Agent Learning experiences as a way to inform and drive better in-classroom utilization. Part of that problem continues to be teachers' lack of sophistication and knowledge about how to effectively use technology within learning. This ongoing lack of deep familiarity influences their opinions, attitudes, and valuations around digital learning, whether that is in the classroom or on the living room couch.

New theories about what constitutes knowledge in the twenty-first century and how that knowledge is acquired are part of this mounting tension between adult authority and student autonomy. While classroom learning continues to be focused on conceptual knowledge attainment, students' self-directed learning places a higher emphasis on problem-solving activities, contextualized experiences that emphasize tangible skill development, and a high valuation on pursuing seemingly random academic curiosities. The chaotic nature of the learning experience in personal usage is inherently nonlinear and thus an alien concept to most teaching practices. As students increasingly have ubiquitous access to information in the palm of their hands and begin to identify with their new roles as content creators, particularly when their own interests drive that content, the formal education community may be losing its grip on the knowledge monopoly, a sign of disruptive innovation at work.

It is long past due that adults realize that the learning experiences that students have in school from 8:30 to 3:00 are not the only (or in some cases even the best) representations of effective learning. Coming to that realization is not for the timid as it strikes directly at everything many educators know and hold dear about school-based learning. An examination of the adoption and adaptation process for teachers using technology within learning provides a foundation for understanding why teachers' continuing conflicted views on the value of digital learning are holding back greater acceptance of the value and potential of Free Agent Learning.

Teachers' Journey with Technology Use within Learning

Since the earliest days of technology introduction in K–12 classrooms, there has been a focus on helping teachers learn how to use an ever-evolving suite of new digital and online tools more effectively to support student learning and their own effectiveness as a teacher. Some of us may remember how truly revolutionary it was for a teacher to have even just one Apple IIe in their classroom. For a generation of students, their first introduction to a digital game was Oregon Trail using either a floppy disk or CD on an Apple IIe in the back of their classroom. As a statement to the indelible imprint of this early educational game on pop culture, many adults today still talk emotionally about the impact of losing their entire game-based family to dysentery before they could reach Oregon.

To support teachers in their use of these emerging technologies within education, a new industry was born to provide educational software and teacher training (companies such as MECC, The Learning Company, Tom Snyder Productions, and Davidson & Associates, to name a few) alongside new professional associations for "educators using computers" in the classroom (such as International Society for Technology in Education, ISTE; California's Computer-Using Educators, CUE; and the Texas Computer Educators' Association, TCEA). Special conferences were held to provide teachers with access to experts who could help them learn about the new technologies and how to use these tools in their classroom; the National Education Computing Conference, which later became ISTE, is a good example. Educators faithfully followed the best practices of regional and national thought leaders as to what works in the classroom.

The early tech pioneers were recognized in their schools as model teachers or tech heroes. These tech hero teachers were the first to get the new Apple Macintosh computers in their classroom and proudly hung up the "One Computer Classroom" poster from Tom Snyder Productions and later the ISTE Standards poster on their class bulletin board. They became passionate early members of ISTE or their local affiliates. Apple anointed these tech teachers as Apple Distinguished Educators, a recognition that brought with it almost a celebrity-type status. Like professional athletes or Oscar-nominated actors, these education technology pioneers also coveted winning the heralded

ISTE "Making IT Happen award" with its requisite recognition jacket (true confession, the jacket proudly hangs in my closet also). For a select group of teachers at the time, these were exciting times to be part of this exclusive club or clique of educators advancing the use of technology in the classroom. They were the early adopters and, like the Oregon Trail narrative, saw themselves as pioneers in a new field that they believed could revolutionize K–12 education.

Researchers studying the emerging use of technology products within education developed theories about the adoption process that mimicked the way business talked about product adoptions. Using a classical normal distribution, or bell curve model, the researchers identified these pioneers as innovators or early adopters and the teachers who were reluctant or slow to embrace these new technologies as laggards. New frameworks and models were developed to chart teachers' progress with their adoption of technology within instruction. School districts embedded these frameworks into their annual technology plans and used them to guide teacher professional learning goals.

Wanting to expand the number of early adopters, federal and state programs, private foundations, and technology company philanthropies focused their efforts on getting more teachers trained on the mechanics of using computers with students. During this time period, millions of dollars in federal funds were channeled to high-need school districts to implement technology in schools, including purchasing devices, digital content, and investing in teacher professional development. The goal of these types of programs was to ensure that every teacher knew how to use a suite of digital tools identified within their district as supportive of their student outcome goals. To facilitate training across the entire teaching staff, the once- or twice-a-year professional development (PD) day for technology became an institutionalized fixture on many school calendars. In that era, I participated in many of those types of PD days for teachers as an instructor and facilitator helping groups of teachers learn the ins and outs of using email or how to set up their class to play the online game Zoombinis at recess.

In working with so many educators over the years, I have often heard both teachers and administrators describe using technology for learning as similar to using a pencil for writing. Their intent is to make the point that both digital resources and pencils are simply tools teachers and students can use to support learning, that they are easy to pick up and adopt for effective usage, and that the impact of that usage is obvious. While this approach gained some traction when teachers were first experimenting with technology use in their classroom, the impact was mostly about tempering down the concerns that teachers had about how technology was conceptually going to change the way they taught. The reality is that teachers did not want to change their instructional practices, and so by using the pencil metaphor, administrators and policy advocates could sidestep teachers' reluctance and sell technology on the grounds that it was as easy and effective to use as the common pencil. That was a mistake for two reasons, described below, and the ramifications of that misguided approach are still being felt today in classrooms and schools nationwide.

As a result of the "technology as a tool like the pencil" metaphor, professional development for teachers has mostly focused on the technical skill development of how to use the tool, rather than how to adapt classroom practices to take advantage of the tool. Generally, this focus on the mechanics of usage has had a strong product orientation: training on how to use a particular product in the classroom. In many cases that training is provided by the product vendor, either included in the product license fee or contracted by the school district. These learning experiences are actualized efficiently with standalone "technology PD days," where company/vendor representatives are trainers, demonstrating the features of their product and how to use that product in the classroom with students. Many education technology conferences continue to take the same approach with an emphasis on "learn this today, and use it in your classroom tomorrow." The overarching preoccupation on developing teachers' product usage skills is exemplified by the abridged listing of the 2020–2021 professional development classes that were available to teachers in a school district in Massachusetts (see Figure 7.3).

This approach to teacher training is fairly typical across many districts. The emphasis on product training supports the hypothesis that if a teacher gains confidence in how to use a digital product (in

---

Topic: Securly

- The new Go Guardian tool we are using in the district is called Securly. Check out how to use this to support remote, in-person, and hybrid learning where you can push websites out to students and keep them on-track while using their technology.

Topic: Organize Your Google Classroom

- This will focus on creating topics to organize your work and materials, how to set up assignments, how to turn off notifications (to save your sanity), email guardians, add co-teachers, use the to-do list, set up docs to automatically make copies, etc. Also how to teach your students how to use Classroom and how to allow for the special edu teachers to add modification to lessons and assign them to specific students.

Topic: Communicating through Class Dojo

- For grades K–5, this will be the primary way to communicate with caregivers. In this workshop you will learn about any new updates, how to set up your class, and what to do if caregivers seem to not be engaging with this platform.

Topic: Flipped Classroom

- In this session catch the bug as we discuss flipped and blended instruction. Topics covered will include videotaped lessons, useful resources, and best practices to begin. Participants will be introduced to the concept of using video for learning (i.e. flipped/blended learning, creating vs. consuming, etc.), discuss common challenges of flipped instruction and their solutions, preview and test resources for video creation, editing and curation, examine best practices for video in teaching and learning.

Topic: Aspen

- This will cover how to set up a gradebook, how to use the communication log, and how to enter grades.

Topic: Zoom Fundamentals

- Trainer will go over how to use the whiteboard, how to create breakout rooms, how to switch hosting/share screens, create polls, and allow for remote control. If you want to learn a bit more about Zoom, this is the place to go.

Figure 7.3 Sample professional development line-up.

this case products such as Securly, Class Dojo, and Zoom), they will be able to use it effectively with their students. Just like with a pencil. The problem with the "technology as pencil" analogy is that it is too simplistic, is incomplete, and does not consider the transformation potential of digital tools. Technology is not just another pencil in the students' tool set for learning. To follow the pencil analogy, technology actually enables not just writing but a totally different form of writing, a process of writing that we cannot do without having access to the technology.

Why Schools Are Not (Yet) Ready to Embrace Free Agent Learning

Unfortunately, this strong orientation to skill-based professional learning for teachers has had a limited impact on motivating teachers or helping them successfully change their instructional practices to include appropriate technology more seamlessly within learning. Effective use of technology most often means reengineering existing lessons or units of study to take advantage of the digital tools. But that heavy lift of additional work requires strong motivation on the part of teachers and an understanding of the value proposition or benefits of doing that redesign work. This focus on skill development first also has not helped teachers see the big picture as to why and how the effective use of technology can support student learning and also increase teacher overall instructional effectiveness.

Project Tomorrow has been collecting feedback from teachers on their use of technology in the classroom since 2004. Additionally, the organization has designed and implemented over 55 different efficacy and evaluation studies on the impact of digital content, tools, and resources on both student outcomes and teacher effectiveness in K–12 education since 2007. Central to all of this work has been a focus on how teachers value the use of digital tools within instruction. What I have learned from these many experiences is that a teacher's personal attitudes toward and valuation of digital learning eclipses technical skill every day of the week when it comes to teachers' effective use of technology within classroom instruction. The ability to roster students in the new math app, assign learning activities to individual students, and access the performance data for the class are important first steps on teachers' journey to using technology effectively, but on their own they are insufficient in creating efficacious or sustained usage. While more recent professional learning approaches now emphasize learning goals first and provide strategies to help teachers understand how to effectively integrate digital tools into their everyday instruction, they still fail to recognize the importance of understanding teacher readiness to teach using technology.

Just as we are often blind to how our students are using technology outside of school and the value they derive from those experiences, we also often miss a critical step in helping teachers use technology more effectively in the classroom by not considering their experiences outside of the classroom.

Most of the popular frameworks, models, and adoption curves do not fully consider how much a teacher's success with integrating technology within everyday instruction depends on a complicated relationship between teachers' skill knowledge with using these digital tools (competency), the ease in which they believe they can implement these tools in their classroom with their students (comfort), and their belief that using technology in this way to support student learning will positively affect the outcomes desired (confidence). The interdependencies between competency, comfort, and confidence influence teachers' attitudes toward and valuation of technology use with students. And every day, teachers' attitudes and valuations affect their sight lines on the potential of technology, both in school and out of school, to support student learning.

Despite huge investments in teacher professional learning over the past 20 years, teachers' comfort and self-efficacy using digital tools to support new learning models and practices is still mostly unrealized. While the pandemic-induced shift to remote learning placed a far greater emphasis on the use of technology as a learning platform, the emphasis continued on the operational aspects of using the technology rather than exploring how to transform the learning experience. Thus, while we can see from the Speak Up research increased usage of a wide range of digital and online resources and content within the K–12 classroom during remote learning, we do not yet correspondingly see evidence of significant changes in teachers' practices. Less than one-third of teachers across all grade levels say they are very comfortable with new learning models and practices such as using digital tools to personalize learning for each student

Table 7.1 Teachers' comfort levels with new digitally enabled instructional practices (2020–2021).

Teaching practices	Percentage of teachers who report they are very comfortable with this practice in their classroom			
	All teachers (%)	Elementary school teachers (%)	Middle school teachers (%)	High school teachers (%)
Using data derived from online tools and apps to inform my instructional practice	38	45	38	33
Personalizing learning within my classroom for each student	37	43	34	28
Allowing students to have choices about how they want to learn	31	29	31	35
Leveraging technology to differentiate instruction	29	30	32	25
Facilitating student collaborations using digital tools	27	25	30	30

Source: © Project Tomorrow 2021.

in their class (37%), differentiating instruction through the effective use of technology (29%), or facilitating student collaborations through the features of various digital tools (27%) (see Table 7.1). Comparatively, in the 2018–2019 school year, long before remote learning, a relatively similar percentage of teachers (23%) said they were very comfortable using technology to differentiate instruction in their classroom.

Expected differences in teachers' comfort levels exist when the data is disaggregated by grade level assignment. High school teachers are more comfortable providing students with choices about their learning paths than elementary school teachers. Elementary school teachers with a smaller number of students to teach appear to be more facile at personalizing learning for their students than their colleagues in secondary schools. The bottom line, however, is the same. Our current professional development approaches may be promoting greater usage of technology, but they are not providing teachers with the inherent capacity to support their adoption of new learning models.

Teachers' attitudes influence their expectations for student technology usage in class and their views on the value of self-directed, technology-enabled learning outside of school. If a teacher is not comfortable providing their students with choices about their learning paths in the classroom, it is unlikely that they will realize or appreciate the value of self-directed learning outside of the classroom. As stated earlier, teachers' personal experiences with using technology to support their own goals and objectives outside of school have a significant impact on their interest and willingness to be more innovative with digital tools in school. The depth and breadth of the Project Tomorrow research on this topic provides context for understanding not just how teachers have adopted technology to use with their students but also the impact of those personal and professional experiences with technology on how and why some teachers have been more successful than others in their assimilation of technology use into their classroom.

In parallel with student technology use, it all starts with teachers' use of smartphones and social media in their personal lives, as depicted in Figure 7.4. The cumulative impact of teachers' seeing increased valuation in their own personal lives with using technology stimulates greater interest for using these same tools in the classroom. The increased access that teachers have to the tools is part of the equation for changing mindsets and attitudes. So, for example, the increased access to mobile devices in the classroom from 2014

Why Schools Are Not (Yet) Ready to Embrace Free Agent Learning

to 2020 helped teachers experiment and gain experience with using these tools to engage their students in learning. For instance, in a 5th grade classroom in Chicago where every student was assigned a tablet, a teacher dipped their toe into leveraging that 1:1 access by having students use Google Earth to seek out locations in China that supported the class's current reading book.

In Teacher 2's classroom, the mobile devices were used to support very specific learning outcomes and goals while at the same time helping the students develop information and media literacy skills. To help her students understand the context of a particular book they were reading in class, Teacher 2 assigned her students to use their tablets to do research on China and then develop a presentation to share with the class. Appreciating that her students may lack familiarity with China, the lesson started with a whole class visit to China via Google Earth. Using their own tablets, the students explored the Great Wall and zoomed in on palaces. The act of personally "visiting China" with their fingertips highly engaged the students in learning more and set the tone for their further research work. The standards for dissemination of information via a presentation were high and students both encouraged and commented on each other's work. The tablets in this case served as both a research tool and a way for students to develop stronger technology skills within the context of their curriculum.[6]

Though the initial intent was increased engagement, the experience provided the teacher with new insights about the additional benefits and value of using technology to support learning and in particular, students' skill development. According to the statistics shared in Figure 7.4, we see that *aha* moments like these are starting to change teachers' mindsets about the value of technology within learning, but it is a process that needs targeted reinforcement and support through administrators' own valuations on those benefits.

Asset: Smartphone adoption by teachers
2008 – 20% of teachers have a smartphone
2015 – 91% of teachers have a smartphone

Asset: Teachers' valuation on the importance of effective technology use in school for students' future success
2008 – 33% say it is very important
2019 – 61% say it is very important

Asset: Greater student access to mobile devices in the classroom
2014 – 20% of teachers say they are teaching in a 1:1 classroom
2017 – 45% in a 1:1 classroom
2020 – 77% in a 1:1 classroom

Barrier: Teachers see primary role of technology as student engagement tool, not as way to support deeper learning, student ownership of learning or skill development

Student engagement in learning
2009 – 51%   2018 – 51%

Deeper exploration of learning topics
2009 – 19%   2018 – 34%

Creating student ownership of learning
2009 – 23%   2018 – 38%

Developing critical thinking and problem-solving skills
2009 – 27%   2018 – 42%

Teachers use technology outside of school in personal life
Setting: Teacher uses technology to support personal life activities and goals
Tools: Email, smartphone, social media
Impact: More effective way to do things they are already doing (shopping, engaging with friends, communications)
Value: Saves time, more efficient, expanded reach

Idea: I am communicating more with other people and feeling more productive. Could I use these same tools in school to support interactions with colleagues and administrators?

Teachers use technology in school to support professional tasks with colleagues
Setting: Teacher uses technology to support communications and engagement with professional peers and colleagues
Tools: Email, smartphone, social media, school portals
Impact: More effective way to do things they are already doing (exchanging info with other teachers, getting office announcements, seeking help with lessons)
Value: Saves time, more efficient, expanded reach

Idea: I seem to be more engaged in what I am doing when using technology. Could technology be used to engage my students in learning?

Teachers use technology in school to engage students in learning
Setting: Teacher uses technology to periodically engage students in learning with video clips, website access or use of a digital device
Tools: Internet, digital devices, websites
Impact: Students appear to be more engaged in learning when technology is used within lessons or learning activities
Value: Increases student engagement

Idea: My students like using technology and I am seeing some positive outcomes from this usage. Could technology be used to enable more differentiated learning and future-ready skill development by my students?

Figure 7.4 Teachers' assimilation of technology in the classroom—the journey from personal to professional usage.

Why Schools Are Not (Yet) Ready to Embrace Free Agent Learning

There is no magic bean here to help teachers gain competency, comfort, and confidence in using technology to support learning in school nor to have a greater appreciation for the value of the Free Agent Learning experiences of their students. But increased familiarity and the development of a personal value proposition where technology yields direct benefits to the teacher are keys to supporting a new mindset about how digital learning can affect student outcomes, especially those beyond engagement. Additionally, though, educators may have to reset their own assumptions about where, when, and how effective learning takes place.

Leveraging Free Agent Learning in the Classroom

A full appreciation of Free Agent Learnership may require educators to suspend prior assumptions, conventional wisdom, or long-held beliefs about what constitutes effective learning for students. I recognize that suspension process may be difficult for some. The futurist Alvin Toffler, in his landmark book *Powershift,* noted the importance of the twenty-first-century skill to *"learn, unlearn, and relearn."*[7] I believe that as we talk about how to improve our K–12 schools, it is imperative that we all understand the value of unlearning some of the bedrock assumptions we have about effective learning. This is certainly the case relative to Free Agent Learning.

To support the unlearning and relearning effort, let's examine how a typical middle or high school social studies unit of study may look differently with a greater appreciation of Free Agent Learning. This side-by-side comparative will help to illuminate the differences between a traditional classroom learning assignment and a lesson where the teacher has embraced Free Agent Learning and is leveraging students' self-directed learning outside of school to support a standard curriculum unit. It will illustrate how an explicit acknowledgment of students' Free Agent Learning proclivities may actually enhance the overall learning experience if teachers are willing to lean into self-directed learning as a meaningful learning modality.

Traditional Learning Assignment

Curriculum unit:	The Articles of Confederation
Assignment:	Write a four-page essay about why the Articles of Confederation was not successful as a form of government in the United States.
Requirements:	Students must cite one primary source reference from a trusted and reputable online source in their paper. Use your textbook as well as your library print and online resources. Don't forget to adhere to all school policies regarding accessing certain sites and tools using your school-assigned Chromebook.
Student actions:	To complete the requirement, the student may do online research to identify a primary source reference about the Articles of Confederation at various repository or collection sites for primary sources such as the National Archives (https://www.archives.gov/), the National Constitution Center (https://constitutioncenter.org/) or through paid subscriptions such as to Gale in Context: US History (https://www.gale.com/c/in-context-us-history).

This type of an assignment may look very familiar to many educators. This assignment follows a traditional pattern with the student writing a report, essay, or paper to represent what they have learned. To add in a technology component to this activity, the student is allowed and/or prompted to include an online resource. With the Substitution Augmentation Modification Redefinition (SAMR) mode of technology integration in the classroom popularized by Ruben R. Puentedura,[8] the use of technology within this assignment would represent a substitution activity, substituting for a traditional printed book or article with an online or digital equivalent. The parameters of the lesson and the cognitive processes used in fulfilling the assignment are not changed or transformed by the use of the online resources. Nor does this assignment address the essential elements of

203

the Student Vision for Learning in any significant way or demonstrate that students' out-of-school Free Agent Learning activities have any bearing on this learning experience.

The following hypothetical learning assignment is built on the same foundation of learning about the Articles of Confederation. The student in this example has a certain level of choice within the assignment but more importantly, the structuring of the assignment empowers the student to take greater control over their own learning process, thus not only supporting many of the aspects of Free Agent Learning but also endorsing in many ways the Student Vision for Learning elements.

Hypothetical Free Agent Learning Enhanced Assignment

Curriculum unit:	The Articles of Confederation
Assignment:	To understand the impact of the creation and failure of the Articles of Confederation on the development of the Constitution as the basis for government structure in the United States, and the long tail bearing of that process on current governance issues.
Requirements:	Students must identify and use appropriate historical and current resources to adequately support your research question and hypothesis. Students should create an artifact of your choosing that represents what you have learned through this research process. As with all of our class assignments, we expect the quality of your work to be appropriate for a college-bound graduate of our school.
Student actions:	1. Develop your own personalized research question to guide your work on this assignment. Based on what we have discussed in class, what do you want to learn more about? What new questions do you have? What are you curious about? To review what was discussed in class about developing a good research question, this YouTube video may be helpful: https://www.youtube.com/watch?v=71-GucBaM8U. Test out your research question with a classmate to get a fresh perspective on whether your research question meets our class standards.

2. To address your research question, investigate different sources for information making sure to employ your digital literacy skills to ensure content validity, reliability, and accuracy. You can use any tools that are most comfortable for you from a personal learning perspective. That includes social media, YouTube, discussion forums like Reddit, websites, primary source sites, etc. Document your research and learning process so that it can be included in the assessment of your work product. The research process is as important to your learning as the final content you produce.

3. Using the research collected, develop your learning artifact so that you can substantiate what you have learned through this assignment. That artifact could be an essay, a slideshow, a video, a blog/vlog post, a newspaper article, or whatever best fits your research question and your learning process. The artifact should be shareable with your classmates either in class or through another online site. Get feedback from your classmates about your artifact and your learning process.

4. Write a short reflection on this learning activity from your perspective. What is your new understanding about the Articles of Confederation and the impact of that form of government on current governance issues? What did you learn? How efficient or non-efficient was your learning process? How did the process of creating an artifact help you develop a greater understanding of this topic and your research question? What would you improve upon if you were to do this assignment again? What are three new questions that you have now about the Articles of Confederation, our form of government, or the impact of activities that happened over 200 yrs. ago on current events? How will you explore those questions in your own self-directed learning?

The contrast between the two different study units illuminates how an appreciation of Free Agent Learning can influence how teachers could approach instruction and, in particular, student assignments. The hypothetical example includes several of the essential elements of the Student Vision for Learning as well as leveraging the lived experiences and expertise of students who are already self-directing their learning outside of the classroom. Those key components include the following:

- Students are playing a bigger role in the self-determination of the learning process in the hypothetical example compared to the traditional example. The students are in control of developing their own research question, thus helping to develop learning ownership while at the same time the learning objectives meet the unit requirements of enhanced learning about the Articles of Confederation.

- Compared to having a limited number of information resources, students have the ability to choose from a seemingly infinite set of tools and content vehicles to support their work. Most notably, students have the ability to use resources that they are already familiar with and have expertise in how to leverage effectively for self-directed learning.

- The hypothetical example appreciates that students want to engage with their classmates and others in social-based learning experiences.

- The learning activity is enhanced by stimulating the student to explore the relevancy of the failure of the Articles of Confederation on current-day governance. This linkage between history and current events provides a contextually rich connection.

- The description of the assessment process specifically acknowledges the process as well as the final deliverable as valuable pieces of understanding student learning.

Additionally, the hypothetical example provides an opportunity for this one assignment to support multiple other learning objectives or goals, simply because it is framed from the Free Agent Learnership perspective. For example, additional learning objectives accomplished through this newly formatted assignment could include:

- Explicit focus on the student's appreciation of their own metacognition through the reflection exercises;
- Development and reinforcement of information and media literacy skills;
- Prompting of extended learning opportunities; and
- Support for the skills and habits of lifelong self-directed learning.

This hypothetical learning assignment is meant to be an illustration on how a different mindset, potentially a more accepting mindset, around Free Agent Learning can support both effective standards-based instruction and the Student Vision for Learning. An interesting professional learning community exercise might be for teachers to take existing lessons and assignments and experiment with the infusion of some of the concepts from this hypothetical example. Can we stretch our muscles to develop new learning activities for students that may help make school-based learning look more like those types of purposeful self-directed learning students are experiencing on their own already?

Barrier #3: How Technology Access Is Changing the Traditional Power Equation in the Classroom

The social dynamics in the classroom between teacher and students are largely influenced by the teacher's own perceptions of their role, their confidence in their own abilities, and the type of power positioning they embrace with their students. Over 50 years ago, the social psychologists John R. P. French and Bertram Raven shared their research on the types of power that influenced human dynamics.[9]

Table 7.2 French-Raven types of social power—in the classroom.

Type of social power	Description—source of power	Classroom adaptation
Legitimate	Position or role	Teacher is in charge of the classroom
Expert	Knowledge or experience	Teacher is the keeper of the learning content knowledge and process
Referent	Perception of caring and mutual respect	Students feel that teacher cares about them and wants them to succeed
Reward	Ability to recognize and reward with benefits	Teacher can provide extrinsic rewards for good behavior, attendance, grades, etc.
Coercive	Ability to punish	Teacher can assign punishments like detention or lost privileges
Informational	Controls access to information	Teacher controls the access to information or resources students want to use

Their research was not focused on classroom dynamics, yet subsequently, other researchers have utilized the French-Raven six types of social power to explain how teachers acquire, retain, and lose authority or influence with their students. To provide context, I have adapted the French-Raven core concepts to fit a classroom setting (see Table 7.2).

Certainly not every teacher is using all six of these power types in their classroom. However, it is interesting to see how teachers view their power positioning relative to providing students with voice and choice about their educational opportunities. I was recently invited to share some of the Speak Up research with a school district community group that was working on developing their Graduate Profile. The group included teachers, administrators, school board members, community leaders, and parents. After presenting some of the research findings about the Student Vision for Learning and how students were self-directing learning outside of school, a 5th grade teacher in the group stood up and told me that they were very opposed to the idea that I was promoting, that students should have more input into classroom experiences because of their learning experiences outside of school. They explained that they were the teacher (legitimate power), the expert on learning and the curriculum (expert power) and would make the decisions about the learning activities that their students would experience in their class (informational power). They also noted proudly that while not a huge believer in the value of technology within the learning process, they did provide their students with time to play online games if they finished their work early (reward power). Given these attitudes about their role, their expertise, and their power over their students, it is understandable why this particular teacher could not see the value of Free Agent Learning. Their reluctance to see that value, however, does not stop their students from exploring and discovering new learning experiences every day outside of school, on their own. I see it though as a missed opportunity for this teacher to engage with their students around their academic curiosities and passions and to help their students develop effective self-directed learning skills.

The effectiveness of the power positioning in the classroom is affected by the student reaction to that positioning. As noted, not every teacher utilizes all six types of social power in their classroom. Also, not every type of social power as described by French and Raven is sustainable over the long term. For example, while teachers may start the school year with legitimate power, that positioning could be diminished if the teacher does not also have expertise in the content area, relies too heavily on coercive power, or is highly limiting with their informational power base. Students will delegitimize their teacher based on how power is used.

Increasingly, students also view that power positioning through the lens of technology usage in the classroom. This includes not only teachers' attitudes about technology use but classroom and school policies that may limit students' access to the digital tools they are commonly using outside of school for their self-directed learning. In that way, teachers' exercising their informational power to restrict student technology use in the classroom may be a barrier to their greater understanding of the value of Free Agent Learning.

Some of the blindness around the valuation of digital tools within learning may be the result of years of unintended negative messaging about self-directed technology use within classroom settings. For example, that negative messaging is often actualized through school policies that limit students' use of their own devices, notably their smartphones, in class. These policies stand in stark contrast to the increased access that students have to such devices and how they are using these tools regularly to support a consistent portfolio of self-directed learning activities every day. The Speak Up research and other research studies such as from the Pew Internet and American Life Project have long documented the increasing access that K–12 students have to personal mobile devices, including smartphones.

The school year 2011–2012 was the turning point in terms of students' ubiquitous and highly convenient access to a world of information and learning resources in their pocket; 50% of high school students and one-third of middle school students reported having their own smartphone. The trend has continued over the past 10 years with increased personal student access to devices that bring learning to the learner directly. Based on Speak Up research conducted during the 2018–2019 school year, 94% of students in grades 9–12, 87% of students in grades 6–8, and 58% of students in grades 3–5 have their own personal smartphone. Almost a majority of kindergarten through second grade students say the same now (47%). When disaggregated by community type (urban, rural, suburban) or home poverty (identified by the school's Title 1 status), the percentage of students with devices does not significantly differ. The Pew Research Center reports similar findings for high school students;

their reports from spring 2019 indicate that 95% of teenagers have a smartphone.[10] Interestingly, 83% of teens said they use their smartphone to "learn new things." Additionally, one in five students in middle school and high school are now sporting a smart watch also, thus enabling even easier access to information at the flick of a wrist.

The defining element of this ready access to content, media, and experts, however, is not the currency of the device. The students may not have in their pocket the latest version of the iPhone or Samsung Galaxy, but the universal denominator is connectivity to the Internet, enabled through both increasingly lower cost data plans and widespread access to Wi-Fi networks.

With such widespread access to technology in students' pockets and backpacks, we might expect to see greater acceptance of students' ability to use these tools to support everyday learning in their classroom. In reality, every student has a computer with them at all times that could be effectively leveraged as a learning tool: their smartphone. Rather, school district policies either outright prohibit student use of their own devices in class (24% of school districts in 2018) or leave it to the discretion of the school administrator (20%) or the classroom teacher to make that decision (41%). The balance of the school districts in 2018 reported limited Bring Your Own Device (BYOD) policies that allowed some students to use personal phones and other digital tools in school, or the districts said that since they were providing devices to students, there was no need for students to use their own phones, for example, in school. Not surprisingly, 36% of high school students and 54% of middle school students say that their inability to use their own personal devices in school is a barrier that affects their learning. One-third say another barrier is that their teachers specifically limit technology use in class. Schools and districts speak eloquently about the need to control personal device access in school to protect students from bad actors, to secure school and district networks, and to reduce distractions in class. Additionally, especially since the sudden shift to remote learning, more and more districts are adopting one-to-one programs, which assign a school-owned device to support student learning. The districts are therefore discouraging personal device usage in lieu of the ready access to school-owned devices. This is evident in the latest Speak Up research from the 2021–2022 school year with only 25% of school district technology leaders saying that they have a BYOD policy.

These are meaningful explanations that certainly have a level of reasonableness. But don't we all prefer to use devices that we have personalized with our own apps, favorite sites, and personal information? Speaking from personal experience, it would be very difficult for me to use a tablet, laptop, or Chromebook to support my professional work that was not configured to my preferences or did not include the apps that help me be most productive. And yet that is exactly what we are asking students to do every day with a school-owned device that is standardized for enterprise management, not personal productivity. That is why even when devices are provided to students to use at home, many students prefer to use their own digital tools to do homework or work on school projects. The students view that choice as one of efficiency: "It just saves time for me to use my own laptop rather than the school Chromebook."

Beyond not having access to sites that a school district may filter or block, students also like having the fluidity of going back and forth from interacting with friends on personal accounts (often prohibited on school-owned devices) and doing schoolwork using their school-prescribed resources. Researchers have long documented how students' experiences online are often a mix of personal and learning activities with a seamless flow from one to another. For example, a student may be watching a Twitch live stream of Pokimane playing Fortnight while also checking their class portal periodically to see if their biology teacher has posted the test grades from Friday. Or a student may be working on an essay about climate change and wants to watch a Greta Thunberg video on YouTube to get her take on the latest UNESCO report on sea level changes to include in the essay. In both examples, using a school-owned device to accomplish all of these tasks may be impossible as filters may block Twitch and YouTube on the school-provided laptop. The expectation is that a student will use one device for schoolwork learning and their personal device for the entertainment activities, relationship development, and self-directed learning that they are doing outside of school. This expectation, however, does not take into account the natural ways that students are seamlessly interweaving their school and personal lives using technology. Nor does it acknowledge that learning for today's students is a 24/7 enterprise of which school-initiated learning is only a small portion. In short, many of our well-meaning school policies and programs fail to appreciate how students are engaging with technology specifically and learning generally when they are outside of the classroom.

Thus, even as the pandemic-induced adoption of virtual learning fueled a shift to putting more technology in the hands of our students than ever before, educators continue to be reluctant to value students' self-directed learning outside of school or to appreciate how students could effectively be using their own digital resources to have highly purposeful and meaningful learning experiences beyond teacher sponsorship. As noted, there may be many reasons for this hesitancy, including concerns about changing the power dynamics in the classroom. Technology has certainly added a new element to the social dynamics in the classroom.

- Educators who are highly invested in their expert power may not want to share that with students who quite possibly may know more about a particular subject area or classroom topic because of their Free Agent Learning experiences outside of school.

213

- Teachers may be limiting student access to technology in school because of a fear that their own lack of expertise in digital learning may negatively affect their social power. Only 27% of classroom teachers say they are very comfortable when their students know more about technology use than they do. Notably, that percentage does not significantly differ by years of experience of the teacher; teachers with 1–3 years of experience are just as likely as teachers with 16+ years of experience to not be comfortable with students knowing more than they do.

- Too often, student voice looks more like student choice than real agency. Possibly in wanting to retain the informational power, educators position student voice opportunities as choices between options. For example, students are given the option of writing an essay or creating a slideshow to substantiate what they have learned about the theme of a particular novel. Or a principal asks input from the student government body about whether student cell phones should be allowable at lunch. The options are binary: allowable or not allowable.

- While many schools and districts publicly espouse the value of student voice and participate in different ways to collect student input about their education (including through the Speak Up surveys facilitated by Project Tomorrow), the opportunities for students to share authentic perspectives are often limited by structure, number of students involved, or topics explored. The ideas and values expressed by the students are also frequently regarded more as curiosities than true assets that can be leveraged to support improvement in school learning. While providing ways for students to have a real voice in their education could be viewed by students as a type of referent power, too often students only see these types of limited experiences as tokenism or an expression of reward power on the part of educators.

To fully embrace Free Agent Learning, educators must suspend assumptions and belief systems about learning that may not be relevant today, evaluate the ways we are effectively positioning technology usage in school, and examine whether the social dynamics of power and authority may be obstructing our ability to see the self-directed learning experiences of our students as a leadership asset that we can use to improve education for all students. Suspending long-held assumptions, evaluating the efficacy of tools we use, and examining power constructs are difficult tasks for many of us. These types of highly reflective activities also require us to understand the differences between change and transformation. Even though *transformation* is becoming a commonly used term in education, it is possible that the nuance of the differences between making a change and implementing a transformation may also be difficult to see. Technologists view these two terms very differently. Maybe it is time that in education, we do the same. In an online article in *CIO Insights* in May 2021, the author illuminates the differences as such:

Change is a response to external influences, where modifying day-to-day action achieves desired results. Transformation is about modifying core beliefs and long-term behaviors—sometimes in profound ways—to achieve the desired results. Mastering change may enable companies to keep up with fast-shifting consumer expectations. But deliberate, planned transformation often redefines what success looks like and how you get there.[11]

Certainly, the events of the COVID pandemic and sudden shift to new learning models resulted in changes in K–12 education that are still having a ripple effect today. The opportunity exists, however, to think beyond those structural changes and explore new ways to modify core beliefs and behaviors and create transformation within our schools so that our students can more fully realize the vision for learning in our practices. In Chapters 8–10, the theme of why Free Agent Learning matters will provide a new foundation for that transformational process.

Connecting the Dots

- Several cultural and structural barriers or obstacles stand in the way of schools embracing students' Free Agent Learning ecosystem as an asset in supporting education transformation. The three key barriers are the following:

  - The long-held belief that student learning only happens (or happens best) in a school setting. This belief prevents some educators from seeing the value of students' self-directed learning outside of school.

  - Educators' perceptions on the value of technology within learning is still evolving. Getting beyond thinking about technology as a tool primarily to engage students in learning is a step in the right direction to aligning with how students view technology as a utility to support personalized learning, skill development, and tangible academic outcomes.

  - Self-directed learning by students, fueled by increased access to digital and online tools and resources, threatens the traditional power positioning of teachers in the classroom.

- To understand teachers' blindness or reluctance to appreciate Free Agent Learning, it is important to acknowledge teachers' journey in their adoption and adaptation of technology within classroom instruction.

- Embracing Free Agent Learning in the classroom will take more than simply reengineering some lesson plans to incorporate

---

students' ideas or choices for learning modalities. Preexisting mindsets and belief systems will need to be altered to more fully appreciate the value of students' self-directed, interest-driven learning, which happens beyond the sponsorship or facilitation of an education professional.

Now, Think about This!

1. Does your Graduate Profile or other means of measuring student graduation outcomes include an explicit appreciation and acknowledgment of student learning outside of school? How can students' self-directed learning experiences influence new metrics that define student success?

2. How can you help your teachers or colleagues develop a new perception or mindset around the value of Free Agent Learning? What do they need to think differently about students' self-directed learning as a meaningful type of educational experience?

3. How are you effectively providing your students with opportunities to develop self-efficacy and agency within classroom learning experiences? How well do those experiences reflect the types of choices students are making every day within their Free Agent Learning experiences?

4. What is one thing that you can do today or tomorrow to change the mindsets of your teachers or colleagues to more fully appreciate and embrace Free Agent Learning as an asset that can be leveraged to transform the school experience for all students?

Why Schools Are Not (Yet) Ready to Embrace Free Agent Learning

Notes

1. http://www.battelleforkids.org/about-us.
2. https://all4ed.org/future-ready-schools/.
3. https://www.claytonschools.net/domain/1261.
4. https://www.amazon.com/Ready-Anything-Touchstones-Future-Focused-Innovative/dp/1947604392.
5. https://www.elsegundousd.net/page/graduate-profile.
6. https://tomorrow.org/publications/MakingLearningMobile3.html.
7. Toffler, A. (1990). Powershift: Knowledge. Wealth, and Violence at the Edge of the 21st Century, 240–241.
8. http://hippasus.com/resources/sweden2010/SAMR_TPCK_IntroTo AdvancedPractice.pdf.
9. https://scholar.valpo.edu/cgi/viewcontent.cgi?article=1312&context= jvbl.
10. https://www.pewresearch.org/fact-tank/2019/08/23/most-u-s-teens-who-use-cellphones-do-it-to-pass-time-connect-with-others-learn-new-things/.
11. https://www.cioinsight.com/it-management/expert-voices/the-difference-between-change-and-transformation.

Chapter 8

Why the Free Agent Learning Ecosystem Matters Today—Student Engagement

When I present the research about the *hows* and *whys* of Free Agent Learning, the first response from many educators is often one of both shock and awe. For many people, including educators, the idea that students could be using a wide range of digital tools including social media outside of school for highly purposeful learning that is self-initiated, not teacher assigned, creates a state of cognitive dissonance. Two assumptions roil their ability to accept the premise of the Free Agent Learner.

In their belief systems, school is where learning happens. Students come to a school building to learn. The learning process is sometimes extended beyond the classroom or school building in the case of homework assignments, field trips, or individualized study plans when students cannot come to school because they are ill or traveling. They will also sometimes acknowledge that learning can take place in after-school settings, summer camps, or special Saturday events such as art classes, museum programming, or career days, but that is more extracurricular than mainstream learning, a sort of second-class learning process. The key sticking point for many is their deeply held conviction that student learning must be directed by trained professionals who are experts in the content areas that students need and well versed in formalized pedagogy to support effective learning. In their worldview, students may dabble in some informal or random learning activities by looking up information online about endangered species in Australia or find a YouTube video about NASA's Perseverance rover, but that is not "real learning." The cognitive dissonance that creates the shock response is about students directing their own purposeful learning without having a trained educator at the wheel.

The awe part of the response comes from a flawed assumption still held by many people, once again including educators, that technology use by students outside of school is generally all about posting selfies, watching cat videos, or playing Fortnite with strangers until the wee hours of the morning. When I explain how the students are using these same types of online and digital tools (social media, multimedia, and games) for purposeful learning, they are often amazed to learn that tools like this can be used for anything other than entertainment or friend interactions.

The Forces Behind Educators' Shock and Awe

It is often recognized in education circles that "everyone is an expert on education because we all went to school at some point." The same philosophy now applies to technology use. People assume that they are experts about how technology can be used for good or bad based on their own experiences. The adult worldview in this case about how students might use online and digital tools is predicated on their own personal usage.

Marc Prensky popularized the concept that students were digital natives and adults were digital immigrants. His treatise explained that while adults needed to adapt their already well-honed practices to accommodate technology, students were more facile with using technology since they did not need to unlearn and then relearn new practices. While some researchers including myself do not buy in

100% to the idea that all students are digital natives, it is human nature to assume that others are using technology the same way you are. Thus, adults see technology usage through the lens of their own experiences.

Teachers in particular seem to transfer their expectations and valuations on the efficacy of digital tools for learning onto their perceptions around student usage as well. Too often that perception of how or why a student may want to use a technology tool is limited by the teachers' views on its utility, which is often narrowly viewed only through their own personal experience. For example, if a teacher is not a gamer and thus lacks experience with playing digital games, they may not understand the value of that experience, particularly from the perspective of learning future-ready skills. This relationship between personal experience and valuation results in the cognitive dissonance: If I as the teacher am not using this digital tool in that way, how could a student possibly be using it to support learning? Unfortunately, the limited perceptions around the potential of technology to support self-directed learning are also influenced by media reports that dramatize predominantly the adverse impact of technology usage especially relative to youth and children and the increasing abundance of ill-informed or misleading research on the topic.

Social media use provides a good example of how an educator's view on students' usage may be affected by their own experiences and valuations. For many years, the Speak Up Research Project has polled students in grades 6–12 about their preferred social media tools and the regularity of using various social media platforms. From our data collected during the 2010–2011 school year, for example, 62% of high school students reported that they regularly updated their personal Facebook site. Just the year before, in 2009, only 42% of high school students said Facebook was their social media platform of choice. It may seem hard to believe now that Facebook was just coming into its own in 2010. This was evidenced on December

27, 2010, when the co-founder of Facebook, Mark Zuckerberg, was named the Time Magazine Person of the Year.[1] The 2010–2011 school year, however, was also the last time that students named Facebook as their most favored site.

As I often say, the death knell for Facebook in terms of youth participation was not when their mom or dad set up their personal Facebook pages, or even when they noticed their teacher was now on Facebook, but rather when Grandma started friending them, the students knew it was time to find a new social media platform. A steady decline in Facebook is noted in the annual Speak Up data from 2010 until the most recent year students were polled, 2019–2020. According to that 2019–2020 school year data, only 25% of high school students and 12% of middle school students say they regularly check or update a personal Facebook site. According to recent news stories, Facebook leadership is now aware of this reality and struggling to find a way to create relevancy for their products among a younger generation of new social media users.

As has been reported by many organizations, including Project Tomorrow and the Pew Research Center,[2] our youth have not given up social media but have simply migrated to other new platforms to meet their personal needs (YouTube, Snapchat, TikTok, and Instagram) or in the case of the Free Agent Learners to platforms that better address their learning goals. Adults have not migrated as quickly to some of these new platforms and thus their experiences in social media and perceptions of value with using such tools are still primarily being influenced by their personal experiences with Facebook almost exclusively. Pew's recent 2021 research shows that 7 in 10 American adults (69%) use Facebook regularly with the largest percentage of users in the age bracket of 30–49 years old.[3]

A comparison of the tools used by high school students today and American adults (which most inevitably includes educators at all levels) highlights the disconnect that may be underlying this cognitive

Table 8.1 Regular usage of various social media tools—US adults vs. US high school students.

Social media tools	% of American adults using this tool regularly Source: Pew Research Center data from Jan–Feb 2021.	% of American high school students using this tool regularly Source: Project Tomorrow data from 2019–2020 school year.
Facebook	69	25
Instagram	40	80
Snapchat	25	71
TikTok	21	53

Source: © Project Tomorrow 2021.

dissonance about student use of technology outside of school (see Table 8.1). The adults unfortunately have a very limited experience with many of the social media tools that students are using as key components of their daily lives. This lack of firsthand knowledge prevents many adults, including educators, from seeing these tools as potentially supporting learning.

As illustrated, students are less than half as likely as adults to be using Facebook but twice as likely to be Instagram or TikTok regulars and almost three times more likely to be Snapchatting than adults.

While it is certainly interesting cocktail party banter to talk about the ways that student use of social media diverges from adult usage, it is more important to note that this divergence will continue as new social platforms emerge and attract the attention of younger users. No one has a Magic 8 Ball to determine what will be the next big social media platform that will dominate the space. However, the real story here is not about the difference in tool usage between adults and students but rather how those differences translate into perceptions and valuations on social media usage and technology use in general and the long-tail impact on student learning in general. It is for that reason that many educators are stuck in a state of disbelief when confronted with the evidence of students demonstrating the behaviors of Free Agent Learning.

For some, they simply do not have the personal experiences that could help clear up the dissonance around the idea of students self-directing their own learning without teacher sponsorship or even the preposterousness of students using technology tools, including social media such as YouTube, Snapchat, and TikTok, as vehicles for learning. For example, while 60% of high school students say they use social media to learn about and connect with people who can help answer questions for them, only 27% of high school teachers use social media in that same way to support their own professional learning. It is understandable that lacking that frame of reference, teachers may have trouble fathoming or appreciating how students are using social media as a learning platform and not just to follow celebrities or influencers, or mimic silly trends and behaviors. It may also be that some educators are simply unfamiliar with or unaware of how students are using technology outside of the school building or classroom walls. That lack of familiarity may lead to a cavalcade of assumptions that are no longer valid. That may explain why 53% of high school principals nationwide say that the best way for them to disseminate general school information to their community, which includes parents and students, of course, is through a posting on the school's Facebook site. While this may be an optimal tool for parent communication (70% of parents agree), 57% of high school students say they never use Facebook and an additional 18% say they use it only rarely. Those well-meaning but potentially uninformed principals are therefore effectively disenfranchising up to three-quarters (75%) of their students through their choice of Facebook for communication about school events such as homecoming dates, school performances or assemblies, or potentially life-changing important information such as graduation requirements, College Board test dates, or visits to campus from military recruiters.

It is totally understandable and acceptable to have an initial shock-and-awe reaction to the information about Free Agent Learners. Many of you probably are still in that mind space now. But the next reaction should be to understand that a deeper appreciation for the Free Agent Learning ecosystem can be an asset for teachers, principals, and district administrators trying to address many of the vexing challenges in education today, notably, students' lack of engagement in school-based learning, how to empower students to be efficacious learners, and the stubbornly persistent inequities in education that transcend time and generations. That next reaction really should be one of excitement about the boundless opportunities that come with embracing Free Agent Learnership as a new tool in your toolkit for transforming education for all students. Students' experiences with self-directed learning outside of school will continue to evolve and grow, with more students taking control of their own education destiny through their smartphone and a personally curated collection of self-discovered apps and learning content. This will inevitably increase as more students, and even younger students, gain new access to emerging technologies such as artificial intelligence, virtual/augmented reality, and the yet to be invented social media platform of next year. Just as the students are not waiting for their teachers to catch up to them in terms of technology usage sophistication, our leaders should not assume that this profile of the Free Agent Learner is a static one. The next frontier is really about how those experiences will inform and influence students' perceptions of the relevancy and value of their in-school learning experiences and what this means for their expectations for new learning environments. This environment has been amplified now by the experiences that many students had in remote virtual learning during the heights of the COVID pandemic. We are clearly in a new era where the voice of the education stakeholder, including your students, matters more than ever. So while some school and district leaders may certainly roll their eyes and say, "So, what?" to this new information about how our students are self-directing learning outside of school, beyond teacher direction, using a wide range of new digital assets, others are already asking the most important question, "So, what is next?"

To answer that question, let us discuss how understanding the Free Agent Learning ecosystem could potentially help educators address the following three key challenges that many are facing as a result of the events of the past two years:

1. How to meaningfully engage students in school-based learning;

2. How to create environments that support student development of agency and self-efficacy as key aspects of a future-ready education; and

3. How to directly address the implicit and explicit inequities in education beyond providing access to a Chromebook and a hot spot for continued learning at home.

The Challenge of Determining What Constitutes Student Engagement

In many ways, student engagement in school-based learning is the elusive holy grail in education. Everyone acknowledges the research-proven relationship between student engagement and academic performance, and yet there is no real consensus on what constitutes effective engagement within student learning, how to nurture or sustain student engagement in a traditional learning setting, or even how to appropriately measure it. As is often applied to other hard-to-define concepts, many educators will defend their inability to comprehensively define effective student engagement by declaring that they "know it when they see it."

The Myth of Physical Cues

Too often, that is distilled down to head or facial cues such as head nodding, smiling faces, and shiny eyes as the proxy for identifying and calculating the level of student engagement. I have had many of these discussions with teachers in particular over the past 20 years who continue to stand by the tried-and-true "eyes on me" approach to compel engagement. Yet, as many students report, eyes on their teacher may not mean the same as it once did. This is not dissimilar to what I see today as a conference speaker. As any current conference speaker will attest, the days of getting physical cues or emotional energy from the audience with eye contact or head nods to indicate buy-in or engagement with your content is in the past. New metrics include evaluating the depth and quality of the backchannel communications that are taking place during your presentation or speech.

Let us get real about this. The long-held belief that eyes on the teacher meant students were engaged in the lesson, lecture, or lab was never really valid. While there are many of the scenes in the 1986 movie *Ferris Bueller's Day Off* that continue to resonate today with students, teachers and parents as representing current classroom norms, one particular scene illustrates the point about the elusiveness of student engagement. The realism of the "Anyone, anyone?" scene in the movie where a teacher played by Ben Stein lectures students on supply-side economics illustrates how students are often bored or disengaged in the learning process in class but may be looking directly at their teacher, even smiling and nodding their head.[4] It should be noted that according to the director of the movie, John Hughes, he cast Ben Stein, a writer and commentator on politics and economics, in this role because "he wasn't a professional actor. He had a flat voice, he looked like a teacher."[5] And while we may hope that a teacher dryly lecturing on supply-side economics is not the norm in most classrooms today, recent data collected by Project Tomorrow through a special study of the classroom practices of history, government, and economics teachers reveals that 93% say that lecturing is the most common instructional practice they use in their classroom. Comparatively, a slightly smaller percentage of high school teachers (76%) said that they regularly engage their students in learning through collaborative group projects.[6] The emerging focus on engaging students through collaborative projects is promising but lecturing particularly in high school classes (and certainly in higher education) is still part of the everyday learning experience for students across all subject areas. And thus, this challenge of defining, measuring, and sustaining student engagement continues to be a timely topic of concern and conversation school-wide.

How Technology Comes into Play

Educators' familiarity with the connection between student engagement in learning and their academic achievement is also often the driving force behind the assessment of the impact of different learning interventions in the classroom, including new products, resources, models, and approaches. Given that, school and district leaders are concerned about the impact of the pandemic and remote learning during the 2019–2020 and 2020–2021 school years on students' ongoing engagement in the learning process. Two-thirds of principals (65%), for example, say that remote learning was less engaging for their students than in-classroom instruction. Many equate the perceived decline in student engagement with a level of learning loss or disruption that needs to be remediated. This creates another cognitive dissonance moment.

Educators have long heralded the use of technology as a vehicle for stimulating increased student engagement in learning. According to longstanding Speak Up research, teachers, principals, and district administrators regularly rank improved student engagement as a primary benefit of providing students with a mobile device to use for learning and/or integrating digital content within the curriculum. In the early days of classroom technology usage, the mere inclusion of technology within the learning process was perceived as a magic bean for elevating student engagement. The theory was as follows: Students like using technology, so if we can include opportunities for students to use technology, even if that usage is limited by time and scope, students will transfer that enjoyment into engagement in the learning content. Given that belief, it is understandable why many educators were confounded by a key reality during virtual learning. From their perspective, students seemed to be less engaged, not more engaged, in the screen-based learning process. They assumed that student engagement in learning would stay the same or might even be elevated during remote learning since students would be using at least conceptually a wide range of digital tools.

This is another false assumption about students' relationship with technology for learning. Student engagement in a learning process that includes technology is not about the ability to simply use a digital tool or even access online content, but rather, it is about how those resources, when used effectively and purposely, create learning experiences that have context and relevancy for the student. This harkens back to our discussion in Chapter 1 about the Student Vision for Learning and how students want learning experiences that are socially based and rich with collaborative learning experiences, learning experiences that are not tethered exclusively to the resources or capacities of their teachers, school, or community, learning experiences that demonstrate a contextual connection to the real world, and learning experiences that provide opportunities for students to self-direct the learning process. Student engagement in learning is therefore tied to how well educators implement the Student Vision for Learning. Technology is a tool for supporting that implementation, but it must be done effectively.

A widely promoted theory from both media and educators has been that a decrease in students' engagement in learning during remote learning as evidenced by students not showing up for virtual classes or not engaging in learning content was the fault of remote learning. The belief is that the virtual learning modality was not effective for most students, and thus, they did not show up for class and/or were not engaging in the learning process during online instruction. While it is difficult to estimate the validity of these claims or the extent to which students were not engaging with online learning, a report published by Bellwether Education in October 2020 estimated that as many as three million K–12 students were potentially not engaging with remote or online learning from spring 2020 through fall 2020. The authors' three million student estimate was based on a compilation of different estimating methodologies with some limitations noted.

The report, however, pointed out several troubling local statistics, including that in Los Angeles it was estimated that *"15–20% of English learners, students in foster care, students with disabilities, and homeless students didn't access any of the district's online educational materials from March through May [2020]."*[7] An update to the report in October 2021 cited decreases in school enrollments for the 2021–2022 school year as evidence of the impact of the pandemic and remote learning on student attendance: *"Nationwide enrollment in public pre-K through 12 schools dropped by more than 1.3 million students between 2018–19 and 2020-21, a decline of 2.7% from 2018–19 enrollment."*[8] And while it is extremely difficult to scientifically prove a causal relationship here between the implementation of remote learning and decreased student engagement in learning or even school enrollments, several in the media and corporate worlds are connecting those dots anyway.

As an example, an article in an education technology publication in August 2021 with an eye-catching headline title of "Remote Learning Kills Student Engagement" shared the results of a study conducted by an education technology company that examined their products' usage analytics to draw a connection between technology use and student engagement. Using the number of interactions students had with their product as their evidence base, the study proffered students using their product in fully face-to-face classrooms were more engaged in learning than students in virtual classrooms during the 2020–2021 school year. According to the study, students in remote learning interacted with their product less than students in fully face-to-face, traditional classrooms, and this was interpreted as indicating a difference in engagement levels in education.[9] However, this conclusion flies in the face of how most educators assess student engagement. When asked to identify how they measure students' engagement in learning, over 60% of school principals in the 2020–2021 Speak Up survey indicated these were their top three metrics: student academic outcomes, student participation in class, and student feedback on the learning experience. Only one-third of the administrators (32%) said that they considered analytics on digital content usage as a meaningful metric for evaluating student engagement in learning.

But is it true? Did remote virtual learning result in more students being less engaged in school than they had been before the pandemic?

Definitely, this live, large-scale experiment with virtual learning during school closures demonstrated that not every student benefited or thrived in their online classes. Many factors may have contributed to this situation, including teachers' comfort, confidence, and capabilities with remote learning methodologies and tools. This is not meant to disparage the efforts undertaken by teachers to support continuity of learning to the best of their abilities. But the reality is that most teachers had no prior familiarity or training on how to implement virtual learning before March 2020. Teacher effectiveness has always been the most significant factor determining the quality of the student learning experience. And this applies to face-to-face instruction as well as virtual learning. Contrary to conventional wisdom and long-held assumptions, face-to-face, in-classroom instruction might not be the best experience for some students. A key lesson learned from the pandemic and the shift to remote learning that we should pay more attention to is that for too many students, school is simply not intrinsically motivating. For many students, before the pandemic, compliance was the most significant driver to go to school, show up in class, and participate at least nominally in the learning activities. Without the compliance factor and the extrinsic rewards associated with going to school, some students lacked the internal motivation to regularly engage with teachers and classmates in virtual classrooms. Remote learning did not create this problem, however. It merely opened our eyes to an existing situation that many schools and communities have simply not addressed previously—the persistent lack of student engagement in classroom learning.

Besides asking questions about students' use of technology to support learning, both in school and out of school, the annual Speak Up surveys also ask students about their learning environments. This data helps school and district leaders understand how their policies and programs may be affecting school climate issues for students. Many districts use their local Speak Up data to meet state reporting requirements. Such is the case for many districts in California that use their Speak Up school climate data results to report on the status of their Local Control and Accountability Plan (LCAP), a three-year plan that describes the school district's goals, actions, services, and expenditures to support positive student outcomes that address state and local priorities. Speak Up data insights based on examining current and longitudinal findings on student views about their school's culture and climate and their personal motivations for learning are informative for this discussion on student engagement.

Students' Engagement in What They Are Learning in School—Speak Up Data Insights

For the past few years, students in grades 6–12 have been asked on the annual Speak Up surveys about their level of agreement with this statement: "I am engaged in what I am learning in school most of the time." Table 8.2 documents the responses from over 87,000 students in grades 6–12 representing a diverse set of schools and communities during the 2019–2020 and 2020–2021 school years. For the 2019–2020 school year, the data is disaggregated into two distinct time periods: (i) pre-pandemic and before school closures in March 2020, and (ii) during the pandemic, when most school buildings were physically closed and remote learning was the modality for learning continuity.

As evidenced in this data, only 54% of middle school students (grades 6–8) in the pre-pandemic time period in 2019–2020 agreed

Table 8.2 Students' levels of engagement with learning in school (2019–2021).

"I am engaged in what I am learning in school most of the time"	% of student agreement and disagreement		
	2019–2020 school year		2020–2021 school year
	Before school closures	During school closures	
Students in grades 6–8			
Agree	54	55	49
Disagree	46	45	51
Students in grades 9–12			
Agree	47	49	50
Disagree	53	51	50

Source: © Project Tomorrow 2021.

that they were engaged in what they were learning in school most of the time; 46% said they were not engaged most of the time. Comparatively, the percentages of engaged and non-engaged students were statistically the same during remote learning (55% said they were engaged, 45% said they were not). The statistics for the high school students are similar for the 2019–2020 school year. For high school students, only 48% of those students said that they were engaged in learning at school on the 2019–2020 Speak Up surveys. Again, there is no statistical difference before and during remote learning. The pandemic and sudden shift to remote learning in March 2020 did not affect students' levels of engagement in their schoolwork. The statistics for the 2020–2021 school year follow the same sobering trend line. Approximately 50% of students in grades 6–12 say they are engaged in learning most of the time when they are in school; another 50% say they are not.

As evidenced by this data, students' engagement with what they are learning in school was the same before remote learning and during remote learning. And that same lack of interest with school learning persisted in this most recent school year as well. The wake-up call for school and district leaders is that the traditional school environment and learning modalities may only be working for half of your student population. Not only is this an important consideration to understanding student engagement but is an indication of some underlying equity challenges as well.

Students' Beliefs about the Value of Learning and School—Speak Up Data Insights

Other attitudinal statements about school also indicate that students' lack of engagement or interest in what they are learning in school runs deeper than what many educators may assume. Again, refuting theories, beliefs, or media stories connecting disengagement with remote learning, many of students' attitudes about school and the value of the learning experience in school has not significantly changed in the past four years. It does not appear that their experience with remote learning, whether that experience was an exemplar of virtual learning or not, affected their attitudes about school.

For this data analysis, I examined the feedback from middle school students specifically. The data displayed in Table 8.3 documents the level of student agreement and disagreement with three key statements about their interest in what they are learning in school and the value they place on that learning using data from 2017 through 2021. Key insights are as follows:

- On average over a four-year time period from 2017 to 2021, only 42% of middle school students (students in grades 6–8) say they are interested in what they are learning in school. This means that 58% of our middle schoolers over the past four years, including pre and post school closures, say that they are not interested in what they are learning in school.

- As an aspirational statement, 49% of the middle school students wish their classes were more interesting.

- Only 49% of the students say that they believe that what they are learning in school is important for their future. This corresponds to the desire students have for their school-learning experience to be more contextually relevant and to directly address what they perceive as their needs in terms of skill development and/or learning experiences for future success, echoing the Student Vision for Learning.

The jaded among us may write off these research findings as the views of typical students who have never liked or valued school.

Table 8.3   Grade 6–8 students' attitudes about school over time (2017–2021).

Attitudes about school		% of student agreement and disagreement with each statement					
		2017–2018	2018–2019	2019–2020 Before school closures	2019–2020 During school closures	2020–2021	Four-year average
"I am interested in what I am learning in school."	Agree	41	41	46	54	41	42
	Disagree	59	59	54	46	59	58
"I wish my classes were more interesting."	Agree	45	46	58	41	48	49
	Disagree	55	54	42	59	52	51
"What I am learning in school is important to my future."	Agree	47	46	53	58	47	49
	Disagree	53	54	47	42	53	51

Source: © *Project Tomorrow 2021.*

Too often I hear from policymakers and business leaders in particular that the problem with today's youth is that they do not like learning. Nothing could be further from the truth. Today's students very much like learning; they just may not like what they are being taught in school. That is a very important distinction.

To further prove or disprove the impact of remote learning on student engagement, it is valuable to examine how students in different learning formats during the 2019–2020 school year reported on their attitudes about learning and school, and the value they placed on their teachers as well. To do this examination, I disaggregated the Speak Up data based on the type of school format in place when the students completed their Speak Up survey. In the survey we offered students the choice of three different formats, the ones most in use during the 2020–2021 school year: a fully online format, a hybrid learning format where students were in a physical classroom a few days a week while also learning online a few days a week, and a traditional, face-to-face in-school format (see Table 8.4). The key findings from this analysis are as follows:

- **Students want to do well in school.** 82% of students in grades 6–12 say this is true for them. But this valuation has not changed as a result of the pandemic nor does it vary significantly across different school formats. In 2016, 81% of students in grades 6–8 and 82% of students in grades 9–12 said that doing well in school was important to them. Students understand the importance of school for their future. Additionally, that valuation was not affected by their school format over the past year. A similar percentage of students in all three formats agreed with this statement about the importance of doing well in school.

237

Student Engagement

Table 8.4 Students' attitudes about learning and school across three school formats—2020–2021.

Value statements about school and learning	All school formats	Fully virtual learning environments	Hybrid learning environments	Fully face-to-face learning environments
	% of students who agree with each statement			
	Gr 6–12 students	Gr 6–12 students	Gr 6–12 students	Gr 6–12 students
"Doing well in school is important to me."	82	78	81	83
"I like learning how to do things."	68	64	67	69
"I like learning about new ideas."	59	57	58	61
"I like learning how to make or build things."	54	50	54	54
"Teachers are important to my learning."	53	48	52	55

Source: © *Project Tomorrow 2021.*

- **Students like learning how to do things and how to make and build things, and they like learning about new ideas.** As with their overall valuation on the importance of doing well in school, students' attitudes about learning do not differ significantly based on their school format. Over two-thirds of students in grades 6–12 (68%) say they like learning how to do things.

- **Students value their teachers.** Educators would probably like to see a higher percentage of students who say that their teachers are important for their learning. The consistency of this data statistic over time and across different community types (urban, rural, and suburban) and school demographics (percentage of students in schools where the majority of students are students of color) speaks to the validity of the finding. As Table 8.4 shows, 53% of students in grades 6–12 said in 2020–2021 that their teachers were important to their learning. Very similarly, in 2016, 52% of students in grades 6–12 agreed with this statement about the importance of their teachers. Equally notable is the lack of statistical significance in the differences based on school formats in the 2020–2021 data.

Students' views on their level of engagement in learning and their views on school and learning in general do not happen in isolation from each other. When students are engaged in learning in school, they like school, they value their in-school learning experiences, and they appreciate their teachers as the facilitators of that engaging learning process. However, the converse is true as well for many students. For those students who are not engaged in what they are learning in school, they also show a marked lack of interest in what they are learning in school, and they do not see value in the school-based learning experience. This is not something new, however. The traditional school structure has never had universal appeal for all students.

Whether we want to admit it or not, I believe many students simply soldier on through the school experience despite not feeling that their school learning is worthwhile or meaningful. That our students may be faking their engagement in school learning may surprise many educators and be difficult for others to accept. This was certainly the case for Thomas as described in Chapter 6. When I think about the students who have expertly learned how to outwardly play the game of school in spite of its inadequacies for their personal needs, I am reminded of what I learned from a frustrated and resigned high school student in the early days of this research.

The student summed up their high school learning experience like this: "School is just a place I have to get through now to get to something better later." While this is not the way all students view their in-school learning environment, the Speak Up research indicates that as many as 50% of middle and high school students are not engaged in what they are learning in school and that this is not the result of the pandemic, or the way remote virtual learning was implemented. But rather, the pandemic and remote learning provides us with a unique opportunity to put aside our rose-colored glasses about the efficacy of traditional school for all students and seriously evaluate why the learning environments in our classrooms, even now with an abundance of digital tools and resources at the ready for student and teacher usage, are not meeting the needs of too many of our students.

In many ways, the experiment with virtual learning in spring 2020 and through the 2020–2021 school year in many communities is a perfect lab environment for understanding the root causes behind the student engagement challenge, and thus seeing the potential ways that the Free Agent Learning ecosystem could help leaders meet this challenge head on.

Learning about Student Engagement from the Challenges of Virtual Learning

Much was written in the early days of the COVID pandemic remote learning experiment about students not showing up for their virtual classes, not keeping their cameras on during Zoom or Google Meet sessions, or simply not being as engaged in their school learning activities. Peter DeWitt, a former K–5 public school principal turned author, presenter, and leadership coach, discussed some reasons why he thought students may not be showing up for virtual classes in an April 2020 *Education Week* opinion piece, "6 Reasons Students Aren't

Showing Up for Virtual Learning."[10] On one level, the six reasons can feel very time-bound to those early days of virtual learning. But scratching beyond the surface, these reasons can also point to some institutional barriers that may be unintentionally resulting in a lack of student engagement in school-based learning. By examining these reasons with this new lens based on what we have learned over the past few years, we could conceptually retitle this piece, "6 Reasons Students Aren't Showing Up Emotionally for Learning Today."

Analysis and commentary on the "6 Reasons Students Aren't Showing Up for Virtual Learning" by Peter DeWitt appear in the following sections.

Students Lacking Access to Adequate Technology to Support Consistency in Virtual Learning

Project Tomorrow has long documented the extent of the "Homework Gap" across the country. "Homework Gap" is a term coined by Federal Communications Commissioner Jessica Rosenworcel to explain how some students do not have access to technology including the Internet when they are out of school to do homework or engage even in self-directed digital learning. This was certainly a significant barrier to student participation in remote learning. Prior to the pandemic, 13% of middle and high school students said they were at least occasionally affected by this Homework Gap according to Speak Up reporting. With significant new federal and state investments in home connectivity to support learning continuity over the past two years, the percentage of Homework Gap–affected students has fallen to 9–11% of the overall student population as of the 2020–2021 school year, representing an improvement in students' out-of-school access but not solving the overall problem.

But why did it take a pandemic to realize that so many students did not have access to technology as a learning resource once they left their school campus? Because while students have long reported how they are using the online content and tools to support schoolwork and homework, in most cases that was self-directed usage, not assigned homework, that was outside of the purview of teachers or administrators. Despite what many believe to be true, teachers have long been reluctant to assign digitally based homework that required out-of-school connectivity for two primary reasons: (i) teachers believed, whether true or not, that at least some of their students did not have access to technology at home and they did not want to prejudice those students by requiring digital homework, and (ii) teachers were not yet using technology as a learning vehicle or platform during their instructional time in class and thus did not have the experiential sophistication to understand how to assign effective or meaningful digital homework or online learning activities.

The big wake-up call for teachers coming from the pandemic was a new awareness that technology could potentially be used effectively to support many aspects of their everyday teaching and learning practices, not just the sporadic or random digital learning episode within a day of traditional instruction. As teachers become even more familiar with how to use technology to support new learning models in their classroom, the need for students to have access to learning-appropriate digital tools and high-speed, consistent online connectivity outside of school will increase. A smartphone and Wi-Fi connection through Starbucks or McDonalds will no longer suffice for learning activities. The fact that too many students (9–11% of students in grades 6–12) still do not have regular, safe, and convenient access to such tools and resources outside of school means that the Homework Gap will continue to be a contributing factor for why students may not be engaged in school-based learning. In Chapter 9 I will further discuss the connection between technology access, equity, and Free Agent Learning.

Students Serving as Essential Workers

In many communities, high school students had to take on new income-producing responsibilities in their family during the pandemic. This was due to other family members losing their jobs or not being able to find work, and the impact of COVID illnesses and deaths in many communities. Surprisingly, virtual learning in many ways opened the door for students to be able to have employment opportunities that are not limited by traditional school hours or limited to just after-school or weekend jobs. With virtual learning assignments being self-paced in many classrooms, students were able, for example, to take a foodservice job during the day and work on their schoolwork in the evenings. Not only did this help meet the economic needs of many families, but it provided students with real-world job experiences and a new sense of self-worth and independence. For some students, the ability to self-direct their school-based learning whether that was at 10 a.m. or 10 p.m. felt more in alignment with the types of learning experiences they were already valuing as Free Agent Learners, following their own interest-driven intellectual curiosities.

Embracing competency-based learning that places a premium on student proficiencies and outcomes over seat time in class is an example of how school and district leaders can address this engagement challenge, acknowledging that non-traditional learning schedules and programs may be a better fit for some students. Additionally, students identify getting work experience as the number one way for them to develop the future-ready skills they will need for college or career. Providing flexibility so that some students can work if desired while also going to school changes this barrier from a negative to a positive: students doing essential work to prepare for their future.

Students Lacking Compliance or Motivation for Attendance

DeWitt notes in his original opinion piece that a school district's decisions to eliminate grading in virtual classes resulted in a decrease in students' engagement or participation in virtual classes. In other words, the extrinsic motivation for student participation was the "stick" of grades, not the "carrot" of learning for learning's sake. In my interviews with students in spring 2020 and spring 2021, this was a common observation on the part of the students also. If teachers were not grading the assignments, why should they, the students, care about doing the assignments or putting forth their best work?

In this case, I think the school and district leaders' concerns about not penalizing students who were having trouble accessing remote learning facilities resulted in an unintended overall devaluation of the students' perceptions of the learning experience. Couple this with the students' perception that their school-based learning was not adequately preparing them for future work success, and it is highly conceivable that the decreased engagement or motivation to go to school was the result of the absence of key extrinsic motivators that are the foundation of traditional school structures. This applies in a post-pandemic environment as well.

It is imperative that we both understand the role of extrinsic motivators in supporting student engagement in learning and at the same time realize that for students to develop the future-ready skills of self-direction and self-learning, we must help them build their own internal intrinsic motivations that value learning without teacher direction or assignment. Relying upon compliance is not a successful formula for increased student engagement in school-based learning, especially in light of the more meaningful learning that students are experiencing as Free Agent Learners.

Students Providing Childcare for Other Siblings at Home

In many communities, including in many immigrant communities, childcare is often provided by older family members such as grandparents who are tasked with watching the preschool children while their parents work. Due to ongoing concerns about spreading COVID, these older family members are today less available to help with childcare. And unlike in other families, the work of many immigrant adults continues to be outside the home even at the height of the pandemic due to the high percentage who are working in service, hospitality, and public-facing jobs. Remote work was not an option.

Older students took up not only the responsibility of childcare but also the responsibility to ensure that their young siblings and cousins were engaging in their own remote learning. Many high school students have shared with me the challenges they faced trying to participate in their own remote learning classes while helping a seven-year-old sister or brother get online for their own daily online class. A high school junior noted that in most cases, her teachers were supportive when she explained that she could not participate in online school if she had to take care of her younger sister.

The virtual learning experiment prompted by the pandemic opened up many educators' eyes as to the family situations of their students and their living conditions at home. Research has long documented how students' home experiences affect their learning potential and their ability to be fully present in school, whether that is because the student in hungry, tired, stressed, or suffering from trauma. The new emphasis on many schools on social, emotional, and mental health supports for students is a critical component of addressing the engagement challenge.

Students Lacking Adequate Space to Support Virtual Learning

While we would like to believe that every student has a learning-appropriate workspace at home to do virtual learning or homework (dedicated desk, ergonomic chair, good lighting, quiet environment, healthy snacks, and adult supervision), that was not the case before the pandemic and certainly not during the pandemic. Nor has the pandemic changed this dynamic for the future. And while it is certainly possible to silently complete math worksheets or do classwork reading while sitting at the kitchen table or on the living room sofa alongside siblings, participation in a virtual class brings to that scenario a host of new challenges, most notably if active participation (answering questions aloud, being part of a class discussion, collaborating on a project via Zoom or a Google Meet) is required.

Providing every student with a Chromebook and a hot spot was a heavy lift for many districts. It was certainly necessary to support the continuity of learning but was unfortunately also insufficient if the student did not have an appropriate physical space to be able to fully participate in online class. A few districts, upon realizing that this was the situation for many students, opened their school doors for students to come back to school and use an empty classroom or library space as their base camp for engaging with online learning.

For too many students, however, a deterrent to participating in online learning was a limitation of space at their home that would work within the parameters of the class. Additionally, some students may not have wanted their teachers or classmates to have a firsthand view of their living conditions either. To effectively engage students in school-based learning, teachers are gaining a new appreciation of the need to know their student more holistically. That includes an understanding of the home environment and what might work or not within that student's different environments outside of school as well.

Students Lacking Meaningful Student-Teacher Relationships

While the previous five reasons why students may not have been engaged in remote learning were primarily structural or institutional barriers, this reason is grounded in a well-documented tenet of effective learning, the student-teacher relationship. An *Education Week* article in 2019 (before the pandemic) summarized the results of an analysis of 46 research studies about the positive effect of a strong teacher-student relationship on key outcomes highly valued by schools and districts.[11] The studies identified outcomes such as "student academic engagement, attendance, grades, fewer disruptive behaviors and suspensions, and lower school dropout rates" and noted that the effect of a strong student-teacher relationship was not diminished when controlling for variables such as student/family backgrounds or even school backgrounds.

And yet despite this strong research basis and an inherent understanding on the part of educators that student learning depends on a two-way street of respect, trust, and empathy between students and teachers, the lack of a meaningful relationship could be a factor in the suppression of students' engagement in learning or wanting to participate in school. According to Speak Up data from 2015 through 2021, an average of only 34% of high school students believe that their school cares about them as a person. This percentage was highly consistent with data from the most recent school year, 2020–2021, following the pattern with 36% of students holding that belief about their school. However, among students who said there was at least one adult at their school they could trust, 49% of those students said their school cared about them. Correspondingly, when students highly valued their teachers within their learning experiences, the percentage of students who said their school cared about them as a person soared to 52%.

Students' beliefs about school appear to be deeply rooted in their relationships with their teachers. For students who say they are engaged most of the time in what they are learning in school, 68% say they feel they are emotionally safe at school, 69% say their teachers are important to their learning, and 70% say their school cares about them as a person. It is understandable that lacking a trusting and supportive relationship with a teacher could result in students not engaging or participating in virtual learning and also having the same response to in-school learning as well. It is worth repeating: Personal relationships between students and teachers in school really do matter.

Leveraging the Free Agent Learning Ecosystem to Augment Student Voice and Address Engagement Challenges

And here lies the conundrum with student engagement in learning today. As evidenced by the Free Agent Learning ecosystem, students are engaged with learning when they can self-direct those experiences on their own time using digital tools and resources to satisfy academic curiosities, develop future-ready skills, explore career or job paths, or support self-identified needs for remediation on school subjects. Their level of engagement is notable due to the frequency of these self-directed, interest-driven behaviors, and the diversity of the students who are Free Agent Learners.

And yet, these same students, who are so engaged in learning outside of school, often find their school-based learning experiences to be less than satisfactory especially in terms of engaging them in the learning process. As noted earlier, only 50% of middle and high school students report being engaged in what they are learning in school most of the time. The issue, however, is not that students do not want to learn or are not capable of being fully engaged in learning. Rather, the secret to understanding how to increase student engagement in learning, whether that learning takes place in second-period geometry class or at home using Minecraft to explore architecture as a career field, is to appreciate the role of purpose and relevancy in students' learning lives.

To fully embrace the recognition of purpose as a key determinant of student engagement, educators need to first appreciate and value the learning experiences that students are having outside of school, self-directing learning that is both engaging and purposeful for their lives. As discussed in Chapter 1, students' Free Agent Learning behaviors are a direct response to and actualization of the key tenets of the Student Vision for Learning:

- **Social-based learning**—students want to leverage communications and collaboration tools to create and personalize networks of experts to inform their education process and to support shared problem-solving experiences.

- **Untethered learning**—students envision learning experiences that transcend the classroom walls to expand their access to knowledge and experts so that their education is not limited by resource constraints, traditional funding streams, geography, community assets, or even teacher knowledge or skills.

- **Contextualized learning**—students desire stronger connections between academic content and real-world issues and events with a goal to drive learning productivity as well as the development of the college, career, and citizenry skills they need for future success.

- **Self-directed learning**—students believe that the types of learning experiences where they can control (at least to some degree) the *what, where, how,* and *why* of the experience will help them develop agency and efficacy as a lifelong learner.

Underpinning each of these tenets within the Student Vision for Learning is a connection to a learning process that has explicit relevancy, context, and purpose in the eyes of that student. Central to Free Agent Learnership is also the opportunity for the student to self-direct the learning experience and to have voice and choice in the path and process of learning. However, the concept of student voice is not analogous to embracing the Free Agent Learning ecosystem as a way to increase student engagement in school.

Over the past few years, a strong emphasis has been placed on the importance of student voice in education. A wide range of organizations have endorsed and written about student voice, including think tanks and policy organizations such as Center for American Progress, an independent nonpartisan policy institute, as well as educator associations such as the National Association of Secondary School Principals (NASSP), the National Elementary School Principals Association (NAESP), and the Association for Supervision and Curriculum Development (ASCD). And most recently, the Collaborative for Academic, Social, and Emotional Learning (CASEL) has explicitly linked student voice to effective social-emotional learning plans in schools. Project Tomorrow's annual Speak Up Research Project is at its core a student voice initiative. I started the Speak Up Project in 2003 because of a strong belief that students' authentic, experiential ideas and views about their learning experiences should be better leveraged by school and district leaders to improve education. I believe this is even more important today.

There is no debate that encouraging student voice within education yields multiple benefits, especially for students. But what do we really mean by student voice? Dana Mitra, professor of education at Pennsylvania State University and researcher on educational policy and student voice, explains student voice in this way: "At the simplest level, student voice can consist of young people sharing their opinions of school problems with administrators and faculty.

250

Student voice initiatives can also be more extensive, for instance, when young people collaborate with adults to address the problems in their schools—and in rare cases when youth assume leadership roles to change efforts."[12]

Mitra points out that true student voice is about more than simply listening to students' ideas; it is really about integrating those ideas and the students themselves into organizational problem-solving and strategy development work in schools to improve education. This potential power-sharing relationship requires that educators embrace two key concepts that may be difficult for some to adopt: (i) students have ideas worth listening to, and (ii) students can have a meaningful role in education decision-making. ShoutOut, an organization that supports student voice in education, has developed a ladder of student involvement that recognizes not only the steps to fully actualize student voice within a school setting but also how student voice can be subverted into forms of tokenism, decoration, or manipulation when these two key concepts are not fully embraced.[13]

The results from the Speak Up Research Project provide a glimpse into how difficult it is for schools to fully embrace student voice as an agent of change. Despite the increased emphasis on student voice as a concept, the reality is that most students do not believe that their views are valued or that they are provided with opportunities to share their ideas with education leadership. On the 2017–2018 Speak Up surveys, only 35% of high school students agreed with this statement: *Administrators and teachers at our school are interested in listening to and acting upon ideas from students about how to improve school and our education.* The impact of this reality extends beyond student voice, however, with implications for how schools can address the challenges of increasing student engagement in school-based learning.

In the various discourses on student voice, many writers and researchers note a connection between educators' support for student voice and student engagement in learning. Educators implicitly make that connection already. When asked to identify the best ways to measure student engagement in learning, 61% of school principals and 54% of teachers say that they seek out student feedback on classroom learning as a viable metric for understanding student engagement. And while many researchers point out that having a regular method of asking students their ideas about school can help students feel a stronger connection to their school, the linkage back to increasing student engagement still feels tenuous.

However, marrying student voice with an appreciation for how students are engaged in learning outside of school has the potential to help educators increase student engagement in school by explicitly valuing students' lived experiences and their views on those experiences. As noted earlier, educators identified various ways that they are measuring student engagement in learning today, including academic outcomes, participation levels, and student feedback. However, less than 1 in 3 principals and teachers say that they look for evidence of extended learning as a metric for understanding student engagement. This is a missed opportunity. Through an explicit understanding for how students are self-directing learning as Free Agent Learners and even encouraging that behavior, educators have an opportunity to bridge the gap between school and home learning experiences and to connect the currently disparate parts of a student's learning life (in school and at home) into a more cohesive and engaging experience overall. The starting point is to appreciate how students are already leveraging online educational content to support what they perceive to be more engaging and purposeful learning experiences that align with the Student Vision for Learning. The following model is not only a noteworthy example but one that could be highly replicable in the typical classroom.

A Replicable Model: Students' Self-Authenticating What They Learned in Class

In my travels to visit schools and classrooms across the nation, I often meet with students in classrooms to listen to their ideas and views on their learning experiences. In one such visit to an eighth grade science classroom in the Houston area, I asked the students in the class if they used online tools and resources when they were at home to support their learning. The students all enthusiastically responded that they did that regularly. Specifically, the students told me that they regularly went online afterschool to check to see if what their science teacher had taught that day was accurate and if it represented the latest theories or ideas about science.

Though I immediately worried that this may be an uncomfortable disclosure for the science teacher, who was in the back of the classroom with their principal and a district administrator from the central office, the teacher quickly assuaged my concern. The teacher explained that they had taught their students to do this self-authenticating of class content (including their lessons) as a way to develop their information and media literacy skills. Additionally, as the teacher explained, this behavior provided a way for their students to be more engaged in the science learning content since it put the process of confirmation and potentially discovery in the hands of the eighth graders directly. The students felt personally invested in ensuring that the information provided in the class represented the most current research not only for themselves but for their classmates as well.

And along the way, the students engaged in the Free Agent Learning behaviors of self-directed, interest-driven learning by extending their vetting assignment to research other new topics in science and even explore science careers. The starting point of authenticating the teacher's lesson was the beginning of their Free Agent

Learning explorations. The students brought back into the classroom the results of their online research (even occasionally "corrections" to the teacher's lessons and content) as well as sharing what they had learned on their own. Each of the four elements of the Student Vision for Learning is represented in this learning experience as well (socially based, untethered, contextually relevant, and self-directed). By incorporating the outcomes of the students' Free Agent Learnership within the classroom experience, the teacher supported student voice, increased student engagement in school-based learning, and helped their students develop an ethos for lifelong learning. By institutionalizing this process as part of the classroom culture and appreciating the value of students' self-directed learning, the teacher effectively turned the table on how to effectively engage students in school-based learning by leaning into the values of Free Agent Learnership and the Student Vision for Learning.

Considerations for Replicating This Model in Your Classrooms

This model that embraces Free Agent Learning can be replicated in most classrooms, spanning a variety of subject areas and grades. To be effective, teachers must reevaluate their role in the classroom, transitioning from being the expert on all learning content to being the facilitator of the learning process, which implicitly involves students' taking responsibility and feeling empowered to authenticate the quality and accuracy of their own learning. This model also provides a unique opportunity for teachers to help students develop information and media literacy skills, especially when using online resources. To facilitate that effectively, teachers may also need to develop their own information and media literacy skills especially around how to authenticate online content and verify bias or prejudice in Internet-based resources. It is important for teachers to position this type of learning activity with their students as an opportunity for them to have a voice in their education but also to develop the skills they need for future success, thus providing a purpose and context for why bridging school and at-home learning is valuable.

The goal of this chapter was to examine how the Free Agent Learning ecosystem can help educators address the vexing challenge of increasing student engagement in school-based learning. In Chapter 9, we extend this discussion about student engagement to examine student empowerment and to answer the question about how to create learning environments that support student development of agency and self-efficacy as key aspects of a future-ready education. Central to that discussion is a comprehensive understanding about the relationship between equity and student agency. The chapter will provide guidance for educators at all levels as to how to leverage Free Agent Learnership to support both student agency and equity in learning experiences.

Connecting the Dots

- Educators' appreciation and acknowledgment of how students are self-directing learning outside of school can be a powerful asset in terms of supporting increased student engagement in classroom learning.

- But to do so, we need to move beyond the myths around student engagement particularly relative to the pandemic and disruptions in traditional in-school learning. With 50% of our students saying they are not engaged in what they are learning in class (both before and after school disruptions), we have to acknowledge that our traditional education processes are ineffective in meeting the needs of too many students.

- Closely examining students' views on the pros and cons of their virtual learning experiences can provide new insights and ideas into actionable steps that educators can take to address the challenges of student engagement.

Now, Think about This!

1. How has your definition of student engagement changed as a result of the new learning models implemented during the pandemic? What are the most effective ways to measure student engagement today?

2. Based on the high level of engagement of students in their Free Agent Learning activities outside of school, what elements of those experiences can educators replicate or mimic in the classroom to elicit a similar level of emotional investment on the part of the student?

3. Where do the lines of student engagement and student empowerment in learning intersect? How can we help students develop self-efficacy as learners in the typical classroom setting?

4. What is one thing that you can do today or tomorrow to help your teachers or colleagues think differently about student engagement in learning, both in school and out of school?

Notes

1. http://content.time.com/time/specials/packages/article/0,28804, 2036683_2037183_2037185,00.html.
2. https://www.pewresearch.org/internet/2018/05/31/teens-social-media-technology-2018.

3. https://www.pewresearch.org/internet/fact-sheet/social-media/?menuItem=4abfc543-4bd1-4b1f-bd4a-e7c67728ab76.

4. https://www.youtube.com/watch?v=uhiCFdWeQfA.

5. https://en.wikipedia.org/wiki/Ferris_Bueller%27s_Day_Off#cite_ref-DVDCommShoot_20-3.

6. https://certell.org/resources/projecttomorrow.pdf.

7. https://bellwethereducation.org/publication/missing-margins-estimating-scale-covid-19-attendance-crisis.

8. https://bellwethereducation.org/publication/missing-margins-estimating-scale-covid-19-attendance-crisis#2021.

9. https://thejournal.com/articles/2021/08/18/remote-learning-kills-student-engagement.aspx.

10. https://www.edweek.org/leadership/opinion-6-reasons-students-arent-showing-up-for-virtual-learning/2020/04.

11. https://www.edweek.org/teaching-learning/why-teacher-student-relationships-matter/2019/03.

12. https://www.academia.edu/2005772/The_role_of_leaders_in_enabling_student_voice.

13. https://soundout.org/2015/02/02/ladder-of-student-involvement.

Chapter 9

Why the Free Agent Learning Ecosystem Matters Today—Equity in Learning

It is too simplistic to think that the equity-based reasons why the Free Agent Learning ecosystem should matter to school and district leaders today are only about technology access, though it is understandable why that view may be the first to come to mind. The events of 2020 and 2021 have put a spotlight on students' access to technology to support school-based learning. But just as the equity in education conversations should not be limited to technology access, the same is true for understanding the implications and opportunities for Free Agent Learnership on K–12 education. The reasons why equity in technology access is top of mind, however, are a good starting point.

In spring 2020, when education, parent, and community leaders around the world were struggling to understand how to continue learning for students when school buildings were suddenly closed due to the COVID pandemic, Robin Lake, director of the Center on Reinventing Public Education (CRPE) at the University of Washington, beckoned us all to look anew at a reality about equity in learning. At that time, schools were in triage mode working round the clock to develop new procedures and systems to distribute their inventory of tablets, laptops, and Chromebooks directly to students to facilitate online learning. While many schools had embraced the concept of personally assigning digital learning devices to individual students, that usage generally was limited to in-school only. According to the Speak Up Research Project, in the 2018–2019 school year, only 4 in 10 school principals said that they allowed school-owned devices to go home with students, and 50% said they had no plans to do so anytime in the near future. That was all obviously before the pandemic and the need to position technology as the primary learning platform and gateway during school closures.

Yet while the world was focused on setting up distribution sites to hand out Chromebooks and mobile hot spots, Ms. Lake was already thinking differently about the long-term impact of this new reality. As she explained to a virtual town hall in spring 2020, while COVID-19 did not create this digital divide for students, the pandemic did force us to "stare [the problem] right in the eye."[1] While much has been written and debated since 2020 about the students' lack of access to appropriate technology tools and safe and consistent Internet access to support learning, what Federal Communications Commissioner Jessica Rosenworcel calls the *Homework Gap*, the problem that is staring us in the eye today is not just about the lack of access. Rather, the new spotlight is on the institutional and cultural factors in our education system that are creating and perpetuating inequities.

From NetDay to the Global Achievement Gap

Over the past 30 years, policymakers have defined the digital divide as the ability of some individuals to have access to technology while others do not. Concentrated efforts in the late 1990s by government agencies, corporations, and philanthropic and community organizations provided significant financial and human capital investments in connecting schools and homes to the Internet, particularly in rural and urban communities. Project Tomorrow, under our previous organizational name NetDay, was conceived originally to help schools get connected to the Internet by orchestrating "electronic barn-raisings" around the country where volunteers from technology companies, government, and community groups would come together on a Saturday morning to literally pull blue Internet cables through ceiling tiles to create new hardwired connection spots in classrooms for computers. The first NetDay held on March 9, 1996, mobilized 20,000 volunteers across the state of California to wire 20% of the K–12 schools in the state. Both President Bill Clinton and Vice President Al Gore were part of that volunteer force on that day.[2] The movement gained steam and was replicated around the country and the world.

As a result of a multitude of efforts, from both private and public sectors, by 2003, policymakers and researchers had essentially considered the war to close the digital divide of access as having been won, especially in terms of school connectivity. The prevailing viewpoint at least until the pandemic has been that while not all students were connected to the Internet at home, the almost universal access in school was good enough. School is where real learning happened, and so as long as the school was connected, we did not need to worry too much about home access anymore. The pandemic and resulting school closures changed that viewpoint overnight.

Even before the pandemic, however, some researchers have started to look beyond the simplistic binary counts of who has access to technology and who does not and examine the differences in how technology is utilized by teachers and students as a new indicator of educational equity, what some call the *second level digital divide*.[3] Researchers examining differences in teachers' familiarity, comfort, and use of technology within instruction have reported on significant differences based on their school's economic factors. Additionally, they are documenting new barriers that limit the utility and impact of the increased access even when underserved students are afforded access to technology tools in school and at home. Education researchers Lauren Chapman, Jessica Masters, and Joseph Pedulla summarized the impact of this new digital divide as follows: "What does it profit students to have technology access if both they themselves as well as those instructing them do not have the training or capacity to utilize this technology efficiently?"[4]

This was certainly the case during the pandemic. Well-meaning but potentially ill-conceived efforts by teachers to replicate the in-school learning experience through a screen are now acknowledged as being less than effective for both students and teachers. Rather than embrace the potential of the technology to support new learning modalities, too many teachers got stuck in the replication process including setting up physical whiteboards in their homes and using their laptop cameras to capture lecture-based lesson delivery.

Additionally, current conversations about the Homework Gap put a premium on the value of Internet connectivity for students at home as necessary for facilitating school-assigned homework or projects and do not address the value or need for students to have that connectivity for their self-directed digital learning activities. Just as many researchers have noted that educators lack an appreciation for the value of students' self-directed learning, it appears that the views of policymakers may not yet have evolved to see the value of students' self-directed learning as important as school learning.

Students' use of digital tools to self-direct learning outside of school because of what they perceive as deficiencies in their current in-school learning experiences is core to many of the philosophies of Tony Wagner. Wagner extends the social justice and educational equity argument beyond simple digital connectivity. As he explains, even our nation's best schools continue to focus on old-world school tasks and paradigms that do not address the development of the types of skills that students will need to thrive and compete in the global information economy and society. Thus, the "Global Achievement

Gap," as Wagner terms it, is increasingly less about resource disparity in our schools and more about a mismatch between what students are learning and what they will need for post-school success.[5] The increasing importance of this issue transcends community type and family socioeconomic indicators.

The research and policy discussions on the second level digital divide and the Homework Gap highlight that students, particularly those in underserved communities and schools, often have to negotiate barriers and obstacles both at home and at school to use digital tools in ways that are relevant and meaningful for their lives and interests. Wagner's Global Achievement Gap broadens the conversation beyond connectivity to a new issue of equity and social justice: How well are we preparing all of our students to compete in the increasingly information-intensive global economy and society? The new equity equation, therefore, means that policymakers as well as educators need to think beyond the old paradigms of schooling outcomes and realize that today's students need a new set of skills to be successful. Equity is not just about access anymore but increasingly about usage and the quality of the digital learning experience for all students, no matter what purpose is driving their learning needs and desires, who is originating that learning process, or where that learning is taking place.

The Four Types of Equity Education Leaders Need to Be Talking about Today

The role of technology as an agent for creating more leveled playing fields for student learning is certainly not new. Technologists have long talked about the potential of digital tools to disrupt and transform the traditional school paradigms. The difference in the conversations today is that there are new motivations that are propelling these conversations to a new height of awareness.

- First, the impetus for this new focus and articulation is the high concern that teachers, administrators, and parents have for "learning loss" or the need for learning recovery or acceleration due to the impact of the COVID pandemic on students. Teachers are especially concerned about their special education students. Almost one in two teachers (49%) per the most recent Speak Up research findings say that addressing their special education students' learning loss or need for remediation is their biggest concern right now. Additionally, 63% of teachers say they are worried about how to support the remediation needs of all students.

- Second, the social justice movements of 2020 and beyond have also contributed to putting a brighter spotlight on institutional infrastructures or cultural habits and norms that are perpetuating inequities in education. Consequently, educators are interested in expanding the ways they are thinking about equity in education and investigating with a new fervor what is needed to support equitable learning in their classrooms. It is simply impossible to look away once the stark realities are exposed.

To get beyond the Homework Gap, the second level digital divide or thinking that you have addressed equity by putting a Chromebook and hot spot in the hands of every student requires a broader view on what we mean by equity in education and learning environments. It also mandates that we move from an abstract view to a tangible plan of action. To support that work, I have identified four distinct types of equity that I believe every school and district leader should be thinking about, talking about, and creating a plan in their school or district to address today. Free Agent Learnership is present already across all four types of equity, through the views of students about their current school-based learning environments and what they are doing every day outside of school to bring the

Student Vision of Learning into this personal learning ecosystem. In that way, Free Agent Learning can be a powerful asset to help education leaders both understand the implications of this expanded definition of equity in education and create tangible action steps to identify inequities and develop new plans to address them. The four types of equity in education are as follows:

- **Equity of student access to learning content and tools:** Students have access to high-quality learning resources both in school and at home;

- **Equity of student learning experiences:** There is consistency in students' learning environments and experiences and teacher quality across classes, grade levels, and schools;

- **Equity of learning opportunities for student success:** Students can learn in environments that are safe, trusting, and supportive; and

- **Equity of student agency and empowerment:** Students are explicitly empowered to take ownership of their own learning and given opportunities to develop lifelong learning skills.

In the following sections, I will discuss each of these equity types in more detail and provide research data and real-world examples to support the potential of Free Agent Learnership as a leadership asset in addressing the new equity challenges.

Free Agent Learning and Equity of Student Access to Learning Content and Tools

As discussed already, the need to ensure continuity of learning during school closures resulted in thousands and thousands of tablets, laptops, and Chromebooks being distributed to students and families from school district inventories. Today, 9 in 10 school principals say that their school provides devices for students to use in school and to take home. To support Internet connectivity, school districts seemingly overnight created mobile hot spot loaner programs and the requisite logistical systems to distribute and manage these devices. In the 2017–2018 school year, only 8% of school districts had such programs in place. By 2021, 85% of districts were in the mobile hot spot distribution business.

While it's often lamented that K–12 education enterprises are like aircraft carriers in their inability to make significant shifts in direction quickly, the efforts to put technology in the hands of all students over the past few years is certainly laudable. However, somewhere in the haze of all of the procurement of devices, the setting up of touchless drop-off and pickup of devices by teachers as well as families, the identification and licensing of online learning platforms and resources, and the almost continuous cycle of creating and revising school opening and closing plans based on community health metrics, educators' views on the value of school-based learning hardened. Driven by a concern about their Children's Internet Protection Act (CIPA) compliance, districts install content filtering systems that extend into student usage at home. Self-directed or highly personalized learning driven by the students themselves is thereby unfortunately discouraged implicitly by the filters that block student access to websites and social media channels that were not considered educational or part of the school's curriculum plan. This helps to validate that the number 1, 2, and 3 reasons for putting technology in the hands of students are to exclusively support school-based learning.

For some students, the work around is easy. Driven again by their passionate motivations to self-remediate, develop new skills, act on curiosities, or prepare themselves for future careers, the students simply use other devices in their home as their gateways for their Free Agent Learning. But what about the students who do not have access to other tablets, laptops, or Chromebooks at their homes to use for their desired Free Agent Learning activities? Is the subtext to the equity of access to learning content and tools really only about supporting learning experiences that are school sponsored? How can we say that we are addressing equity through our distribution of technology into children's homes if the usage for learning is only limited to school-based or teacher-sponsored or -sanctioned activities? As noted in earlier chapters, today's students see learning as a 24/7 enterprise, not just what happens between 8:30 a.m. and 2:30 p.m.

From 2012 to 2015, I evaluated the impact of a mobile learning project that was implemented in four fifth grade classes in an elementary school on the northwest side of Chicago. At the time, the school served a very-low-income, immigrant population. Ninety-four percent of the school families were identified as low income. Ninety-three percent of the students identified as Hispanic/Latinx, and 45% qualified as English language learners. Every student received free lunch at this school every day. Very few families had technology at home to support learning and fewer still had Internet access. While 54% of students in grades 3–5 nationwide at the time reported having access to high-speed Internet through a home computer, only 39% of the Chicago school student cohort said the same. The study project provided each fifth grader with a tablet computer and home Wi-Fi access to support the continuity of learning after the school day ended. The project was groundbreaking in Chicago at the time because at that point, no school in Chicago Public Schools was sending devices home with students. The project included professional learning for the teachers on how to effectively leverage these always connected devices within instruction as well as access to high-quality online content. A special content filtering system provides an automatic way for the devices to shut off the fifth graders' access to the Internet at 9 p.m. each night. For this cohort of students and teachers, the 1:1 assignment of the devices in the classroom was a brand-new experience. They had never had that type of technology access in class, let alone at home.

My evaluation of the project included examining for both the typical anticipated outcomes, as well as keeping my eyes wide open for new revelations, surprises, or unintended outcomes. On the side of the anticipated outcomes, I reported on the changes in teachers' proficiency with using the tablets within instruction and the changes in their personal valuation on digital learning. Based on my prior and subsequent evaluation work, this was a totally anticipated outcome. Given the mentoring and training provided by the program, the high level of support of the school administration, and the teachers' personal interest in becoming more proficient with technology, it was logical to expect to see growth in skills and comfort with the tablets over the life of the project. The teachers' skills and attitudes evolved over the three years of the project. Some progressed more quickly than others as would be expected. Their sophistication in creating new ways to use the devices to help students in English language arts, math, science, and social studies was very impressive. And while the project is a good case study for understanding how teachers adopt and then adapt digital tools in the classroom, the most notable finding for me was the emergence of students' self-directed, interest-driven learning empowered by their new access to the tablet and Internet at home.

Among the many examples of this emerging Free Agent Learnership stands out a story about how a fifth grade boy learned to play the piano using his school-provided tablet. Diego had always wanted to learn how to play the piano, but his immigrant family could not afford to buy a piano or to pay for piano lessons. Armed now with his new tablet, Diego on his own researched and found an app that could convert his tablet screen into a piano keyboard and an online site where he could learn basic piano skills. Over the course of several months using these tools at home after school and in the early evening, he became increasingly proficient playing a wide variety of music on his tablet. I was lucky enough to be at the school on the day that Diego asked his teacher if he could do a concert for the class. Diego recruited his friend Pablo to be the vocalist, and the two gave a 20-minute impromptu concert, Pablo singing several songs in Spanish accompanied by Diego on his tablet piano. This was all a surprise to the teacher; she had no idea that he was using the tablet to learn how to play the piano at home, nor that he would be so proficient as to hold the class of naturally limited attention fifth graders spellbound for 20 minutes. The class gave Diego and Pablo a standing ovation at the end of the concert.

Like most Free Agent Learners, Diego took advantage of the technology access he had to pursue his passionate motivation to develop new skills, in this case, to learn to play the piano. That was all in addition to using the tablet at home to submit his homework assignments online through Edmodo and to practice his math skills using Raz-Kids. The key learning here is that the tablet and at-home Internet connectivity not only facilitated school-based learning but also provided a very important way for Diego to develop self-efficacy as a learner and develop confidence in his ability to tackle a difficult learning challenge, learning to play the piano.

The teachers' increased awareness about how their students were using the tablet and the at-home connectivity to support self-directed learning started to change the way the teachers thought about their classroom instruction and how to best meet the needs of their students. For example, one teacher told me that one of her students started every school day by running up to her at the classroom door to share what she had learned the night before on her own using her tablet and the at-home connectivity. The learnings, driven by her fifth grade level intellectual curiosities, ranged from research about animals (coyotes, polar bears, mountain lions) to locating where her family was from in Mexico on Google Maps. The student's excitement for learning and enthusiasm for sharing what she had learned was infectious in the class. The teacher ended up institutionalizing "what did we learn last night at home using our tablets" as a regular part of their class morning routine, thus recognizing the value of the self-directed learning and encouraging it within her students. The teacher told me that simple shift in her mindset, to provide her students with agency and space to share their self-directed learning experiences, was the best change she made in her classroom that year. And that mindset change paid off in dividends as it helped this teacher to see how her students' access to technology at home could transcend and extend what she was doing in the classroom every day. Rather than minimizing her role, she astutely understood that her increased awareness about her students' at-home learning could support her classroom efforts for whole-child learning.

There are obviously many ways to address the challenge of ensuring all students have equitable access to high-quality learning content and tools. But it is important for school and district leaders (and teachers) to recognize that how students are self-directing learning on their own, outside of school, is part of the learning process also. Self-directed learning is a vital component of education today. And the tools that we are providing to them for school-based learning activities (homework, projects, continuity of learning) are also vehicles for ensuring that all students have the ability to follow their academic passions, to self-remediate, develop new skills, explore their future college or career paths, and even to be Free Agent Learners in fifth grade. Conversely, the ways that students are engaging with these tools outside of school, to learn about polar bears or how to play the piano, are important insights for all educators to appreciate as it contributes to a better understanding of our students' needs, what motivates them, and how to engage with them in the classroom. When we think about the equity of student access to learning content and tools education, leaders should broaden their perspective and include empowering students' self-directed learning as a significant outcome of the increased access.

Free Agent Learning and Equity of Student Learning Experiences

If we truly buy into the long-held belief in education that every student deserves and is entitled to a high-quality education, then we have to examine the consistency of our student learning experiences across different classrooms, schools, and districts. Despite best intentions and investments that are meant to alleviate differences in learning experiences such as federal funds from Title 1, variances in the access to instructional resources, academic materials, human capital, and social capital still persist across communities. These differences have a long tail that affects not only students' learning experiences in school but also at home.

The Speak Up research data has chronicled the points of divergence between schools that serve a student population that is majority students of color versus schools that serve primarily white students. Some of those points of contrast are attitudinal, and some are based on structural limitations. Obviously, the attitudinal differences are the more difficult to change. For example, 54% of teachers who teach in schools where the majority of students are students of color say that inequities in education is a significant personal concern. However, only one-quarter (24%) of teachers in majority-white schools hold the same opinion. Interestingly, teachers in schools with students of color (57%) are also more likely to see increased personalization of the students' learning experience as an important outcome of using technology effectively compared to their peers in majority-white schools (48%). Possibly, heightened cultural awareness and/or a higher sensitivity to equity considerations provides the teachers in the schools with students of color an added impetus to using digital tools more effectively.

The challenge, however, is that the Speak Up research also indicates that schools serving students of color continue to be under-resourced when it comes to technology. Each year on the Speak Up surveys, teachers are asked what they need to be able to use technology more effectively to support student learning. Table 9.1 provides the results from the 2020–2021 school year with data from classroom teachers disaggregated by both school student demographics and community type. As depicted, 72% of teachers in schools where the majority of students are Black, Hispanic/Latinx, Asian, or Native American say that they need more consistent and reliable high-speed Internet connectivity to support students' learning. However, only 59% of teachers in schools with white students say the same. The teachers in the schools serving students of color are also almost

Table 9.1 What teachers say they need to implement digital learning more effectively

Teachers' wish list	Percentage of teachers who agree				
	Schools where majority are students of color (%)	Schools where majority are white students (%)	Urban schools (%)	Suburban schools (%)	Rural schools (%)
Consistent, reliable, high-capacity Internet bandwidth	72	59	75	69	54
Classroom set of devices for every student to use	59	32	62	55	34

Source: © Project Tomorrow 2021.

twice as likely as their colleagues in primarily white schools to say that they need a classroom set of digital learning devices.

The Speak Up data reveals similar discrepancies in terms of usage of online curriculum, collaboration tools, and other digital resources in the classroom. The lack of resources in some schools may limit the types of learning experiences that students are having despite the best intentions of their teachers or even their teachers' increased awareness or sensitivity to those inequities. Consequently, understanding and embracing new knowledge about Free Agent Learnership can be a powerful asset to support efforts to address inequities in the learning experiences of all students. Here is why.

As discussed in earlier chapters, Free Agent Learning is a representation of the Student Vision for Learning. The four essential elements of the Student Vision for Learning—socially based, untethered, contextually relevant, and independently driven—are naturally inherent in many of the purposes and motivations of the Free Agent Learners. Likewise, the students' Free Agent Learning activities support their personal attainment of the goals espoused within self-determination theory, which are competence, autonomy, and relatedness. For example, a student who has a curiosity about the Black Lives Matter movement may use various social media channels to learn what other people are doing or thinking about relative to the movement and then transfer that new knowledge into action by reading primary source content from the National Archives about the history of Black social movements in the United States. This student's Free Agent Learning behavior incorporates each element of the Student Vision for Learning: leveraging socially based learning through the social media interactions, the untethered nature of accessing learning content that is beyond local resources, the contextual relevance because of the student's personal interest in the topic, and the independently driven nature of the activities.

Whereas we continue to see inequities in school-based learning experiences, either because of a lack of resources as documented in Table 9.1 or differences in teachers' attitudes or competencies, students' Free Agent Learning experiences appear from the eight years of Speak Up research to be universal, and not significantly differentiated by community or school population demographics. Students of color or students in communities of high poverty are just a likely as white students from more affluent communities to be Free Agent Learners. This is an important defining characteristic of Free Agent Learning.

As depicted in Table 9.2, for example, 76% of students in grades 6–8 nationwide report that they regularly watch an online video to learn how to do something. There is no statistically significant difference in that percentage when disaggregated by community type (urban, suburban, rural) or by school student demographics (schools serving primarily students of color and schools serving primarily white students). The same is true for all of the Free Agent Learning behaviors I have identified in this book; the disaggregated percentages for the most popular middle school student behaviors are included in Table 9.2 (also represented as Table 5.2 in Chapter 5). The results from the analysis of the high school students' data follows the same trend.

It would appear that while students may not be experiencing equitable learning experiences in school, their experiences self-directing their own learning seem to be very consistent across a variety of settings. The driving force is the powerful combination of students' quest to have a different type of learning experience from what they are having in school on a regular basis (thus the Student Vision for Learning) and their increased personal access to a wide variety of digital tools and resources that enable the self-directed learning activities. This information can be very valuable for school and district leaders seeking new ways to ensure that their students'

Table 9.2 Grade 6–8 students' Free Agent Learning behaviors—disaggregated by community type and school student population.

Free Agent Learning behavior	Percentage of grade 6–8 students who report these Free Agent Learning behaviors					
	Nationwide (%)	Urban communities (%)	Suburban communities (%)	Rural communities (%)	Schools where majority are students of color (%)	Schools where majority are white students (%)
Watch a video to learn how to do something	76	75	77	76	79	76
Research information on a website to answer a question	72	69	73	72	72	72
Play an online game or augmented/virtual simulation activity	61	65	60	60	56	61
Watch other people play online games	57	61	59	54	58	57
Use social media to learn what others are doing or thinking about relative to an interested topic	46	48	48	45	46	46

Source: © Project Tomorrow 2021.

in-school learning experiences are equitable for all. It may also be especially enlightening to teachers to understand that despite potentially a lack of equity in resources (certainly not every student has the latest iPhone or access to high-speed connectivity all the time), students from all backgrounds and circumstances are still creating meaningful learning experiences for themselves following their interests and passions. This again proves that educators', researchers', and policymakers' views on the irrelevance or unimportance of students' out-of-school learning lives may no longer hold water. Additionally, this new insight about the universality of Free Agent Learning across different demographics and settings provides a unique impetus for exploring how to incorporate the Student Vision for Learning within your school's everyday curriculum and instructional practices.

Free Agent Learning and Equity of Opportunities for Student Success

Just as the COVID pandemic and resulting disruptions to traditional schooling did not create the digital divide or the Homework Gap, remote learning can also not be wholly responsible for the concerns today about students' social, emotional, and mental health and well-being. Many educators have been talking about the need for a whole child approach within K–12 education for a long time. ASCD (Association for Supervision and Curriculum Development) defines the concept as follows: "A whole child approach to education is defined by policies, practices, and relationships that ensure each child, in each school, in each community, is healthy, safe, engaged, supported, and challenged."[6] At its heart, the whole child approach encompasses the equity of opportunities for success. Are we providing students with learning environments and a school culture that will help them be as successful as possible? Do those environments ensure emotional safety, engender trusting relationships, and support all students on their journey to success? The recent conversations about students' well-being bring all of these questions to the forefront again.

Over the past few years, the Speak Up surveys have started asking K–12 students more questions about school culture and climate and how existing environments affect their learning potential. The data findings help school and district leaders understand the effect of their actions on their students' well-being and opportunities for success. Many leaders use these local Speak Up results for state compliance reports or community information and engagement. The findings also demonstrate the ongoing disconnect in many cases between the assumptions that many educators make about students' interest or engagement in school and the other social and emotional factors that may influence students' school experiences. Students' motivations for Free Agent Learning are examples of such assumptions.

Just as some may easily misinterpret students' Free Agent Learning activities as students just wanting to use technology for everything, others may think that the students exhibiting those self-directed learning behaviors must be less interested in traditional school than other students or may be having a negative in-school experience. That is not the case at all. While many of the Free Agent Learners talk about how traditional school is not meeting their learning needs, they continue to value the importance of school. Over three-quarters of students in grades 6–8 (79%) and 84% of students in grades 9–12 say that doing well in school is important to them personally. This statistic has not varied significantly since the Speak Up surveys started asking that question in 2015. There is also no variance or difference for students who report regular Free Agent Learning activities. Similarly, my analysis of the views of students on other school climate and culture issues also indicates no statistical differences whether the students are regularly participating in Free Agent Learning behaviors or even within the types of self-directed activities they are engaged with.

277

Equity in Learning

The reality is that too many of our students say they are not interested in what they are learning in school. They do not believe that their school cares about them as individuals, and they also equate school with stress and anxiety. Table 9.3 examines the feedback on five key metrics on students' social-emotional well-being in school, disaggregated by the same most popular Free Agent Learning behaviors identified in Table 9.2.

The reality that 64% of our middle school students (and 74% of high school students) identify school as a source of stress should be a wake-up call to everyone interested in students' social-emotional well-being. The percentage of students for whom this is their reality was relatively the same in the 2019–2020 school year as well. Additionally, as schools and districts contemplate how to implement social-emotional learning programs or bring more mental health resources onto campuses to support students' needs, it is essential that we look internally at our school cultures, policies, and structures that are in place, given that only 43% of students in grades 6–8 believe that their school cares about them as a person. There is no significant variance, in either the positive or negative direction, for the students who are Free Agent Learners. Additionally, these widespread views among middle and high school students predate the pandemic and remote learning.

But the silver lining is that with the information in hand, our school and district leaders have the background to start planting seeds of change. It may be unreasonable to expect students to be engaged in learning when they do not believe that their school cares about them individually, but that also does not make it acceptable. As noted earlier, our discussions about equity must be about more than providing students with a Chromebook and a hot spot; we must seriously evaluate the culture of our school and its related effect on the quality of the learning experience and how well those experiences support opportunities for success for all students.

Table 9.3 Grade 6–8 students' beliefs about school—disaggregated by the five most popular Free Agent Learning behaviors.

Students' belief statements about school	All students (%)	Percentage of grade 6–8 students reporting this type of Free Agent Learning behavior				
		Watch a video to learn how to do something (%)	Research information on a website to answer a question (%)	Play an online game or augmented or virtual simulation activity (%)	Watch other people play online games (%)	Use social media to learn what others are doing or thinking about relative to an interested topic (%)
I am interested in what I am learning at school	41	42	45	41	44	40
I believe that my school cares about me as a person	43	45	46	42	46	41
I feel emotionally safe at school	40	47	43	40	42	40
School sometimes makes me feel stressed or anxious	64	65	66	71	66	66
There is at least one adult at school that I trust	58	59	61	60	61	58

Source: © Project Tomorrow 2022.

Free Agent Learning and Equity of Student Agency and Empowerment

I recently had the opportunity to hear the mother of a very successful and well-known esports athlete talk about her son's experiences in school and what propelled him in his career playing competitive video games. As a student, her son had many extracurricular interests including basketball and playing video games in addition to his schoolwork. His personal video game play soon evolved into multiplayer games, and he began getting recognized beyond his friends for his innate abilities in his game of choice, League of Legends. Suddenly, he was being recruited to be part of a competitive League of Legends team. At that time, he was the only high school student on this team of professionals and being able to compete at this high level required sacrifices by himself and his family.

As with other athletes in more traditional sports, it often takes a parent or family member to provide the resources that enable the student to participate in their chosen sport while still balancing schoolwork, teenage life, and family activities. This was the same for this esports athlete and his mother. Not unlike hockey parents who drive their children to get ice time at 5 a.m. or baseball parents who make the trip to Cooperstown for summer baseball camps, this mother shuttled her son to gaming events and training sessions every weekend for several years, sometimes up to two hours away from their home. As the most junior member of the team, her son had a lot to learn about competitive play and often felt discouraged or embarrassed by his lack of prowess and skills. But both mother and son persevered because the coach told them he saw potential in this athlete, potential that they needed to give time to develop. Additionally, this game play was the passion in this athlete's life, it was the motivator for all of his actions at that time. And he had agency to be able to fulfill his goals. Some of that agency was certainly enabled by his mother and his coach, but it was also part of his own personal motivation for his goals that drove his perseverance even when faced with adversity. After many years of competitive play, this athlete stepped away from the game play and is now a professional streamer on YouTube creating new videos every day. His YouTube channel has 1.75 million subscribers.

The Organisation for Economic Co-operation and Development (OECD) addressed student agency in its "Future of Education and Skills 2030 Concept Note."[7] In that document the international organization framed student agency around the "principle that students have the ability and the will to positively influence their own lives and the world around them." They further defined student agency as the capacity of students to set goals for themselves that result in changes. OECD postulates that agency is about the students' ability to set their own direction and path, rather than having that direction or path determined by others. The organization says that within a learning environment, "When students are agents in their learning, that is, when they play an active role in deciding what and how they will learn, they tend to show greater motivation to learn and are more likely to define objectives for their learning."

Free Agent Learners are agents in their own learning, directing the path and pace of the learning process around their own motivations and objectives. When a student decides to watch a YouTube video about auto mechanics or read an online research paper about a new cancer treatment breakthrough, they are exercising their agency as a learner. In many ways, Free Agent Learnership is the actualization of student agency in its purest sense. Correspondingly, since students are exercising their agency as learners through their self-directed learning activities outside of school, they are also very much aware of how limited their own personal agency is within the walls of their classroom.

This disconnect between student agency and school experiences is most evident when examining students' abilities to self-direct learning in school. It is notable that when asked about the value of virtual learning during the pandemic, 67% of students in grades 6–12 identified that the virtual learning modality provided them with the ability to learn at their own pace. Similarly, students say that the number-one outcome of effective technology use in schools is that they have a greater opportunity to self-manage the learning process and follow their own path. Students also highly value when they can be in control of when and how they learn, additional components in the OEDC definition. And yet, only one-third of classroom teachers say that they are very comfortable providing their students with any choices about how they learn.

Here we have a dilemma. Students want more choices within their in-school learning experiences as a result of the ways they are regularly exercising those agency reflexes as part of their Free Agent Learning activities. These self-directed, interest-driven learning experiences are empowering them as learners, helping them build self-confidence and develop the types of skills they will need as lifelong learners, including the ability to seek out their own learning resources. And then they walk into their classrooms and are struck over and over again by the reality that they have no agency in many of these environments. Two-thirds of their teachers are not comfortable with providing even the simplest manifestations of choice within the learning process in their classroom. It is no wonder that 45% of high school students said on the most recent Speak Up survey that they worry that they are not learning the right skills in school to be successful in the future.

It is certainly true that some teachers do an exceptional job of helping their students develop self-agency as a learner. Those teachers know that they are not the only learning expert in the room and that helping their students develop their own skills as learners is the most important task every day. But when we talk about the equity of student agency, we cannot rely on the belief that there are enough mothers out there driving their sons to gaming events every weekend or enough teachers that are allowing their students to determine their own individualized learning path. Nor can we assume that just because students are Free Agent Learners, they are developing enough agency capacity to compensate for the lack of the same during the school day. Not every student has access to the resources including family support or attentive teachers to help them develop the skills they need for future success. Thus, it must be the responsibility of every school and district leader to ensure that empowering student agency is part of the playbook for every classroom. Providing teachers with professional learning experiences that develop their comfort and confidence with relinquishing control over the instructional process is a good place to start.

Connecting the Dots

- Equity is about more than handing every student a Chromebook and a mobile hot spot.

- The four types of equity that every school and district leader should be addressing today are as follows:

  - **Equity of student access to learning content and tools:** Students have access to high-quality learning resources both in school and at home;

  - **Equity of student learning experiences:** There is consistency in students' learning environments and experiences and teacher quality across classes, grade levels, and schools;

- **Equity of learning opportunities for student success:** Students can learn in environments that are safe, trusting, and supportive; and

- **Equity of student agency and empowerment:** Students are explicitly empowered to take ownership of their own learning and given opportunities to develop lifelong learning skills.

- Free Agent Learning can be a powerful asset to help education leaders both understand the implications of this expanded definition of equity in education and create tangible action steps to identify inequities and develop new plans to address them.

Now, Think about This!

1. How are you addressing all four types of equity in your school or district? What are the most effective ways to ensure that your students are benefiting from your equity efforts?

2. Using this new, broader definition of equity in education, can you see where there may be new motivations or incentives for transforming the classroom experiences for your students?

3. Based on the learning experiences that students are having on their own as Free Agent Learners, what elements of those experiences can educators replicate or mimic in the classroom to help students develop greater agency or feel more empowered to be successful in school?

4. What is one thing that you can do today or tomorrow to help your teachers or colleagues think differently about empowering student agency in classroom learning?

Notes

1. https://www.edsurge.com/news/2020-06-16-covid-19-has-widened-the-homework-gap-into-a-full-fledged-learning-gap.
2. https://en.wikipedia.org/wiki/NetDay.
3. https://eric.ed.gov/?id=EJ966923.
4. https://www.learntechlib.org/p/76521.
5. https://www.amazon.com/Global-Achievement-Gap-Survival-Need/dp/0465002307.
6. https://files.ascd.org/staticfiles/ascd/pdf/siteASCD/policy/CCSS-and-Whole-Child-one-pager.pdf.
7. https://www.oecd.org/education/2030-project/teaching-and-learning/learning/student-agency/Student_Agency_for_2030_concept_note.pdf.

Ten Things Education Leaders Can Do Today to Support Free Agent Learnership

An emerging thread in education discussions and research is a new understanding of the potential value of tapping into students' learning experiences with technology to instigate transformational change within traditional K–12 education. Several research studies examine the impact of digital learning experiences where the student is the driver of that experience, rather than a teacher or another adult. The value of those experiences focuses on enhancing a student's self-efficacy as a learner and the development of highly contextualized workplace-ready skills and literacies. Through this new field of research, the goal of translating students' personal experiences into new classroom practice has significant implications for school and district leadership and their abilities to address emerging social justice issues inherent in both school and home technology access.

As discussed in Chapter 9, however, the social justice and equity argument extends beyond simple digital connectivity. As Tony Wagner explains, even our nation's best schools continue to focus on old-world school tasks and paradigms that do not address the development of the types of skills that students will need to thrive and compete in the global information economy and society. Thus, the Global Achievement Gap, as Wagner terms it, is increasingly less about resource disparity in our schools and more about a mismatch between what students are learning and what they will need for post-school success. The increasing importance of this issue transcends community type and family socioeconomic indicators.

Free Agent Learnership provides new insights into the value and efficacy of using technology in school to support student engagement and skill development (the "why technology matters" value proposition) and the potential of how students' out-of-school experiences can prepare them for post-school success. An awareness of the Free Agent Learner ecosystem and appreciation of the centrality of purpose driving students' use of digital tools, content, and resources outside of school to self-direct their learning, be it for self-remediation, skill development, curiosity, or career preparation, has important implications for education leaders as well as policymakers today. Given the pandemic-induced disruptions to traditional school since 2020, the twin challenges of improving student learning outcomes and changing school cultures to support education transformations are top-of-mind issues for most education leaders.

Evidence of students' interest-driven digital learning, such as identified through this book, validates the need for education leaders to think beyond traditional learning settings and to appreciate the ways that students are self-directing meaningful learning experiences without the sponsorship of teachers and other adults as an asset for thinking about addressing the new challenges in education. Beyond the classroom and school building walls, our Free Agent Learners are developing their own learning ecosystems that highly value collaboration, knowledge sharing, and peer mentoring. An opportunity exists to leverage those student experiences and the Free Agent Learning ecosystem to support education transformation.

To support those efforts, I have identified 10 innovative ideas for how school and district leaders can support Free Agent Learnership in their schools and realize benefits from that embrace in terms of creating new learning experiences for students. This is not an exhaustive list of ideas, but my hope is that this list serves as a jumping-off point for your own reflection and thought on leveraging Free Agent Learning within your school or district.

Here's a summary list of 10 new ideas for how you can support Free Agent Learnership in your schools:

- Get to know the Free Agent Learners in your school or district;
- Discover the power of asking students about their Free Agent Learning activities;
- Support more effective and equitable Free Agent Learning through information and media literacy skill development;
- Integrate Free Agent Learning strategies and tools into everyday classroom instruction;
- Empower students with the ability to exercise Free Agent Learning during the school day;
- Enable students' Free Agent Learning activities when they are outside of school;
- Recognize outcomes from Free Agent Learning in your Graduate Profile or Portrait;
- Provide academic credit for learning outcomes derived from Free Agent Learning;
- Encourage teachers and administrators to be Free Agent Learners with their own professional learning; and
- Create a culture around Free Agent Learning concepts and principles within your district.

Get to Know the Free Agent Learners in Your School or District

The goal of this book is to introduce education leaders to a new and emerging phenomenon, Free Agent Learning. The chapters provide you with rich, research-based insights about the activities and motivations of students who are self-directing learning outside of school to satisfy very specific needs around self-remediation, future-ready skill development, curiosities, or to explore a future career or job. But what are the specific motivations of the Free Agent Learners in your schools, your district, your community? What types of self-directed activities and behaviors are they using most often? What are the outcomes from those experiences and how are those experiences affecting their expectations for their in-school practices and opportunities?

The Speak Up Research Project has always had a bifurcated mission: (i) to provide national research (such as about Free Agent Learnership) to inspire and stimulate new discussions around how to improve education for all, and (ii) to provide local school and district leaders with easy and efficient access to the views of their stakeholders so that local decisions are better informed and aligned with community needs. The Free Agent Learning experiences of your students are information assets that can be valuable in your quest to improve education in your schools. But first, you need to understand the lived experiences of your local students. Therefore, I would highly encourage you to get deeply involved with learning about the activities, motivations, and outcomes of your own students' Free Agent Learning experiences. There are multiple ways to do that.

Participation in Project Tomorrow's Speak Up Research Project is available to any K–12 school or district that would like to learn more about the views of their students, parents, teachers, and administrators on a range of education issues, most notably about digital learning in school and out of school. The annual student surveys include questions about the frequency of self-directed learning and the motivations for those activities. Having your students complete the annual Speak Up survey is a good first step to understanding your local edition of Free Agent Learning. Access to the Speak Up surveys is free and all reporting on the results is provided to school and district leaders with comparative national data.

You might learn, for example, that your eighth graders are more likely than their peers nationwide to be frequently tapping into online writing sites to get third-party input into how to improve their writing skills, or that your 11th graders are regularly seeking information about ways to get involved in social justice issues through social media sites. From this information, you could deduce that your eighth graders might also value more input on their writing skills from their teachers or may feel that they are not getting enough writing experiences to ensure that their skills are proficient. That information could be translated into actionable knowledge for your eighth grade English language arts teachers as to ways to improve their classroom activities and experiences for students. Correspondingly, knowing that your high school students are actively seeking social justice activities could inform new conversations with your high school administrators about how to support those interests within the student body and whether the information and media literacy training provided by teachers and librarians is sufficient to ensure that students are good evaluators of online content authenticity.

There are other ways as well to learn about the lived experiences of your students relative to Free Agent Learning. Each year I facilitate 20 or more student focus groups, panel discussions, or interviews to better understand the current ways students are using technology to pursue their curiosities about the world. Several key elements are essential to make experiences like a focus group meaningful for both students and adults: active listening, suspension of assumptions, leave bias at the door, and do not judge.

A few years ago, I was asked to facilitate a large discussion session with graduating seniors from a local high school. Contrary to the typical process, the students chosen for this activity were not exclusively the top scholars or student leaders, but a very deliberate process was undertaken to bring in a diversity of views and high school learning experiences. After establishing that this was a safe space for open dialog, the students shared poignant examples of both the pros and cons of their high school experience. The process was invigorating for the students who said that no one had ever asked them to speak candidly about their perceptions of their school culture, classes, or interactions. But it was very difficult and uncomfortable for the teachers and administrators to hear that their efforts, always well-meaning, may have missed the mark for years with these graduating seniors. Unfortunately, rather than actively listen and think about ways to improve school, some chose to instead believe that the students' views were fringe and not representative or that the students had misunderstood their intentions or the reasons for certain policies and procedures.

If you want to really understand the lived experiences of your students, both out of school and in school, it is essential for leaders to be courageous enough to suspend their assumptions and actively listen to the authentic feedback. And to model that posture for others as well.

Discover the Power of Asking Students about Their Free Agent Learning Activities

Imagine how powerful it would be if every teacher in your school or district started class time by asking their students this one small question: "What have you learned on your own in the past 24 hours?" As we have discussed, for today's students, learning is a 24/7 enterprise, and what happens in class, in school, is just a small part of that overall learning experience. Your students are learning all sorts of things, all the time. But for the most part, what happens outside of school is blind to their teachers. Not because the students do not want to share but because the teachers are not asking them about their self-directed learning activities or outcomes.

Now initially when your teachers ask this question, the students may be stumped. Just like our teachers, some may be socialized to only think about "real learning" as happening in the school day or may have internalized that their own self-directed, interest-driven learning is not at the same level of value or quality compared to teacher-directed, in-classroom learning. Thus, there will need to be a culture shift in the classroom that explicitly values all kinds of learning, whether the student reads a textbook chapter about the 1921–1923 Teapot Dome scandal in New York in their fourth period AP American history class, or watches a YouTube video from Explore Always at home, on their own time, to learn more about other scandals in American political history. To actuate this culture shift, however, our teachers need to move beyond the assumption that they are the only content or knowledge experts in the lives of their students.

There are multiple reasons why teachers asking their students about their Free Agent Learning activities and outcomes is a good idea.

- First, it validates that we are sincere when we talk about personalized learning and that we are willing and able to meet students where they are in terms of not only their competencies but also their interests.

- Second, it also provides a way for teachers to get to know their students better. Students value and want a good relationship with their teacher. And as one former superintendent explained to me, the foundation for effective social-emotional learning in schools is a bonding relationship between teachers and students and a sense of shared community.

If teachers are empowered with knowledge about their students' interests as typified by their Free Agent Learning activities, they are better equipped to both provide more engaging and meaningful learning experiences and to help develop a stronger connection with their students. In Chapter 6, we learned about how Thomas's Free Agent Learning activities have evolved into a career in digital media. Like most students, Thomas had other interests beyond YouTube and learning media creation skills when he was a high school student. When Thomas was in high school, his math teacher learned that he was very interested in basketball. Leveraging that knowledge, she sought ways to engage him in math learning activities through basketball. Taking a page from the Student Vision for Learning (see Chapter 1), the teacher created an opportunity for Thomas to design a new basketball court for the school, thus providing him with contextually relevant learning that by necessity required him to internalize math concepts and calculations more deeply. Understanding how and why your students are engaged with Free Agent Learning activities outside of school can be a powerful asset for understanding how to engage them in more personalized learning experiences in school.

The motivation or driving passion for Free Agent Learning around self-remediation is also one that deserves teachers' attention. For example, let us think about what the teacher's reaction should be if their students respond to that one small question, "What have you learned on your own in the past 24 hours?" with an explanation that they spent hours watching Khan Academy videos to address what they did not understand from yesterday's math or science lesson. The teacher may want to evaluate their current instructional practices or look for new ways to reach the students who needed remediation. The teacher may also want to check out the Khan Academy videos to learn about why the approaches in their lessons had a better result on their students. Or they may even want to think about incorporating the Khan videos into their own instruction. These are all good actionable steps based on the knowledge of how their students were self-remediating outside of school and effective ways for teachers to bridge the knowledge gap within their students. With that realization about the Free Agent Learner ecosystem taking place in their class, the teacher is now more empowered than before to address the individualized or personalized learning challenges of their students. But what if they never asked that small question?

Support More Effective and Equitable Free Agent Learning Through Information and Media Literacy Skill Development

Inherent to Free Agent Learning is obviously students' abilities to discern the authenticity of the online resources they are using to support their self-directed learning activities, and to be able to detect bias or opinion versus fact. According to the 2020–2021 Speak Up research findings, only 53% of high school students and 41% of middle school students say they know how to determine whether what they are reading or watching online is accurate. Relative to detecting bias or opinion, 61% of students in grades 9–12 and 45% of students in grades 6–8 believe that they effectively know how to do that when viewing content online. The information and media literacy skills of students across different types of communities varies as well. Only 43% of high school students in rural communities, for example, say they know how to evaluate the accuracy of the content they are engaging with online; 57% of their same grade level peers in suburban communities say they are proficient with that skill (see Table 10.1).

Students whose Free Agent Learning activities include social media usage and reading online news articles are slightly more likely than other students including those engaged with other Free Agent Learning behaviors to rate their information and media literacy skills higher. But in general, the overall assessment of our students' skills,

Table 10.1 Students' perceptions of their information and media literacy skills—disaggregated by community type.

Information and media literacy skill self-assessment	Percentage of all students nationwide		Percentage of students in urban communities		Percentage of students in suburban communities		Percentage of students in rural communities	
	Gr 6–8 (%)	Gr 9–12 (%)	Gr 6–8 (%)	Gr 9–12 (%)	Gr 6–8 (%)	Gr 9–12 (%)	Gr 6–8 (%)	Gr 9–12 (%)
I know how to detect bias or opinions in the information that I read online	45	61	45	73	51	79	41	66
I know how to evaluate the accuracy of information I find online	41	53	40	48	46	57	38	43

Source: © Project Tomorrow 2021.

especially those of students in middle schools or in rural communities, needs improvement. This opinion is echoed by school librarians. According to the Speak Up survey from the 2019–2020 school year, school librarians place a very high premium on the value of students understanding how to authenticate online resources for accuracy (92% said this was a priority) and having the ability to detect bias or opinion in what they are reading or watching (78% said this was a priority). On the same poll, only 30% of the librarians said that students at their school were at the proficient level with information and literacy skills; 70% identified student skills as only basic or below basic. This lack of digital literacy is important for in-school learning as well as Free Agent Learnership. Whereas schools have prioritized digital citizenship training, notably student safety measures, over the past few years, they have not focused on the types of information and media literacy skills that are essential for the effective use of online and digital instructional materials being used by students and teachers. That needs to change.

This is one of those potential "teaching moments." If school and district leaders believe in the value of students' self-directed learning pursuits outside of school as the means to develop agency or engage students in informal learning, more needs to be done to support their development of information and media literacy skills for all students. As one education thought leader explains, if schools will not fill this void with appropriate teaching, then someone else will. In the case of the Free Agent Learners, that void may be filled through a TED Talk or a YouTube video. Those online sources of information may certainly be accurate and worthwhile, or they may be filled with inaccuracies or incomplete explanations. Given that information and media literacy is a future-ready skill that students need to develop to be proficient with information in college, jobs, or in a future career, it seems relevant to have those skills developed alongside content knowledge and digital citizenship.

As discussed in Chapter 9, equity of learning opportunities is important to ensure that all students have access to the quality learning experiences that will prepare them for future success. As proffered in this book, that should include the opportunity to use online and digital tools outside of school to pursue academic passions and curiosities successfully and effectively. If we are serious about encouraging students to be Free Agent Learners, and in particular to use school-provided devices to do so, it should be a school responsibility to teach them how to authenticate the accuracy of the online resources and content they are engaging with and be able to detect bias and opinion in those sources. The starting point for this effort, however, may be to teach these same skills to our teachers.

Integrate Free Agent Learning Strategies and Tools into Everyday Classroom Instruction

The four key attributes or characteristics that define Free Agent Learning as described in Chapter 2 are:

1. **Place independence.** While traditional learning is situated typically in a physical classroom or similar formalized learning environment, Free Agent Learning activities typically take place outside of school, beyond the classroom or that traditional learning environment.

2. **Power ownership.** The Free Agent Learning activities are wholly self-directed by the student and are not driven or sponsored by a teacher or another adult in the student's learning life. The student is in the power pole position within the learning experience.

3. **Purposeful technology usage.** The use of digital tools, content, and resources to support Free Agent Learning is highly

purposeful to effectively support the personalized learning goals of the student.

4. **Passionate motivations.** The fourth defining attribute of a Free Agent Learner is the intrinsic passion, drive, or motivation that is propelling students to tap into a wide range of digital tools to support their learning goals beyond the sponsorship of their teachers.

While it may not be possible to wholly replicate these attributes in total in the classroom environment, it is certainly possible to extract essential qualities inherent in the definition of Free Agent Learning to bring the classroom experience closer in alignment with the Student Vision for Learning. As a reminder, the Student Vision for Learning introduced in Chapter 1 puts a premium on socially based learning, untethered learning, learning that is rich in contextual relevancy, and learning where the student has a role in directing the individual activities. Several new learning models in education provide good environments for bringing some essential aspects of Free Agent Learning into the classroom. Here are two different ideas to consider as you work to integrate the values of Free Agent Learning into day-to-day curriculum.

1. According to PBLWorks, a leading national authority on the implementation of project-based learning within instruction, project-based learning or PBL is defined as "a teaching method in which students gain knowledge and skills by working for an extended period of time to investigate and respond to an authentic, engaging, and complex question, problem, or challenge."[1] PBLWorks includes two key components within their Seven Essential Project Design Elements that support the concept of Free Agent Learning and the Student Vision for

Learning. Those two components are providing opportunities for student voice and choice and ensuring that the project represents an authentic challenge that combines real-world context and relevancy with academic learning experiences and skill development.

2. According to the Speak Up statistics on Free Agent Learning activities and behaviors, the playing of digital games ranks as one of the most popular. Additionally, many students are also now watching others, digital games as a learning activity. The students indicate that both the game play and the game watching help them develop important future-ready skills, including critical thinking, communications, collaboration and teamwork, and creativity. For the students it is all about the strategic play experience and less about the interactive elements that adults focus on. The explosion of esports over the past few years, both in society in general and within school environments, is a recognition of the popularity of these activities. A key turning point for esports in schools was the recognition in 2018 by the National Federation of State High School Associations (NFHS) that esports could be an official school sport. Since that recognition, more than 8600 high schools have started video-gaming or esports teams.[2] Participating on an esports team satisfies several aspects of the Student Vision for Learning—it is socially based and at the same time allows for independent decision-making. It is also a good representation of how technology can be used purposely and effectively to support students' skill development. Beyond competitive esports teams, teachers are also increasingly exploring the use of digital, online, and video games within classroom instruction. Luckily for the teachers, they have experts on how to use games to support effective learning already sitting in their

classrooms. Letting their students take the lead on how to leverage these tools most effectively is another way to recognize and value students' Free Agent Learning experiences.

When teachers validate the use of technology as an effective tool for learning, they are also signaling the importance of out-of-school learning experiences. Conversely, when teachers limit the efficacy of technology as a learning tool in school, they are implicitly (though maybe not intentionally) devaluing the students' desire to be in control of their learning destiny. I am reminded of a student who was part of a panel I facilitated for the Los Angeles County Office of Education a few years ago. The student panel discussion was focused on how digital tools and resources can support student learning. The experts of course were the five students from high schools around in the Los Angeles metro area who were sharing their lived experiences.

One student talked about how frustrating it was to not be able to use her smartphone in class to support her academic needs. She shared a story about her English class that was studying Shakespeare's *Hamlet*. As many of us have probably experienced ourselves, sometimes the Shakespearean prose and verse can be confusing. Many high school students are stupefied trying to figure out what Hamlet is talking about when he says, for example, in Act 1, Scene 2, "O that this too solid flesh would melt." Too often the lack of comprehension prevented my panelist from grasping the key concepts, and as the class progressed, the lack of understanding was compounded. Once at home, this Free Agent Learner searched for online sources to gain a better understanding of the passages read during class but at that point, that class experience might have been 12 hours previously. The value of the online sources was limited after so much time had passed.

The student knew, however, of a perfect solution to fix this problem. As she explained, whenever she could, she would carefully sneak out her smartphone to use in her lap under her desk to find an online resource that could provide quick context for the passage in *Hamlet*, right at the same moment that the class was discussing the meaning of the text. This just-in-time support was highly effective for keeping her on track with the reading and developing a stronger level of comprehension and also confidence in her ability to keep up with the class discussion. But unfortunately, her teacher did not allow students to use their own devices in class and too often, the student was caught using her phone in class. The nuance that the student was using her phone to support self-remediation for improved comprehension of *Hamlet* was not valued. The policy of no phone usage overrode the efficiency and practicality of the student using the device to support learning. As we look for ways to integrate the essential elements of Free Agent Learning into classroom instruction, it may be necessary to examine policies and assumptions that may inadvertently limit students' natural inclinations to use technology to support learning.

Empower Students with the Ability to Exercise Free Agent Learning During the School Day

A new learning model concept that is gaining more and more traction each year is competency-based education (CBE). The Aurora Institute has been a national thought leader in advocating for CBE for many years. They define it as an education system whereas:

- "Students are empowered daily to make important decisions about their learning experiences, how they will create and apply knowledge, and how they will demonstrate their learning.

- Assessment is a meaningful, positive, and empowering learning experience for students that yields timely, relevant, and actionable evidence.

- Students receive timely, differentiated support based on their individual learning needs.

- Students progress based on evidence of mastery, not seat time.

- Students learn actively using different pathways and varied pacing.

- Strategies to ensure equity for all students are embedded in the culture, structure, and pedagogy of schools and education systems.

- Rigorous, common expectations for learning (knowledge, skills, and dispositions) are explicit, transparent, measurable, and transferable."[3]

Implicit in the definition of a CBE is the valuation that the student has agency and self-efficacy as a learner. Fully actualized, CBE provides school-level scaffolding to support students' pursuits of their academic interests and the development of appropriate competencies to support their future success. In many ways, therefore, CBE provides a natural foundation for schools to incorporate the concepts of Free Agent Learning within the school day, especially as it pertains to student choice and defining their own educational path. Unfortunately, the adoption of CBE often requires changes in state policies that currently measure the hours and days students spend in school rather than measuring evidence of subject or content area mastery or skill development. Changes like that despite the well-meaning advocacy efforts of the Aurora Institute and many others take time.

But short of adopting a CBE model in your schools, there are also other ways that schools can take steps to provide ways for students to exercise their Free Agent Learning goals. A recent study conducted by REL Central about an innovative program at Legacy High School in Bismarck, North Dakota, piqued my curiosity about how schools may support Free Agent Learning on campus. Legacy High School had implemented a class schedule that allowed students to have a certain percentage of each day as non-scheduled or flexible time (called flex-time). For the most part, students could choose how to spend that time. In some cases, teachers directed that time usage. The REL Center study examined how students were using the flex-time, whether it was for academic or nonacademic activities.[4] The study findings concluded that while students had an average of 80 minutes a day for flex-time, only 19% of that time was spent on "academic tasks." However, the definition used by the researchers for academic tasks was very narrow. The survey students used to report on their use of flex-time only provided three options for the students (see the actual survey item below).

Survey question: How did you spend your minutes of unscheduled time today?

- Doing school-related activities (for example, learning center, classwork, counseling, art/music);

- Doing non-school-related activities (for example, relaxing, lunch, at home, job, appointments);

- Doing both school-related and non-school-related activities.[5]

Academic tasks were narrowly defined as only relevant to traditional schoolwork or in-school learning activities. Non-school-related activities did not include any references to self-directed, interest-driven learning. It is conceivable that students may have used their flex-time to pursue self-remediation, develop future-ready skills, explore an academic curiosity, or do research on colleges or future careers. In other words, they may have used that time to do the same types of Free Agent Learning activities that they do regularly outside of school. While some may not consider that type of learning "academic," learning for today's students is not bound by school-day hours or even the formal or traditional definitions of school-based learning. And for the students, that type of self-directed, interest-driven learning may actually be more meaningful or valuable than what happened today in first period algebra class or sixth period English lit. Unfortunately, the data on how students may have been using their flex-time for Free Agent Learning was not collected. Not the fault of the study; they probably did not know about the Free Agent Learners as you do now.

Beyond the limitations of this study, the concept of providing students with flex-time at school to pursue Free Agent Learning is particularly interesting. As discussed in Chapter 9, students may be inevitably limited in their ability to pursue Free Agent Learning if their access to technology and the Internet is limited when they are outside of school. Providing an explicit block of time for students to use the school Internet connectivity, digital devices, and online resources for self-directed learning pursuits would alleviate that equity concern. Additionally, by explicitly encouraging students to use their flex-time for self-directed learning (which may include self-remediation through school-provided tutors or an on-campus learning resource center), administrators and teachers are helping students develop an ethos for lifelong learning. Taken one step further, schools could provide student mentors ("Master Free Agent Learners") who can help fellow students identify online resources they need to satisfy their "academic" curiosities or pursue learning quests around their passions, be it to learn more about quantum mechanics or the best colleges for naval architecture. While changing master schedules are often fraught with unexpected potholes for a school leader, the opportunity to incorporate a few key elements of CBE as well as supporting the validation of Free Agent Learning may be worth the extra effort.

Enable Students' Free Agent Learning Activities When They Are Outside of School

Whereas there were many aspects of the virtual learning experiment during the COVID pandemic that were less than positive for students, teachers, and families, many students liked how their teachers during that time created videos of class lessons, lectures, and labs that students could access whenever they wanted. Nearly a majority of high school students (46%) said that one of the positive outcomes from virtual learning was the ability to review class materials as many times as they wanted to ensure satisfactory comprehension. Anna, the Free Agent Learner profiled in Chapter 3, hopes that teachers will continue and even expand upon that practice. Watching a video to learn how to do something is a Tier 1 Prevalent Free Agent Learning behavior (see Chapter 5). Therefore, it makes sense that the students want to use that learning modality to support schoolwork as well. Many students are already seeking remediation support from videos on YouTube or Khan Academy. A natural extension of this would be for teachers to create their own personalized collection of videos that their students can use for remediation support as well.

A few years ago, prior to the pandemic, I facilitated a focus group with teachers about using videos in their class instruction. The discussion focused primarily on how to use video effectively especially to stimulate discussion or present different points of view. For the most part, teachers were interested in sourcing high-quality videos for classroom use and seeking input from peers about valid and credible video sources. However, an interesting outcome from the conversation was that among the teachers who had been using videos for several years in their classrooms, such as from Khan, NASA, National Geographic, and others, they were increasingly starting to create their own videos. As one teacher explained, he found that while his students benefited from watching a Khan online video at home about how to work with polynomials, they preferred the home-grown videos he created for his math students where he could reference class discussions or the exercises they had worked on in class.

The goal was the same with both types of videos, the publicly available video or the teacher's iPhone-created video: to provide a way for students to have information to help with their self-remediation at home. The teacher-created video, though not expertly produced with perfect lighting and high-quality audio, had a bigger impact with his students because it contained the type of contextual relevancy the students craved. According to the latest Speak Up research, one-quarter of teachers are now saying that they would like professional learning about how to create their own videos to support instruction, both in class and for students to use on their own. The development of a class library of teacher-created videos could support students' Free Agent Learning goals around self-remediation and also open the door for students' extended learning outside of school.

Similarly, schools could enable students' Free Agent Learning activities outside of school by providing access to additional resources or serving as a curator for self-directed, student-led learning experiences. This is not a far cry from what many schools do now in terms of providing parents with lists of recommended after-school tutoring programs or summer camps. The focus here, however, would be on the types of online resources and tools that students could use to pursue their passions for academic knowledge, career preparation, or self-remediation. Many high school students in my analysis of their Free Agent Learning activities talk about taking online courses such as from Coursera to learn about topics of interest especially around career preparation, even earning certificates of proficiency in different topics or subjects.[6] I recently learned how even elementary students are taking online courses through Outschool.[7] Other young students also talk about tapping into online writing sites to get feedback on their writing such as through the NaNoWriMo Young Writers Program.[8]

The common denominator currently within the Free Agent Learning student ecosystem is that the students need to find these sources on their own to satisfy their desires for interest-driven learning. Some are being supported by parents interested in expanding their children's learning opportunities. The implications here for equity are obvious. Some students, due to their own resourcefulness, access to more online resources, or through enabling parents, have greater access to some learning opportunities while other students may not have those same opportunities. Creating a school or district repository of resources for Free Agent Learning would not only help many more students find meaningful self-directed learning experiences but to do so conceptually more efficiently and effectively. Additionally, it would be a positive way for schools to acknowledge that their students' Free Agent Learning activities are meaningful aspects of the overall learning process. Embracing Free Agent Learnership may mean redefining and extending school-to-home connections to support students' self-directed learning.

Recognize Outcomes from Free Agent Learning in Your Graduate Profile or Portrait

As discussed in Chapter 7, many districts are now embracing the idea of creating a Graduate Profile or Portrait (or Learner Profile for many elementary focused districts) to represent the student outcomes from the education process offered by the local schools. Suzette Lovely in her book *Ready for Anything: Four Touchstones for Future-Focused Learning* shares an example of a Graduate Profile from Carlsbad Unified School District where she is the former superintendent. The five key components of that Graduate Profile include (i) effective communicator and collaborator, (ii) lifelong learner, (iii) critical thinker, (iv) college- and career-ready scholar, (v) ethical and responsible citizen, and (vi) self-directed individual.[9]

While the intention of most Graduate Profiles is to categorize the outcomes from in-school learning experiences, students' self-directed, interest-driven learning outside of school obviously influences and supports those outcomes as well. For example, the Free Agent Learning experiences of students are driven by their intrinsic motivations for acquiring knowledge or skill expertise or learning about post-graduation opportunities. Through those actions they are developing the academic muscles and attitudes that support lifelong learning. Many students identify that they are developing critical thinking and communications skills through their Free Agent Learning activities including through online multiplayer game play. And through their self-remediation activities as well as pursuing different curiosities, the students are supporting their own development as a college- or career-ready scholar through self-directed inquiry and self-reflection on their academic needs.

Given what we have learned about the reasons student engage in Free Agent Learning activities and the types of outcomes they are realizing through those experiences, guiding documents like a Graduate Profile should consider the self-directed learning experiences that students are having as well as the teacher-led, in-classroom experiences as inputs influencing those outcomes. Additionally, if schools embraced Free Agent Learning by not only valuing the experience but encouraging it and integrating those student-led knowledge and skill development activities within a more holistic approach to learning, the Graduate Profile would more accurately represent the totality of a student's learning outcomes, not just what was in the narrow purview of the in-class experience.

It may also be helpful to think about how to align the Student Vision for Learning with the outcomes from the Graduate Profile. For example, within the Student Vision for Learning, students want more socially based learning experiences where they can collaborate on contextually relevant projects with peers, their teachers in co-learning spaces, students beyond their school, and experts worldwide. The value of the socially based learning when executed effectively is that it can provide multiple benefits beyond simple student engagement in learning. Chelsea Waite, a researcher formerly with the Christensen Institute, notes, "Classroom collaboration, done well, not only enhances academic learning and social and emotional skills, but also develops students' social capital."[10] Unfortunately, too often, teachers assume that simply setting up group projects and having assignments where students need to collaborate with each other will yield these supplemental benefits. The process of developing collaboration skills is more complicated. In my interviews with students who are on esports teams, they often talk about the need to learn new collaboration skills as part of their gaming activities. This is because the interplay within a gaming competition requires more advanced proficiencies than simply deciding on roles within a group project.

In many ways, today's students because of their experiences with collaborative learning, both in their classes and in their out-of-school, self-directed learning, have a more astute view on the skills required and the developmental process for those types of skills than their teachers. For example, as explained previously, students often question me about why their teachers only assess the value or quality of their group projects based on the final deliverable, and not on the interim collaborative processes. Given a class project, for example, to develop a group slide deck that compares and contrasts the plot, setting, and characterizations in two Gary Paulsen novels *Hatchet* and *The River*, students believe that the real value in the learning experience is in their collaborative efforts, not just the content and design of the final slide deck. Students say that it is the small decision-making processes that they do as a group (for example, who is going to be responsible for the evaluation of setting in both novels, how are we going to come to agreement on the contrasts in plot, what is the best way for us to divide up the work) that best represents their collaborative success or failure, not whether the final product meets the teacher's rubric. This experiential understanding is based on their own experiences, to the good and the bad, with other collaborative learning environments, and that includes their self-directed pursuits beyond school sponsorship.

As education leaders develop their local Graduate Profiles it is important to think beyond the often-repeated phrases that signal to their community that they understand the importance of college and college readiness or the development of workforce-ready skills and explore how those outcomes will be realized for students. That includes appreciating that our students are already developing capacities and social capital to support those Graduate Profile outcomes outside of school, on their own time, using their own tools to follow their own individualistic interests.

Provide Academic Credit for Learning Outcomes Derived from Free Agent Learning

A key outcome emerging from my analysis of the impact of the pandemic and the disruptions in traditional school environments during that time is a greater appreciation today of what constitutes effective or meaningful learning. For many years, educators and education thought leaders have advocated for more personalization of the learning process for students, providing ways for education to be customized to meet the individual needs of each student. The internationally recognized education thought leader Sir Ken Robinson is often quoted in those contexts with this statement: "The answer is not to standardize education, but to personalize and customize it to the needs of each child and community. There is no alternative. There never was." With this statement, Robinson accurately explains that personalized learning is really nothing new and that an effective education system is built on a bedrock of appreciating each individual student's needs and providing learning experiences that are tailored to those needs. In one of my favorite TED Talks, Robinson also discusses how too often traditional education "dislocates people from their natural talents" and "does not feed their spirit or passion."[11] As discussed in previous chapters, it is logical to see how this type of education environment may not meet the needs of today's students who are actively feeding their spirts and passions through their self-directed learning. The pandemic and resulting school disruptions, however, provide a new opportunity to get beyond the platitudes of personalized learning and to seriously contemplate what needs to happen in our education systems to realize the full potential of personalized learning for every student. For inspiration, I would highly recommend checking out https://www .sirkenrobinson.com/ to learn more about the ideas of this late, great innovative thinker.

As discussed in Chapter 2, Tony Wagner's work on the Global Achievement Gap identifies some of the barriers to changing the current education systems to provide students more effectively with the learning experiences they need for future success. According to Wagner, the traditional classroom rewards individual achievement rather than the success of collaborative efforts, is organized around communicating specific subject content rather than exploratory learning skills, and relies upon extrinsic motivations such as grades and test scores rather than the intrinsic motivators such as play, passion, and purpose. These same environmental factors limit the ability for education institutions to recognize the value of students' individual learning experiences, which are often highly personalized to their interests and abilities. The focus on academic outcomes as prescribed by state standards or approved curricula makes it virtually impossible for a student, for example, who has taken an online class on their own and/or done extensive self-directed reading and study on astronomy to receive graduation credits for that work. Independent study programs offered by schools are often just alternative setting for traditional schoolwork.

A new model for K–12 education may be the ways that some colleges are now recognizing the value of prior learning in awarding college credits. The City University of New York (CUNY) provides a way for students to petition for college credit based on individual prior learning.[12] In the evaluation process, CUNY states that they are willing to examine four types of experiences as satisfying the requirements for certain courses including (i) military training or occupations, (ii) industry certifications, (iii) results from standardized tests, and (iv) an assessment of a student-developed portfolio, which may include job experiences or self-study. CUNY states on their website that they value this credit for prior learning approach as the means to address inequities in higher education. I think that a similar model that recognizes students' Free Agent Learning experiences could also address some inequities in students' access to learning experiences in K–12 settings but also help to support the value of the types of personalized learning that students are engaging with outside of school. As has been stated repeatedly in this book, for today's student learning is a 24/7 enterprise and their in-school experience is only a small part of that learning enterprise. If we are serious about valuing new learning modalities in a post-pandemic world, then it is imperative that we also consider how to provide our students with recognition of their self-directed learning and provide appropriate credit where they have developed proven skills and competencies that potentially they could not develop through the traditional means of school and in-class instruction.

Encourage Teachers and Administrators to Be Free Agent Learners with Their Own Professional Learning

In many ways we are all Free Agent Learners today. Just as the students have more access to digital and online tools to support self-directed, interest-driven learning, so do adults. Every time we search for that YouTube video to learn how deep a hole to dig for that new rosebush in our yard or for a website where we can learn about the pros and cons of electric bicycles, we are self-directing our own learning. The ubiquitous access we have now to online information and knowledge has dramatically increased our abilities to be learning all the time.

And yet, too often in education, we continue to focus on time- and place-dependent professional learning for our teachers, administrators, and staff. The professional learning modality continues to be more passive than active learning, most notably in terms of the origination of the learning process. A quick scan of any school or district calendar will inevitably result in the identification of specific calendar days designated as a Teacher PD Day on Wednesday or Principals' Institute in August before school starts. Many collective bargaining contracts stipulate that the school district provide a certain number of professional learning days for their members. The challenge is not about the compliance with participation but with the sustainability of the impact. Changing professional practices is not a simple process. Even a highly effective PD experience is not a magic bean that will automatically transform the way a teacher approaches instruction.

The same is the case with sending educators to professional education conferences. The learning process may be intensive over the two to three days of the conference, generating enthusiasm and optimism for using these new techniques or tools in the classroom, but in reality, the long-term impact may be minimal as teachers get back into classroom routines and have no support network to implement the new ideas. As with the students, the extrinsic motivations (continuing education credits, compliance per district requirements, a nice lunch, a trip to a conference location) may not be enough to create the desired sustainable impact of the professional learning process. Self-directed learning around areas of interest and which provides tangible value to one's professional work may provide the necessary intrinsic motivation to actively seek out relevant learning experiences and also result in greater "stickiness" in terms of impact.

Since 2009, Project Tomorrow's Speak Up Research Project has polled teachers and school site principals about their self-directed professional learning activities that are not part of school or district provided PD days or events. In many ways this is the companion question to the Speak Up item about students' Free Agent Learning experiences. Table 10.2 identifies the ways that teachers and principals are leveraging digital and social media tools as well as new online learning modalities to support their own professional learning. The table also compares the most recent results from the 2020–2021 school year with what educators reported on in the 2016–2017 school year. As indicated, educators, use of social media and social networking sites for professional learning has had the greatest increase over the past four years. Whereas only 19% of teachers, for example, were following education experts on social media in 2016, 49% said that following those experts and reading their posts were a regular part of their self-directed professional learning in 2020.

The ways that educators are self-directing their own professional learning, thus exercising their abilities to be Free Agent Learners also, has the potential to deliver benefits for students as well. When

Table 10.2 How teachers and principals are using online, social, and digital tools to support self-directed professional learning.

Self-directed professional learning activities	Percentage of teachers		Percentage of principals	
	2016–2017 school year (%)	2020–2021 school year (%)	2016–2017 school year (%)	2020–2021 school year (%)
Participate in a webinar	29	52	59	78
Find information online to support my professional tasks	70	79	71	73
Sought help from other educators through my social networking sites	25	46	32	56
Follow education experts on social media	19	49	39	55
Watch TED Talks or other videos on education topics	42	43	58	48

Source: © Project Tomorrow 2021.

a school or district encourages their staff to pursue self-directed professional learning, and provides support and capacity for those efforts, they are validating the students' Free Agent Learnership as well. Additionally, if teachers and administrators have experiences with self-directed learning to meet their own education needs, they may be more receptive to the motivations of students for similar activities and also understand the habits of the Free Agent Learners in their classes or at their school. It is also more likely that given this greater appreciation and firsthand knowledge of these experiences, teachers in particular will incorporate more self-directed learning experiences within classroom instruction. It is also conceivable that given similar experiences, such as with social media as a tool for self-directed learning, educators may change some mindsets about the value of digital tools in the hands of students, both at home and in school, and how to align classroom practices more effectively with the Student Vision for Learning.

Create a Culture Around Free Agent Learning Concepts and Principles Within your District

As the old adage goes, culture eats strategy for breakfast, lunch, and dinner. The earlier-identified ideas for how school and district leaders can support Free Agent Learnership address changing current school environments from both the inside out and outside in. However, as we have all seen many times before in education, the rise and fall of new initiatives, new learning models, new instructional strategies, or even the use of digital tools in the classroom are highly dependent on the school and district culture. Creating a culture that values and supports the concepts and principles of Free Agent Learning is not going to happen overnight. But there are steps that you can do to plant the seeds today to develop a new ethos within your community for the appreciation of how your students, empowered with online access to a world of learning resources, are purposely self-directing their own learning around areas of interest and passion. And then, how to use that knowledge to rethink and reengineer current instructional practices so that they can align more effectively with the Student Vision for Learning, typified through the Free Agent Learning activities students are engaged with everyday beyond the sponsorship of teachers or schools. Here is one seed of an idea for potential germination in your school or district.

Over the past decade, many schools and districts have developed new cultures within their community for the appreciation of students having increased exposure to science, technology, engineering, and mathematics (STEM) fields through academic courses as well as community engagements and informal learning experiences. Quite often those STEM movements or initiatives started with a small group of leaders seeding efforts within their schools or across their community. The initial efforts focused on explaining the *why* behind the movement and demonstrating value through pilot efforts. As positive results became evident, more people wanted to be part of the effort to realize similar benefits. In many cases, that ground-level campaign eventually resulted in the institutionalization of a STEM focus within many schools and districts evidenced by its inclusion in mission, vision, and value statements as well as dedicated funding to support expansion. STEM has now become an integral part of many school and district cultures with students, teachers, administrators, and parents all understanding the value of a STEM-focused education and providing community support for its sustainability.

A similar effort could be undertaken to develop a new culture around Free Agent Learning. One former superintendent recommended to me that districts interested in developing a new ethos within their community around Free Agent Learning could jump-start the effort with an invitational summit for educators and community members to learn more about the Free Agent Learning ecosystem and to brainstorm small, easy-to-implement ideas for integrating the essential elements of the Student Vision for Learning within classrooms. Key to this effort is to make participation voluntary. Getting the early adopters on board who may already be familiar with students' self-directed activities or may value their own personal access to online resources for professional learning can help create a cadre of supporters. There is also high value in having school-based teams at the summit to build local capacity and sustainability for the work, like putting together a relay team to share the efforts. Workshop-style support for the invitational members including potentially a book study can build capacity for understanding the challenges in terms of changing people's mindsets around the traditional models of student learning and the purposeful use of technology in the hands of students.

But to quote the great basketball coach John Wooden, "Never mistake activity for achievement." With a goal to nurture a new district culture around Free Agent Learning, the invitational summit activities must be sustainable and lead to tangible outcomes. That requires consistent leadership support and commitment and a stated assessment from district leaders that the work of the summit participants is valuable and has a good chance of improving educational opportunities and outcomes for students. Seeds do not sprout leaves overnight, and correspondingly, infusing Free Agent Learning into a school or district culture will take time. But every new step forward starts with someone leading the way.

The findings shared in this book about Free Agent Learners provide education leaders with evidence to support the development of new school cultures that recognize the value of students' out-of-school experiences using technology tools for learning. Contrary to some assumptions, students who are using digital tools for self-directed learning are purposeful in these behaviors. They are pursuing these self-directed learning behaviors to self-remediate where they believe they have academic needs or deficiencies, learning skills that can help them in school and in life, following academic curiosities often sparked by a classroom discussion or activity, and preparing themselves for the future by exploring careers and colleges. Awareness and recognition of these activities and the purposes driving students' self-directed learning may help education leaders change the perceptions of their teaching teams and start new conversations about how to leverage the students' proficiencies and competencies with these digital tools within the classroom.

It is also important for educators to realize that today's students are not waiting for them or their teachers to transform the classroom learning experience to best fit their needs for skill development, to help prepare them for an uncertain future, or even to answer all of their questions about science, history, or politics. That ship has sailed. Armed with Internet connectivity in their pockets, backpacks, or palms of their hands, students have the capacity now to self-direct learning around academic passions or personal curiosities about their world. They are using a variety of digital tools, content, and resources and developing a host of new learning behaviors to support these interest-driven activities. At the center of this self-directed learning is a series of highly developed purposes that are propelling today's students to take their educational destiny into their own hands, literally. An opportunity exists for educators to learn from these student experiences and use that knowledge to spearhead a new morning in education, a morning that values students' self-directed learning experiences and aims to create in-school experiences that are innovative, relevant, and purposeful.

From a strengths-based perspective, it is imperative that today's education leaders tap into the rich experiences that students are having outside of school with technology to support and maximize the in-school learning experience. Students' use of emerging technologies such as games, social media, and mobile devices to pursue self-directed, interest-driven learning beyond educator sponsorship or direction provide a treasure trove of competencies and information that can be better leveraged both to increase student engagement in learning and to support student and teacher skill development. The significant leadership challenge, therefore, may be for educators to develop the will both to envision the future and to create new learning environments that position students for success in the globally information-intensive economy and society.

The critical significance of this book, therefore, is to provide education leaders with a new understanding about the 24/7 learning experiences of today's students. It is my hope that our education leaders will leverage this knowledge to support the development of school cultures and the types of learning experiences that all students need to fulfill their potential to become our world's future leaders, innovators, and engaged global citizens.

Notes

1. https://www.pblworks.org/what-is-pbl.
2. https://www.nea.org/advocating-for-change/new-from-nea/esports-see-explosive-growth-us-high-schools.
3. https://aurora-institute.org/our-work/competencyworks/competency-based-education/?cn-reloaded=1.
4. https://ies.ed.gov/ncee/rel/Project/4615.
5. https://ies.ed.gov/ncee/rel/regions/central/pdf/REL_2020031_appendices.pdf.
6. https://www.coursera.org.
7. https://outschool.com/#abl0y2og3a.
8. https://ywp.nanowrimo.org.
9. https://www.carlsbadusd.k12.ca.us/mvg2.
10. https://www.nea.org/advocating-for-change/new-from-nea/building-culture-classroom-collaboration.
11. https://www.youtube.com/watch?v=kFMZrEABdw4.
12. https://www.cuny.edu/academics/academic-policy/credit-prior-learning.

Index